NATO in Afghanistan

NATO in Afghanistan

THE LIBERAL DISCONNECT

Sten Rynning

Stanford Security Studies
An Imprint of Stanford University Press
Stanford, California

Stanford University Press
Stanford, California

Printed in the United States of America on acid-free, archival-quality paper

Library of Congress Cataloging-in-Publication Data
Rynning, Sten, author.
 NATO in Afghanistan : the liberal disconnect / Sten Rynning.
  pages   cm
 Includes bibliographical references and index.
 ISBN 978-0-8047-8237-1 (cloth : alk. paper)
 ISBN 978-0-8047-8238-8 (pbk. : alk. paper)
 1. Afghan War, 2001– 2. North Atlantic Treaty Organization—Afghanistan.
I. Title.
 DS371.412.R96 2012
 958.104'7—dc23

                                                      2012014294

Special discounts for bulk quantities of Stanford Security Studies are available to corporations, professional associations, and other organizations. For details and discount information, contact the special sales department of Stanford University Press. Tel: (650) 736-1782, Fax: (650) 736-1784

Typeset by Thompson Type in 10/14 Minion

In memory of my father
Svend Erik Rynning

CONTENTS

ACKNOWLEDGMENTS

THE ROOTS OF THIS BOOK can be traced back to 2006–2007 and my ambition to get a grip on the fundamentals of Atlantic Alliance cohesion. My original idea, inspired by the rise of neoconservative confidence as well as Europe's incoherent response to it, was to analyze power shifts and the politics of managing them. This problem of power shift is real but abstract, I realized. Allied statesmen manage power in relation to events, and for about a decade Afghanistan has been *the* event for the Alliance. Thus, I undertook to write a book about the war in Afghanistan and what it tells us about NATO. The world will change, and because Afghanistan has been bruising allied statesmen will be eager to turn the Afghan page. Yet Afghanistan is where the rubber meets the road. It is my hope that NATO statesmen and officials in addition to observers of security affairs will not only enjoy this book but also be provoked to ponder what it is that NATO now must do to reinvent itself.

The research for the book was supported by a grant from the Danish Social Science Research Council (FSE), 2008–2010 (project no. 275-07-0253, "Whither NATO? An Assessment of the Vitality of the Atlantic Alliance"). This was a critically important grant, which I gratefully acknowledge. My partner in crime in the project has been Jens Ringsmose, a top-rate colleague. Jens, along with Birthe Hansen, Rolf M. H. P. Holmboe, Casper Sylvest, and Peter Dahl Thruelsen, met with me to review and criticize the full manuscript before its submission. Peter Viggo Jakobsen likewise commented on the full manuscript, and Theo Farrell and Anders Wivel on portions of it. I am deeply grateful for all these efforts and constructive criticisms. I should also like to thank the two anonymous reviewers as well as Geoffrey Burn, my editor at Stanford University Press, for making the review process a constructive affair.

In the course of the research for the book I have talked to many people connected to NATO's Afghan campaign. A fair number remain anonymous or on background; those speaking on the record are cited in the text. I am immensely thankful for their time and assistance, without which this project would have been impossible. From every conversation I drew benefit and insight. Some conversations took place in Afghanistan in the fall of 2009 as I joined NATO's boldly labeled TOLA (Transatlantic Opinion Leaders, Afghanistan) tour. For a rewarding trip, I thank TOLA interlocutors as well as the Professors' Brigade. Other conversations could not have taken place without the help of key people who made the connection possible. Special thanks go to Jakob Nielsen of the Danish NATO delegation as well as Rolf M. H. P. Holmboe of the Danish foreign service, whose accessibility and diligence have been a superb help, as well as to Per Poulsen Hansen, Thierry Legendre, Daniel Lafayeedney, Andreas Rude, Ryan Brown and David M. Abshire, and Peter Michael Nielsen. For their repeated availability and broad and stimulating thinking, I would like to thank Morten Fløe Henriksen, Jamie Shea, Theo Farrell, and Peter Dahl Thruelsen. Finally, I offer my thanks to the group of students who followed my NATO and Afghanistan class in the fall of 2009 and whose querying minds refined my insights into the issue.

My family must have experienced the writing of this book as a kind of insurgency that regularly wrecked our common lives. Christilla bore with it, admiringly; read portions of the manuscript; and in a flash of insight gave me the title. Emil, Axel, and Clement grew older and must have wondered about adult life. For their patience, endurance, and support, I am forever thankful.

NATO in Afghanistan

INTRODUCTION

THE ALLIES OF THE NORTH ATLANTIC TREATY ORGANIZATION (NATO), along with partners, have for more than a decade been fighting a dogged and brutal war in Afghanistan. What was once a small security operation has become a major war effort involving, at its height in mid-2011, 131,000 troops from forty-nine troop-contributing nations led by the United States.[1] The war is dynamic and defies easy control and conceptualization. The allies have tinkered with various mission headers, such as counterterrorism, stabilization, and security assistance; in the end, settling on counterinsurgency, though transition to Afghan leadership has brought a new focus. The killing of Osama bin Laden, Al Qaeda's leader, on May 2, 2011, is a victory of sorts, but it is now widely understood that outright campaign victory is off the books. The 2009–2011 International Security Assistance Force (ISAF) surge led by the United States hit the Taliban hard but was a prelude to transition and thus a strategy for drawing down force engagements and encouraging Afghan reconciliation and regional engagement. The end game will be difficult, and the outcome remains uncertain. Still, it is clear that the Atlantic Alliance must come to grips with the wider geopolitical lessons of a campaign that has accelerated a global power shift and revealed a deficit in the Alliance's collective purpose.

During the Cold War, NATO's purpose was easy to identify. Lord Ismay, NATO's first secretary general, summed it up eloquently: NATO is here to keep the Soviets out, the Americans in, and the Germans down. This was Europe-centric NATO. But what is NATO's purpose now that questions of security in Europe have evolved and integrate with security issues in other regions and indeed the world? This was a question already posed in the early

1990s. NATO toughed it out, defying political death and busying itself with the reordering of the NATO borderland from the Baltic to the Balkans. The question is not going away, though, as Afghanistan so vividly reminds us. When confronted with the question, NATO's current Lord Ismay—Secretary General Anders Fogh Rasmussen—ventures that NATO's purpose today is to keep "the Americans in, the Europeans engaged, and new threats out."[2]

It is a balancing act between the old and the new—between a Europe-centric NATO that the United States must remained involved in and a global-centric NATO that Europeans must engage. NATO's new Strategic Concept of November 2010 embodies the balancing act stringently and with a degree of vision, and yet it remains a roadmap that struggles with political reality. This reality is notably defined by the tension between coalitions of the willing who drive campaigns and provide leadership on the one hand and collective and formalized institutions such as NATO that provide support and backup. The intervention in Libya—Operation Unified Protector (OUP)—that unfolded through 2011 is a case in point. It was not run by "political NATO" but rather "command-and-control NATO" because the United Nations defined the "Responsibility to Protect" mission, and a coalition of the willing—attached to the Libya Contact Group that later morphed into Friends of Libya—dealt with the high politics of the campaign. NATO was left with military execution, by and large. That campaign had positive effects in terms of Libya's incipient regime transition and Colonel Qaddafi's demise and death but also highlights, therefore, NATO's challenge of political impact and relevance. It is the story we will encounter in Afghanistan as well. If coalitions gain all the political purpose as defined by particular campaigns, if NATO is reduced to a military toolbox because the allies fail to agree to a collective engagement beyond Europe's peripheries, then NATO will be the loser of today's wars. Put differently, NATO is faring badly in Afghanistan because a deficit in political purpose translates into inadequate strategic thinking about ends, ways, and means, and NATO must now confront this deficit.

This book is the first comprehensive assessment of NATO's involvement in Afghanistan and what the war in Afghanistan means for NATO as an alliance. Books on NATO do deal with Afghanistan, just as books on Afghanistan do deal with NATO, as the book review in Chapter 1 demonstrates, but no book has to date focused primarily on the two—NATO and Afghanistan—and the implications of their coming together. This book is about NATO as a Western alliance and a pillar of international order and about what war in Afghanistan has done to this pillar. It offers insights into what NATO is, how it evolves, why it sometimes does not, and what NATO will likely become. It is based on the author's years of engagement with the issue and notably builds on insights generated from discussions and interviews with key NATO actors—statesmen, generals, and other Alliance officials—in Brussels, Kabul, and elsewhere. And it appears at a propitious moment because we know the allies' Afghanistan exit strategy following a decade of war and diplomatic engagement. The exit strategy is contained in the so-called *Inteqal*—from the Dari and Pashtun word for transition—document that the U.S.-led troop surge is designed to realize. The *Inteqal* was negotiated and then embedded into allied strategy in the course of 2010. Thus we know that the Atlantic allies are set to terminate the combat mission within a few years, which naturally raises the question: What is next? What do we learn from the Afghan campaign, and what will NATO evolve into?

LESSONS FROM AFGHANISTAN

It is useful to distinguish between lessons that apply to the NATO experience and the future of the Alliance, and lessons for observers of international affairs more broadly. There are several lessons regarding NATO. The first one is that NATO is failing—and has consistently failed—to provide a purpose for the fight in Afghanistan that connects the ground effort to NATO's wider international effort. It is one thing to say that NATO is in Afghanistan to assist the Karzai government or to counter Al Qaeda; it is quite another thing to justify it with reference to a wider Alliance purpose. NATO's wider purpose is either Eurocentric or only tenuously related to Afghanistan: Combating terrorism is vaguely defined and buried in references to cyberwar, deterrence, and antipiracy missions off Africa's Horn. Assisting Afghanistan is a noble cause in and of itself, but the cause has come to demand such a massive level of engagement that Afghanistan should be situated at the heart of what the Alliance is about. NATO's best answer is to point in the direction of global security management and the need for multiple organizations to cooperate in the management of new threats. It locates NATO at the heart of a wider liberal order and attaches it to the United Nations, which likewise seeks security management. NATO has developed a doctrine to this effect—the Comprehensive Approach. As a tool for organizational cooperation it is appropriate, but as a political agenda for an alliance it is a misfortune.

NATO has in effect retreated into liberal wishful thinking. The assumption that a wider liberal community is ready to act if it can only be organized—via the Comprehensive Approach—is just that, an assumption. It is not warranted by events on the ground, though the assumption must be politically comforting. If the mission spins out of control, we appeal to the community while getting on with our business. If things go wrong, the diffuse community is there to pin the blame on. But the comfort is deceptive because comprehensive cooperation is just a tool: It does not confer purpose, and it does not result in strategy. The liberal ideal has thus become disconnected from reality, and NATO is one of the main culprits of this—the liberal disconnect.

This is not an argument against liberalism but for liberalism's rooting in geopolitical reality. NATO once managed this balance with ease because values and interests coincided. This was during the Cold War. Unsure of its interests in the post–Cold War era, NATO took to cultivating its inherent liberal values as a source of cohesion and a blueprint for external action. It continued to manage the value–interest balance with success, though, because it did not cave in to liberalism's universal impulse and worked predominantly within realistic geopolitical—Euro-Atlantic—confines. It became, in effect, a "benevolent alliance"—still an alliance but also a provider of progress. The terrorist attacks of 2001 and the war in Afghanistan challenged the compromise behind the "benevolent alliance," thrusting it onto the world stage where other actors and issues clamor for influence and attention. Bewildered in terms of interests, NATO has committed even further to liberal values. It thus lost its balance.

Not all is yet lost for the Alliance, though. Afghanistan tells us that the Alliance is capable of change. In 2006–2007, when the insurgency took off in earnest and threatened NATO and ISAF with campaign failure, NATO managed not only to stay together but also to change course. Change began with the collective recognition that this was a real fight and that NATO as a collective body could not handle it. Instead, NATO prepared to support a lead nation—the United States—on the security side and draw in a variety of political and civil means to advance the broader campaign. NATO might not be a strategic actor—one capable of commanding and controlling ISAF in a real fight—but NATO could be a strategic enabler, supporting a lead and gaining a say in the overall strategy. This was an important turn of events, which began in 2007–2008 and continues to this day. It showed that NATO is adaptive. What NATO now needs to do is carry this momentum of change into the wider political arena. In Afghanistan, NATO picked a fight it was not ready for, and it wisely settled for supporting a U.S. lead. Beyond Afghanistan, NATO must maintain the political ability to set priorities when challenged. NATO cannot predict the future and plan strategically for it, any more than other actors, but it can retain its capacity to react thoughtfully and vigorously—strategically—to the changing fortunes that campaigns put on offer. The Comprehensive Approach has become a cover for a deficit in strategic capacity. It provides for an ongoing liberal disconnect. The war in Afghanistan is thus tied to a war for the West. NATO can muddle through in Afghanistan, but it needs to win the latter, and it will require that NATO comes home. To come home is not to redefine Russia as a regional threat or to build a firewall around NATO territory; it is to rediscover the political purpose of the Western alliance in the twenty-first century.

This brings us finally to some more general observations that the reader will be able to take away from the engagement with this book. They will be substantiated by the analysis and will therefore be briefly presented here. The first observation is that there is no antithesis between liberalism and realism, which is otherwise a much-deployed confrontation in the academic literature. Writer and analyst Edward H. Carr once observed that the utopian will fail to find refuge from reality because reality will refuse to conform to utopian standards but also that the realist will find no resting place in pure realism because it fails to provide goals and inspire action.[3] Politics is the art of balancing utopian thought and realist analysis, of infusing into geopolitical analysis the kind of purposive thought that will advance the management of power without wrecking its foundations. This remains the case. It follows that political artists— statesmen—must be cognizant of two challenges. One is the balance between leadership and organization—between heroic initiative and routine. A political community needs both, but in contested operations the schism between coalitions building on initiative and institutions marked by routine can grow dangerously. Though Afghanistan may show that allies can operate a coalition of the willing without endangering the collective Alliance, it has been a rough ride.[4] The coalition—Operation Enduring Freedom (OEF)—was hotly contested by some allies, and it took a long moment of campaign crisis in 2006–2008 to make for a cohesive allied approach, which was the Obama-led surge and transition strategy. The balance between Alliance leadership and allied organization is tenuous, therefore, and the balancing act will continue beyond the transition target of 2014 and beyond Afghanistan itself. Another challenge and balancing act concerns the tension between network and actor.

This is the story of national and allied power versus globalization and global governance. Any one actor can do only so much, and the power of global networks can be immense. However, networks are leaderless. Spoilers can easily exploit this lack of leadership, which we see in respect to Afghan governance and development. Global governance visions have been out of sync with Afghan reality, in other words. To an extent, NATO has been slow in recognizing that it had to provide the overall campaign leadership—not just for security but for the whole range of efforts—and the issue of leadership remains a contentious one in the wider context of NATO–U.N. relations.

The sum of these observations is that NATO has had a deficit of leadership, a strategy building on organizational routine, and a hope that global governance would solve its problems. It was the downside of the benevolent outlook that was nourished through the 1990s. NATO's political leaders have been engaged in the Afghan campaign, for sure, but they have lacked in alliance convictions. Once the Taliban had been chased from power, which happened very quickly, NATO's mission expanded to nation building without the Alliance leadership questioning the appropriateness of this mission end point. Organizational routine then took over, and politics became a question of engineering as opposed to making hard choices: Confronted with vast social and political problems in Afghanistan, the engineer will choose a vast and comprehensive solution. NATO to an extent failed in its responsibility to design policy according to consequences, a classical ethical yardstick. In recent years NATO leaders have come to realize that engineering is a problem, not a solution, and that global governance in situations of war is theory, not practice. The result is a tentative return to political leadership and the type of conviction that could provide renewed purpose to NATO. It could turn NATO around but is, as mentioned, a work in progress.

THE STRUCTURE OF THE BOOK

Chapter 1 takes stock of the debate on NATO. NATO has been around for so long that it is not possible to point to any one source of Alliance continuity. It could be the balance of power or democracy. It could be both, and it could be something else. The ambiguity spills over into the assessment of NATO and Afghanistan. A number of analysts claim that NATO is finished as an effective alliance and that Afghanistan shows it. This is the NATO-is-dying school, and it is countered by another school of thought that believes NATO is doing the right thing but too little of it. This is the NATO-should-globalize school.

This book takes issue with both these positions in terms of how they interpret the record of NATO and Afghanistan and also in terms of their tendency to look at NATO from the outside. To properly grasp NATO we must get inside it. NATO has not only disparate national interests but also collective meaning, as German sociologist Max Weber would have argued. It leads to a third school of thought that finds NATO viable, as opposed to dying, but in need of a more distinct regional, as opposed to globally networked, identity. NATO has people, machines, and missions but also, and critically, a Western character. This book argues that NATO's future depends on its ability to confront and renew this character as it extracts itself from Afghan warfare.

Section I provides overviews of both NATO's recent past and the Afghan conflict. Chapter 2 offers an overview of what NATO had become by 2001 following out-of-area experiences, notably in the Balkans, and what NATO looked like on September 10, 2001. Chapter 3 outlines the kind of government Afghanistan gained following the overthrow of the Taliban regime in late 2001 and how the international community initially set out to assist this new government. It also locates the key points of decision making that shaped and deepened NATO's Afghan engagement.

Section II is composed of three investigative chapters that account for NATO's entry into Afghanistan, its near-death experience as a strategic actor but also its comeback as a strategic enabler, and its dangerous flirtation with the agenda of global governance. Chapter 4 deals with the period 2001–2005, when NATO was at first sidetracked and then pulled in to take the ISAF lead. A number of original sins were committed to the effect that by 2005, when NATO decided that its lead should extend to the entire country, it was not the strategic actor it pretended to be. Chapter 5 covers NATO's encounter with the brutal and difficult campaign in southern and eastern Afghanistan. The campaign shocked the Alliance and left it bereft of leadership. However, NATO managed in these years, 2006–2008, to redefine its role to that of strategic enabler. NATO lost the sense that it could take the military lead, but it gained a policy for handling civil-military matters more coherently. Chapter 6 covers 2008–2012 and thus the struggle to recover purpose and fight the war in Afghanistan to a successful end. There are telling signs of renewal because the allies are cohering around the transition strategy. However, the renewal is incomplete, and NATO must continue to develop its response to critical events in and around Afghanistan and indeed in the wider Middle East.

The conclusion takes stock of NATO and looks to the future. NATO holds potential. NATO remains a valuable gateway for the United States to influence key Eurasian developments and thus manage the international order, and NATO gives European allies a seat at the American table. To realize this potential, the Alliance must face the fact that its tendency to be visionary but not realistic has to do with the "benevolent" mind-set that was nourished through the 1990s. It must balance ideas of benevolence with ideas of Western alliance and purpose, which requires a sustained effort of political leadership. Continued NATO engagement in Afghanistan will be the right policy and not only because it would contribute to Afghan and South Asian stability: It could be the catalyst for NATO's rediscovery of itself.

1 THE NATURE OF THE ATLANTIC BEAST

THROUGH HISTORY AND LITERATURE we typically encounter two Afghanistans. One is a type of roundabout for commerce and cultural transactions that originate in East and West and meet in the plains surrounding the Hindu Kush Mountains, notably to the north in the region once known as Bactria. The forebears of Western civilization come from this region, writes Adda Bozeman, and it was a land of crossroads "where conquest was transmuted into coexistence" and "cultural interpenetration and political cooperation."[1] It is a source of inspiration for Afghan politicians today, among them President Karzai. Another Afghanistan is the country impossible to conquer, most vividly illustrated by the January 1842 massacre of the 4,500 British forces retreating from Kabul and the first Anglo–Afghan war and hoping to reach the safe haven of Jalalabad. Legend has it that Ghilzai guerrillas allowed one soldier to live to tell the tale, and though the legend exaggerates British losses it has nourished the idea that foreign powers are destined to fail in Afghanistan.[2] It matters enormously whether we frame NATO's Afghan campaign in light of one of these Afghanistans. If Afghanistan is truly the graveyard of empires, it should not surprise us that NATO has encountered problems, and we should in fact applaud it for doing so well for so long. If Afghanistan holds potential for coexistence and cultural interpenetration, one might instead ask why NATO has made such a mess of it.

It is possible to assume that both Afghanistans are real and important and then to look to NATO's own history to judge the Alliance's performance. From the vantage point of NATO there was no question that operational pressures from the Balkans had caused the Alliance to change.[3] "This ain't your daddy's NATO," is how Lord Robertson, secretary general of NATO from 1999 through 2004, put it. This history tells us that NATO was adaptable, at least to an extent, but it does not suffice as a yardstick for the Afghan campaign. His- torical differences are simply too great, even though Balkan and Afghan op- erations both somehow fit into the wider business model of crisis management and conflict resolution. In the Balkans, NATO began with a peace plan; in Afghanistan, there is no peace agreement. In the Balkans, NATO began with a grand deployment—60,000 in the case of Bosnia in 1995–1996—and drew down this number over time as belligerents grew less belligerent; in Afghani- stan, NATO began with a few thousand only to build up beyond 100,000. The Balkans are right next door to NATO territory and logistics; Afghanistan is landlocked and thousands of miles of away.

Some of the best books on the Afghan war that began in 2001 are cog- nizant of the dual nature of Afghanistan, its potential and pitfalls, but they pay scant attention to NATO. One of these books is written by the regional expert and journalist Ahmed Rashid.[4] It is not an upbeat assessment. The international community, including NATO but with a notable focus on the United States, has not grasped Afghanistan's potential for progress and as a consequence has nourished the forces that make Afghanistan a graveyard of empires. Rashid's message is that Western policy needs to be less focused on hunting bad guys and more focused on empowering good guys.[5] This liberal message reverberates through Seth Jones's equally insightful work on the Af- ghan campaign.[6] Seth Jones focuses on the United States, though, and Jones is not particularly happy with his country's ability to handle Afghanistan. NATO is present in the book but not centrally so, and it appears mainly in the context of allied disputes and bickering. It is one face of NATO but far from the only one. Two big overview books should be mentioned: Jason Burke, a *Guardian* correspondent, brings together a number of campaigns, conflicts, and tensions in what he calls the 9/11 wars, and Peter Tomsen, former spe- cial envoy to the Afghan resistance, provides an admirable overview of Af- ghanistan's wars. Neither makes the Alliance his subject matter but both are excellent books.[7] Tomsen's book tends to read history to derive policy implica- tions for the United States, though, and Burke's book is more contemporary and wider in its gaze and assessment and ultimately of greater importance for observers of the Atlantic Alliance.[8] Britain's former ambassador to Af- ghanistan, Sherard Cowper-Coles, is fond of allied disputes and especially the frustrations that American planning—or the lack thereof—can engender among allies and himself in particular, perhaps.[9] Cowper-Coles's strong message is that counterinsurgency (COIN) is a means, not an end, and that the COIN surge of 2009–2010 did not sufficiently define the ends of the campaign. His book deals squarely with the predominance of American thinking that came with the surge, as well as British Afghan politics, and it has become a reference point in the debate on what is wrong with the campaign, but it does not tell us why the United States, much less NATO as a whole, has failed—by Cowper-Coles's yardstick—to grasp the nature of the campaign. Tim Bird and Alex Marshall, British lecturers of defense studies and history, seem to tackle NATO head-on in their book on "how the West lost its way."[10] It is a smooth narrative of the war up to 2011 and a stinging critique of Western strategy. Like Cowper-Coles, they take the Western allies to task for mistaking means and ends—COIN is not strategy—and claim, moreover, that NATO has been obsessed by its own internal affairs as opposed to Afghanistan. This part of the story is incomplete. NATO has been able to focus on Afghanistan and in fact strengthen its grasp of the campaign. Moreover, NATO shortcomings result not so much from allied disagreement—often noted—but from the way in which they have framed the campaign mistakenly, which in turn has to do with how common liberal values have become *the* means for managing Alliance diversity and, in consequence, how NATO's campaign has developed within a fixed conceptual space ill suited to the realities of Afghanistan and the dynamic and innovative character of the adversary.

WHAT IS NATO?

NATO was never a congregation of fully aligned nations. It remains an amalgamation of nations with long histories and national interests within distinct geographical confines—be it the Arctic, the Baltic, Eastern Europe, the Balkans, North Africa, the Atlantic, or the Pacific, for that matter. NATO is therefore a geopolitical patchwork that has been kept together by skillful political management. This management relates to interests as well as values. Following the founding treaty of NATO, the values are liberal but rooted in transatlantic soil. The treaty is liberal yet geopolitical. In terms of visionary ambiguity, it is a beautifully crafted document. It demands of NATO statesmen constant attention to the political art of balancing hope and realism but also leaves them scope for action. The community of NATO observers is divided, tending to emphasize a particular factor such as either liberal values or geopolitics. In the search for understanding we would do well to remember that we shall not arrive at a truth about NATO but perhaps improved knowledge. It will come about as we confront the empirical record and assess how well our concepts guide us in the effort to understand NATO and Afghanistan's impact on it. There are two distinct views of NATO. Both are illuminating, but neither one hits the mark.

When Trouble Is Destiny: The NATO-Is-Dying School

Much of the ongoing commentary about NATO and the Afghan war flirts with the idea of Alliance death. It has in fact become an enduring theme. The aforementioned Ahmed Rashid was frank when NATO prepared to expand ISAF into Afghanistan's south and east: The Alliance was setting itself up for "abysmal failure," a view echoed by *The Economist*, which noted that "short-sighted European politicians" were putting "the world's foremost Alliance" at risk given their lack of commitments.[11] Other observers noted the tendency of European allies to "fill up lots of air space at policy conferences talking about Europe's readiness to play a prominent role in global affairs," concluding that Europe's bluff is easy to call.[12] "NATO is flunking," echoes John Feffer, who notes that the "stunning lack of success on the ground" is "the real nail in NATO's coffin."[13] NATO has proved inept at all the fundamentals of strategy, we learn elsewhere: political direction, the generation of military capabilities, funding for the war, and cooperation with other organizations such as the United Nations.[14] NATO may simply be unable to negotiate the contested "rules of the game" that peace-building operations require, according to academic analyst Alexandra Gheicu, and the outcome is ineffective multilateralism, militarized strategy, and an "unrealistic war," adds Luis Peral, another analyst.[15] It all lends credence to the observation that NATO "will prove less and less valuable to its members with each year."[16] When Azeem Ibrahim of Harvard University asks, "If we were designing an alliance most suitable to face the threats of the future, would it look like NATO?" the obvious answer is "No, it would not."[17] James Goldgeier of George Washington University concurs, "If the North Atlantic Treaty Organization (NATO) did not exist today, the United States would not seek to create it."[18] British General Richards, who commanded ISAF during the first critical phase of southern and eastern expansion in 2006, finds that NATO suffered from both political and military inertia and was in fact "quite sclerotic."[19] Canadian General Rick Hillier, ISAF commander in 2004–2005, is perhaps NATO's most outspoken critic: "It was crystal clear from the start that there was no strategy for the mission in Afghanistan." NATO is now a decomposing corpse, Hillier continues, and someone needs to breathe lifesaving air through its "rotten lips into [its] putrescent lungs, or the alliance will be done."[20]

The alleged transatlantic divorce is rooted partly in distinct values and the drifting apart of Europeans and Americans. History and culture are taking their toll and nourish worldviews that can no longer be fitted into one alliance framework. Andrew Bacevich, a professor of history and international relations and a vivid commentator, sees little potential in the transatlantic alliance. "NATO is failing," Bacevich argues, and to think of it as a great alliance is "sheer nostalgia."[21] The problem is that Europe has become pacified and lost its "martial spirit" and that this trend is irreversible. It is time therefore to leave NATO to the Europeans who can use such a downsized alliance to shield themselves against Russia while the United States gets on with its global business.[22] Bacevich's point resonates. Michael Cox, also a professor of history and international relations, concludes that NATO is yesterday's news: "What existed once exists no more."[23] Another professor, Donald Puchala, identifies a transatlantic value gap and cannot see why it should diminish.[24] Nor can Robert Kagan, whose argument that Americans are from Mars and Europeans from Venus stirred great debate some years ago.[25]

The divorce is motivated also by hard power and the rise and decline of nations, the argument continues. Analysts who believe that states tend to balance each other now see European efforts to soft-pedal against the United States and maybe even outright oppose it in critical diplomatic contexts.[26] To these analysts, transatlantic relations have transformed into U.S.–EU relations, and there is no raison d'être for integrative institutions such as NATO. The United States should therefore agree to transfer NATO bureaucratic assets—the military command and headquarters in particular—to the EU and give up on "rigid" international institutions in favor of "flexible coalitions of similarly interested [. . .] states."[27] Part of the reason is that U.S. power can best be preserved if it scales back "onshore" engagements in Eurasia and instead adopts a more selective "offshore" policy that is both less costly and controversial but also in the long run more effective.[28]

Although it seems correct to say that the transatlantic relationship is experiencing the gravitational pull of diverse regional experiences and power transitions, it is ultimately not a satisfactory account of what has happened in the Afghan context. It offers a degree of satisfaction *if* the purpose is to make sense of all the things that go wrong, and many things do. What one must do is then simply to amass evidence—NATO's performance last year in Herat or this year in Helmand, or NATO decision making in Brussels last year and the capacity of the chain of command to carry out these decisions this year—and pull it together in the plotted narrative: The string of failures shows that NATO is dying. The plot is deceptively appealing because it aligns with some trends that are clearly visible and it allows us to make sense of an extraordinarily complex operation.

The plot may simply be wrong, of course. Sarah Chayes, a noted expert on Afghanistan who has worked variously as a journalist, community organizer, and adviser to ISAF, has argued that "NATO didn't lose Afghanistan." The Atlantic Alliance has in fact been a marked improvement compared to the years of U.S. leadership, 2001–2003/4, when the United States pretty much lost Afghanistan, according to Chayes. This may not help NATO win the war, but it causes Chayes to admonish to her fellow American citizens that "the least we could do now is offer gratitude and support, rather than blame our friends for our own follies."[29]

If the Western Alliance were to falter and fall apart, the plot could still be wrong. It certainly offers no account of the reason that NATO was able to make the transition from failed strategic actor to fairly successful strategic enabler. This transition will be presented in this book, and it tells us that if the Western Alliance gets the lessons of Afghanistan wrong and fails to reinvent itself, as this book also argues is about to happen, then it is because the Alliance leaders are mismanaging a real potential for change. In short, death is a framework that provides coherence and meaning, but it also numbs us to reality, providing comfort of illustration where critical analysis is needed.

The World Is a Stage and NATO Must Play Its Part:
The NATO-Must-Globalize School

Other analysts do perceive a need for NATO in the twenty-first century, and they argue that NATO has run into trouble in Afghanistan because it has applied old medicine to new problems. NATO needs to evolve and change, and, if it does, it has a future. This argument comes in two distinctively different versions.

One harks back to the power analysis mentioned in the preceding pages. Some power analysts believe that the transition to a unipolar world of U.S. supremacy spelled the effective death of the Atlantic Alliance, as mentioned, but other analysts of power contend that unipolarity fundamentally alters

NATO's role while not threatening its survival. A unipole such as the United States will seek to perpetuate its dominance and maybe even extend the reach of its policies and principles, and an alliance such as NATO can serve as the handmaiden of these ambitions. The key difference compared to the past is that the United States today is freer to demand certain things of NATO allies without paying for them: The asymmetry of power means that the European allies and Canada cannot use the threat of alliance withdrawal to extract concessions from the United States. NATO has therefore become part of the U.S. policy of shaping the international system: NATO has enlarged, it has taken on rogue states such as the Taliban's Afghanistan, and it has engaged in the business of exporting democracy.[30]

The driver in NATO's transformation is the U.S. global agenda and the inability of allies to really check U.S. policies. The allies lack the power to resist and must therefore adapt. They could of course leave the Alliance and take care of their own security, but strategic uncertainty speaks against this option. At first the allies will try to restrain the United States with reference to NATO rules and norms, but when they discover that such restraint has limited reach, as in the case of Afghanistan, they must opt for a division of labor according to which they do the peacekeeping (ISAF) while the United States sets the strategic framework and does the hard part of countering the Taliban insurgency.

There is great appeal in this account of events because it is self-evident that the United States calls many shots in the Alliance and that the allies lack the power to define an alternative. However, it tends to overstate the degree to which the United States is able to get its way. In Afghanistan, the United States proved unable to control events to such a degree that it was happy to bring in NATO, in 2002–2004, and later to fold most of its coalition operation (OEF) into NATO and ISAF. What began as a cherry-picking approach to NATO has ended up as a strategy of relying on NATO to provide support and legitimacy. And to make an institution work in its favor, the United States cannot merely rely on power: It must enter the fray of Alliance politics.[31] In short, the United States is dependent on—or entrapped in—NATO in ways that the power perspective neglects to highlight.

This brings us to the other argument that foresees a NATO future, only this time in terms of policy rather than power. In Afghanistan, NATO has applied the right medicine but in insufficient doses and only at a late stage in the conflict, this argument goes. NATO is right to think comprehensively and to work with a host of other organizations and actors to create a web of support for Afghan security, development, and governance, but it is probably happening too late to make a difference in the Afghan case.[32] The thrust of this case is liberal, though the liberal case sometimes merges into a sociological assessment of international risk society and the demands it places on NATO.[33] The point remains, though, that with the proper policies states can overcome barriers to security cooperation: Fortunately, NATO offers both an arena of trust and collective assets for cooperation.[34]

This is the conclusion of the one major work to address NATO and Afghanistan. It is a RAND publication that concludes that NATO must become better at networking with other organizations, creating partnerships, and doing strategy in cooperation with the United Nations, the EU, and others.[35] The potential for reward and stability is thus there even if the allies have been poor at cooperating and confused about their purpose in going to Afghanistan. Afghanistan is in fact an opportunity because success here "guarantees NATO's continued relevance to both the US and Europe."[36] Part of NATO's potential has to do with the division of labor also invoked by the power analysts above and according to which NATO can provide unrivaled and much needed reconstruction and stabilization capacities.[37] But there is more to it than this. NATO must "become a global centre for the training of coalition and indigenous forces for a wide range of military and civilian COIN [counterinsurgency] operations"—providing "educational and training opportunities not just for the military, but also for multinational police, the private sector, agencies involved in infrastructure-building, and non-governmental organizations all of which need the coordination that NATO can provide"—partly to solve the issues that prevent effective cooperation between NATO and the EU.[38] NATO can thus teach other actors—NATO partners, third countries, and other international organizations—not only how to coordinate policies but what it means to be part of a liberal-democratic community.[39] NATO can help engender a new framework of thought, in other words, although it should be continuously cognizant of the need to refresh its own thinking that tends to collapse into Euro-American disputes and not just in relation to Afghanistan.[40]

The plot in the story is that the liberal community must be extended and given the opportunity to operate in earnest. The world is the stage, and NATO is just one part of it. The plot has appeal because it resonates: NATO cannot solve Afghanistan's problems on its own. Still, the plot involves a leap of faith. It identifies a complex problem—security, development, and governance in

Afghanistan—and matches it with an equally complex solution in the shape of comprehensive and networked governance at the international level. It may work in theory, but it does not in practice. There is no track record for claiming that the United Nations can take the lead in organizing solutions to armed conflicts. The United Nations typically mandates interventions and coordinates reconstruction efforts in postconflict societies, but it has no experience, much less a successful track record in running reconstruction and governance efforts while running or coordinating a war. NATO should have seen this, one might note, focusing on added value in concrete operational contexts instead of being swayed by the promise held out by the multifaceted and comprehensive approach.[41] The plot lives on, though. Its identification of a complex problem is spot on, but its solution is not.

Whatever advances have been made on the Afghan ground by the international community have come from a number of NATO allies with the United States in the lead. Mistakes have been legion, as mentioned, but it is this set of allies and not the U.N. mission in Afghanistan (UNAMA), not to mention the EU or other actors, that has defined and redefined strategy and invested resources. Strategic leadership is the vacuum in the liberal theory of comprehensive governance, and differences in allied perception of this problem account for NATO's most important political challenge.[42] There is certainly an affinity between the comprehensive approach in action (that is, NATO's political–military plan for Afghanistan) and the comprehensive approach as architecture (that is, the model for international governance writ large). But the conventional liberal wisdom has it that one will lead to the other— that Afghan action will lead to an international architecture—and it probably will not.

A CLASSICAL APPROACH TO THE WESTERN ALLIANCE

Legend has it that Archimedes, an ancient Greek mathematician, once impressed on his benefactor, King Hiero of Syracuse, "Give me a place to stand on, and I can move the earth." The ambition of this book is more modest, but it is nonetheless in need of a place to stand. Its platform is made up of three pillars that form one coherent line of thinking that we can trace through time and that is known as the classical approach to the study of world politics.

The first of these pillars is the literature that addresses NATO as an evolving Western alliance. It puts the emphasis on the "Atlantic" part of the Atlantic Alliance and does not see this Alliance's death as preordained. If the

Atlantic Alliance breaks down, and it might, it is because political leadership fails to realize the potential for Alliance continuity that we can identify in geopolitical terms. Zbigniew Brzezinski, former U.S. national security advisor, believes the United States has an enduring interest in Eurasian engagement because offshore and isolationist policies, detaching the United States from the great landmass, could mean that Eurasian power politics will come back to haunt the United States.[43] One entry point into Eurasia is NATO, and it is in the U.S. interest not only to maintain it but to promote its evolution, Brzezinski contends. NATO should be pulled from its regional confinements, but equally it should avoid the temptation to become the champion of ideological causes—crusading for democracy—that will stir trouble. NATO should be concerned with global governance, and this type of governance does not happen via the United Nations but as a dialogue among the great powers and their alliances.[44]

Where some analysts claim that the "West" was an invention of war—roughly 1939–1989, World War II and the Cold War combined—and that its time has now passed, others thus believe that its roots and relevance go beyond this confined period.[45] The Alliance finds its roots in the eighteenth century when European ideas and values were transplanted to North America. Thus, according to Henry Kissinger and Larry Summers, "The fundamental purpose of that alliance . . . reflects interests that preceded the Cold War, and that remain no less vital now that the Cold War is over."[46] Post-Afghanistan NATO will be less ambitious and more focused on members' national interests, Karl-Heinz Kamp finds, but the West will continue as a "reality in international relations," and NATO will be the face of it.[47] Ideas and values take on distinct flavors in Europe and North America, respectively, observes David Calleo, but their contrasted expressions only enhance the need for the Alliance. U.S. foreign policy builds on the ideas of Thomas Hobbes that power is best exercised in unison and from a vantage point, which informs its so-called unipolar view of world politics; whereas Europe's foreign policies are wedded to the ideas of Montesquieu that power is best dispersed and exercised in a complex and inclusive balance of power, which is the experience of the European Union (EU). Calleo's point is that both worldviews are real but also limited and one-sided and that Europe and North America are better off in an Atlantic Alliance where they can balance out each other's institutional pathologies.[48] To this we may add the irony that the United States builds on Montesquieu as far as its own political system is concerned and that some European states have come closer to realizing the Hobbesian ideal than has the United States. Calleo's point remains, though, that NATO is a useful vehicle for garnering the type of balanced international leadership that the complex transatlantic experiences can inspire but only under the right conditions.

This brings us to the second pillar of the book. However strong the potential for alliance, it must be realized by people in charge of making policy decisions. "Decision makers" is an often-used epithet, but it is avoided in the classical approach because it denotes a technical or functional approach to politics whereby people calculate the best return on policy investments and then make a decision. The big decisions of world politics are too complex, too mired in history, culture, and power's social context to be thus computed and calculated, which is why classical scholars prefer the epithet "statesmen." Statesmen (and women) must grasp the "historical luggage" of their nations as well as that of other actors on the international scene and, by virtue of intuition and experience, define the realm of possible actions.[49] As Hans Morgenthau, a classical scholar, once wrote, the making of policy is an art, not a science, that requires a combination of political wisdom, moral courage, and moral judgment.[50]

This emphasis on statesmanship runs counter to both the NATO-is-dying and the NATO-must-globalize schools of thought. These schools of thought look at NATO from the outside in. They begin with a structural condition—a power gap and globalization, respectively—and deduce their positions: Because the gap is growing, NATO must be dying; or because globalization happens, so NATO must globalize. People, including statesmen, become the pawns of history and grand movements. Politics becomes mere computation: a question of following the demands of structure—no more, no less.

Classical scholarship has consistently sought to rescue politics from such structural or mechanical onslaughts on policy deliberation and choice. Policy is as much a result of people's reaction to history and culture as to power distributions and the scientific engineering of rational solutions. This position defines the core of the classical tradition: It originates in a reaction to the growth of liberalism in the nineteenth and early twentieth centuries and its argument that social and political progress can be engineered by intelligent—enlightened—computation. It thus established the classical criticism of the Enlightenment idea. Later it labored in opposition to the heavily structural bias of scientific theory that came to dominate much of international thinking. Politics is not an empty vessel whose course is set by external stimuli.

Politics is a domain of its own where real people contemplate culture, history, and power before making political choices. If you want to understand politics, you cannot deal in stimuli: You must enter its domain.

This brings us to the third and final pillar, which concerns the method of inquiry. How do we study politics and here statesmanship and its impact on NATO and Afghanistan? Like most classical literature, this book relies on the method devised by German sociologist Max Weber (1864–1920) and known as "ideal-typical concept-construction." The basic idea is simple, although it is usually wrapped in a highly complex debate on methodological ambition and pitfalls. It is that we begin with a general concept such as an "alliance" and then infuse it with the meaning that alliance leaders ascribe to it. The word *alliance* describes NATO from the outside; what we need to do is to interpret what NATO means from the inside. The fruit of our labor will be the assessment of what it means to be NATO: Max Weber decoded the "spirit" of Protestant capitalism; we may hope to unearth the "spirit" of NATO.

Concepts are often developed logically and rationally and for the purpose of generating the kind of general knowledge that is the aim of scientific theory. For instance, alliances are often studied with the use of such concepts as balance of power, balance of threat, bandwagoning, or buck passing. These are class concepts or generic concepts that refer to like phenomena—things we can observe across time and space. Within this scientific tradition we may do large-scale comparisons using data sets and computation, study a limited number of cases to compare them in depth, or simply compare a general theory (balance of threat theory, for instance) and a single case to understand this case in relation to the typical or average pattern. These methods are varied but have as a common denominator the ambition to explain politics with the help of averages.

Max Weber—like all classical scholars—did not believe that averages could generate much insight into social and political reality.[51] Because reality and not theory is our objective, we need a different method of understanding. Weber therefore proposed that we twist class concepts to serve a "genetic" purpose—to get at the genesis or origins of a historical situation and trace its meaning and implication through time. We may take the concept of "alliance" and use it to uncover the genesis of a particular alliance such as NATO and assess what NATO means today to those able to make choices on its behalf. An alliance is thus defined in terms of both power and purpose.[52] The concept "alliance" becomes ideal-typical when it makes "clearly explicit not the class or average character but rather the *unique individual character* of cultural phenomena."[53] The aim is not a "single case study" (which implies that there are several like cases) but to "conceptualize complicated historical patterns" in such as way that we bring out their *"cultural significance."*[54]

The ideal-type or genetic concept of this book is "benevolent alliance." The ideal-type emphasizes NATO's transformation from a mutual-assistance alliance designed to contain an adversary "with incidental effect on international stability" to an alliance committed to provide just that, international stability, and this to a greater number of people.[55] The ideal-type grows out of the work that has gone into this book. It is an inductively generated concept, a genetic concept, capturing NATO's unique individual character. It has been developed in a process, as Weber described it, of abstracting and accentuating certain parts of a historical phenomenon and then bringing these parts together in one "internally consistent system"—a coherent "complex."[56] The "benevolent alliance" is such a "complex." It is derived from the author's engagement with NATO's history and current reality using standard methods of inquiry, including the process tracing of decisions. The classical approach is not foreign to modern methods of inquiry, but it simply refuses to let method guide the inquiry. There can be no privileging of any one set of accessible data, therefore, such as economic indicators or statistics of war and peace that would be comparatively easy to compute and correlate. Interviews with decision makers and NATO "people" are central, of course, but they will be completed by whatever material is available—or can be made available. To explore political choices, writes Lawrence Freedman in the introduction to his grand book on the United States and the Middle East, "I know of no better approach than to consider the available evidence in an effort to sort out the sequence of events and the influences on decisions."[57]

CONCLUSION: A BENEVOLENT ALLIANCE MEETS AFGHANISTAN

In the next chapter we shall encounter the ideal-type of "benevolent alliance" that NATO embodied. NATO had become increasingly convinced that its purpose was to do good in the post–Cold War world and was able to act in unison, though with difficulty at times. It prevailed against critics and set out to extend the benefits of liberal ideas to its neighbors in Eastern and Central Europe, which it did via partnerships and outright enlargement, to Central Asia where states were offered partnerships but not membership, and to the

Balkans where Yugoslavia's disintegration involved NATO's operational role in convincing new, untested, and sometimes virulently nationalistic regimes that the liberal path harbored greater promise. When Serbia refused to agree, NATO went to war against it. Russia balked, as did China, and the United Nations watched with wary eyes as NATO took the lead in defining Europe's order and ways and means of upholding it. It was not easy for NATO to uphold its unity under these circumstances, as we shall see, but the purpose was a noble one, and it maintained the congregation. NATO was the Western alliance in action. It was righteous and determined. It was a benevolent alliance.

The ideal-type is not meant to depict NATO as an ideal alliance bereft of dispute and beset by steely and aligned statesmen, which is an idea that the empirical record does not support. Nor is the ideal-type a normative admonition—a type of yearning for people to support NATO because it is considered good. An ideal-type is an analytical construct. It tells us that it was not just any alliance that confronted Afghanistan in 2001 but an alliance with a certain idea of itself—a winner of the Cold War that had put liberal progress in motion in the Euro-Atlantic area. It is a guide for comparing the past to the present and thus for identifying significant change. The conclusion to the book will offer an assessment of how likely NATO is to prevail. There will be an admonition but no predictions.[58] The admonition is this: There is a need to reinvent the Alliance strategically if it is to avoid its dissolution—the dissolution of the Western alliance and thus also of NATO—into a perhaps inspiring but ineffective global agenda of networked governance.

OVERVIEW

Section I

2 A BENEVOLENT ALLIANCE

NATO'S SURVIVAL PAST THE COLD WAR was not predestined. The Alliance's patron, the United States, certainly favored its continuation, but, to prevail, U.S. policy needed to outsmart political alternatives and navigate upsetting events. At one point France, having embraced a unified Germany in a new European Union, hoped that crisis management in the context of Yugoslavia's disintegration would breathe life into the EU's policy ambitions, but this proved impossible. NATO stepped in but looked equally out of breath. Serb assaults on Bosnian enclaves had the North Atlantic Council dither, and it was not unlikely that the NAC would cut NATO's losses and run. From his sickbed at a hospital in Aachen, Germany, NATO's dismayed but also cancer-struck secretary general, Manfred Wörner, a staunch Atlanticist in favor of an expanded operational role for the Alliance, rose, removed his intravenous support, and had himself transported to NATO's decision-making chamber to weigh in on deliberations.[1] On that day, April 22, 1994, the NAC decided not to run but to dig in, and, in time, Bosnia became an engine in NATO's post–Cold War transformation.

National designs, events, and sometimes dramatic interventions like Wörner's drove NATO beyond the confines of the Cold War. It not only survived but acquired a new role as the primary vehicle for bringing peace, democracy, and stability to the Euro-Atlantic region. It was in many ways a perfect blend of old and new tasks, allowing the allies who felt concerned with Germany's newfound power in Europe's midst or Russia's peripheral power to embed the Atlantic Alliance as a framework of security but with reference to progressive tasks that would build a better future for all. The allies did not have to define what they were against or to designate an enemy because they could all subscribe to the progressive vision that promised an end to enmity. Serbia unwillingly became the catalyst of the vision, being the rogue state from Europe's past that stood between the allies and Europe's future. The allies at first coerced Serbia in Bosnia, then bombed it over Kosovo. This did not happen without qualms or quarrels, but in the end it gave new meaning to NATO.

In this chapter we shall trace the making of this benevolent alliance. There are three steps to the demonstration. The first is to sketch out the fundamental liberal purpose that NATO invoked in going to war over Kosovo in 1999. The next is to lay bare the extent to which NATO was at odds with the United Nations, otherwise the natural caretaker of the global and humanitarian mission that is liberalism's. The final step is to engage the debate on EU–NATO relations and behind them French–American rivalry, which is sometimes seen as evidence of an Atlantic divide that belies the Alliance. I shall argue that in light of the first two demonstrations made here this rivalry is important but secondary. A quest for prestige and influence sometimes puts France and the United States at odds, but the quest does not deny the Atlantic framework.

A LIBERAL HEGEMON

In retrospect, in light of what was about to transpire in September 2001, the years 2000–2001 may seem like a peaceful if deceptive pause in the affairs of war and peace. A storm was gathering, but NATO, like most others, was unaware of it. Yet war was on NATO's mind. NATO had fought a war against Serbia over its province of Kosovo in 1999, and the effort reverberated through the Alliance as it took stock. The former Yugoslavia not only caused NATO's first big air war in 1999; it was also the cause of NATO's first out-of-area mission, which began in 1993 in Bosnia-Herzegovina and which by 1995–1996 resulted in the deployment of a large land force to police the Dayton peace accords. The Balkans thus fed NATO's growing ambition to become the guarantor of stability in the "Euro-Atlantic" area.[2]

In some ways, NATO had merely reacted to a deteriorating situation in the region and sought to arrest the slide into civil war and genocide. It had reacted while its members disagreed on many important issues, such as NATO enlargement (should NATO risk antagonizing Russia?), the geographical scope of its operational role out-of-area (should NATO simply go global as a matter of principle?), its growing portfolio in the context of new missions (how far should NATO go in the provision of governance and development?), and its relationship to the United Nations (should NATO always seek Security Council authorization?). To a point, NATO was muddling through.

But as NATO muddled through the various policy issues, its thoughts and actions produced new meaning within the Alliance. This was liberal NATO, the benevolent alliance. It did not happen by accident in a type of uncontrolled action-reaction chain, as the muddling-through perspective suggests. The NATO allies had in fact willingly urged the development at the very outset of Europe's transformation. Liberal values had prevailed in the Cold War, and such values, being universal, cross boundaries. In the new Europe, the institutional home of liberal cooperation might therefore naturally be an institution that cut across the old East–West frontier, and this is what NATO urged in June 1990: It wanted the Conference on Security and Cooperation in Europe (CSCE) to be strengthened and become a home for truly collective cooperation.[3] And so it happened. In November 1990 the CSCE Paris Charter, signed by thirty-four countries, including most European countries and also the Soviet Union and the United States and Canada, espoused human rights, democracy, and the rule of law as "the bedrock on which we will seek to construct the new Europe."[4] The CSCE was thus called on to help manage the new Europe, and in December 1994 its members decided to upgrade the conference to an organization—the OSCE, or Organization for Security and Co-operation in Europe.

This development was in NATO's interest because the CSCE/OSCE would reflect the values espoused by NATO and for which it had fought the Cold War, and it could become the vehicle for implanting the values in the soil of the former adversaries. Two debates soon opened, however. One concerned questions of institutional primacy within Europe, and it involved—and involves—France (the Europeanist), Britain (the Atlanticist), Germany (the fence-sitter), and the United States (NATO's patron). This debate on NATO–EU relations is important but not as important as the other debate on the principles of order, which concerns the delicate balance among sovereignty, intervention, and self-determination. It is in the latter context that we see the contours of a new liberal order in which Western powers were in alignment on the big issues.

The Western allies singled themselves out by propelling a new approach to the liberal principles celebrated in the Charter of Paris. The culmination came during the Kosovo crisis of 1998 and with the Kosovo war of 1999 (March–June). As Serb security forces clamped down on Albanians in Kosovo, killing scores of them and driving many thousand into refugee camps in neighboring countries, the United Nations condemned the situation but did not authorize armed intervention. NATO acted nonetheless. In October 1998 NATO made clear its determination to act even if the United Nations hesitated by issuing a so-called Activation Order (ACTORD) on October 12, 1998, ordering military forces to prepare for air strikes within ninety-six hours. An "October agreement" with Serbia entered the next day called off the intervention but led only to suspension of the ACTORD. As peace talks through February and March broke down and the situation on the ground deteriorated, NATO unleashed its air power on March 24, 1999 (Operation Allied Force).

This was a benevolent alliance in action. It acted without explicit U.N. Security Council authorization and in opposition to Russia and China. It acted on behalf of liberal principles of order that were universally valid—and therefore of global concern to countries such as Russia and China as well as others—and it acted where its interests were strong. It acted to restore order, but an order it had mostly defined. And it acted with military force, using its combination of national force structures and collective command-and-control systems to intimidate, exhaust, and bend the Serb adversary. What were these liberal principles that held the Alliance together and that justified a war on Serbia—the rogue regime par excellence in 1999?

First of all, and in respect to the aforementioned balance among sovereignty, intervention, and self-determination, the allies were in agreement that the international order based on sovereignty should evolve to give more emphasis to humanitarian standards of good governance. Outside powers such as Russia and China were camped on traditional interpretations of sovereignty, which in their view precluded any humanitarian intervention at all. This was not the view of the Western powers who gathered the warring parties (Serbs and Kosovars) for peace talks at a chateau in Rambouillet, France, February 6–23—and, following an interlude, March 15–18, 1999, to negotiate on terms largely defined by themselves, the Western powers. True to form, the peace talks were shaped by a degree of transatlantic jealousy, but the key matter concerned the substance of these terms:[5] The allies sought to promote liberal change but also to prevent relations to Russia and China from deteriorating dangerously.

The balancing act in Kosovo was this. On the one hand, the agreed-to position was that Serbia had lost its right to full sovereignty because it had violated a minority group within its territory. International supervision was a necessary component, therefore, in the creation of local autonomy for the Kosovo Albanians (Kosovars), and the Western powers were setting the terms for this supervision. On the other hand, they did not want to unnecessarily violate Serb sovereignty and certainly not to the point where the Kosovars were granted the right to self-determination. In respect to the international *acquis* on self-determination, the allies were conservative: Only colonies could succeed from tutelage and gain sovereignty; for everyone else the only option on the table was enhanced local autonomy, which in this case meant Kosovo autonomy within Serbia.[6]

The Atlantic Alliance managed the balancing act quite well. China, whose embassy in Belgrade was hit by three NATO missiles on May 7, 1999, strongly condemned the attack and the violation of its sovereignty, but a wider crisis was avoided.[7] Russia, a traditional ally of Serbia, was involved in the peace negotiations running in parallel to the intervention and its strong-arm tactic of preempting NATO's peacekeeping force (KFOR) in mid-June with a surprise deployment to Pristina airport of some of its forces in Bosnia was managed diplomatically and widely seen as ineffective and contrary to Russian interests. The United Nations, which had been sidelined (given Russian and Chinese objections), was brought back in from the cold by NATO. The U.N. Secretary General Kofi Annan was always inclined to support NATO's intervention because he feared a repeat of the Bosnian tragedy where diplomatic deadlock let civil war run apace. Back in 1993, when he was U.N. undersecretary general for peacekeeping operations, Annan saw an "imperative to explore new avenues of cooperation with regional organizations such as NATO."[8] As secretary general, Annan coordinated policy on Kosovo with NATO, meeting with NATO leaders in Rome in June 1998 and again in Brussels, in NATO headquarters, in January 1999. Emphasizing the presence of "horror" in Kosovo, Annan in January 1999 asked "that we all—*particularly those with the capacity to act*—recall the lessons of Bosnia."[9] In the end, NATO did act.

NATO suspended its air strikes on June 9, 1999, and the next day the U.N. Security Council adopted a road map for Kosovo security and stability—Resolution 1244. Did it tip the scales back in favor of the United Nations? Resolution 1244 singled out the U.N. secretary general as the one who should appoint a special representative for Kosovo and establish an international civil presence to provide for an interim administration (which became the U.N. Interim Administration Mission in Kosovo, UNMIK).[10] There was no direct mention of NATO in the resolution, as notes Lawrence Kaplan, and putting the United Nations in the driver's seat, making NATO an auxiliary organization, was controversial in some quarters, with Richard Holbrooke, the architect of the Bosnian peace accord, being the most vocal opponent.[11] All this makes NATO seem secondary. In addition, the Rambouillet talks were coordinated by the so-called Contact Group—a club of great powers including Russia—rather than the North Atlantic Council, and the peace plan that ended up as Resolution 1244 was the product of a G8 (Group of Eight) effort, the G8 being a club of industrialized nations including Japan and also Russia. Still, the core membership of both these alternate groups was Atlantic. It may not have been the North Atlantic Council that was the lieu of decision making, but the steering wheel was in the hands of Western allies. Moreover, the United Nations was allowed to take the driver's seat because NATO agreed it was appropriate. It was expedient to turn things back to the United Nations, and NATO never sought a rupture with the world body. What it clearly had sought was a confirmed status as a preeminent political force and security provider.

SIDETRACKING THE UNITED NATIONS

Kofi Annan's predecessor as U.N. secretary general, Boutros Boutros-Ghali, was on the face of it an ideal agent of U.N.–NATO cooperation. An international lawyer by training, he saw liberal ideals and the role of democracy as fundamental to peace and justice, as did NATO. His first publication "focused on the role of regional organizations in the pursuit of peace in the international system," and his view of international law and the U.N. Charter was to move beyond customs and purposefully adapt to new conditions.[12] He knew how to put ideas into practice, having been part of the Egyptian team negotiating the Camp David peace accord with Israel in the late 1970s. Later, as secretary general, and in response to a tasking by the Security Council, he wrote the June 1992 *Agenda for Peace* that called for a more active United Nations in crisis management and a subcontracting policy by which the United Nations could draw on member states' assigned military forces.[13]

There was a catch, though, and it derailed U.N.–NATO relations and ruined Boutros-Ghali's international leadership prospects: While members would do the hard work, the U.N. secretary general would be in command. Boutros-Ghali lost this fight with NATO, had to relinquish his control of the Bosnian operation in 1995, and then lost his bid for reelection as secretary general. In the process, NATO became a security agent working on behalf of the United

Nations but outside most of the usual constraints. NATO may have foreseen U.N. primacy of sorts in 1949, but by 1992–1993 that had been a long time ago.

NATO's enduring view of the world is found in its treaty. It supports the U.N. Charter (preamble); establishes NATO as a self-defense organization in accordance with the U.N. Charter's Article 51, whose armed response to an attack will "immediately be reported to the Security Council" and will cease once the Security Council "has taken the measures necessary to restore and maintain international peace and security" (Article 5); and it finally explicitly refers to the Security Council's "primary responsibility" for peace and security (Article 7). However, NATO does not define itself as a "regional security arrangement" under the U.N. Charter's Article 53, Chapter VIII, which would have been logical from the perspective of the U.N. Charter but not from the vantage point of 1949 when the allies refused to grant the Soviet Union political influence in NATO affairs.[14] Nor does NATO fully trust the Security Council to provide for peace and security: If it did, the treaty and its call for an "individual and collective capacity to resist armed attack" (Article 3) would not be justified.[15] It may appear an ambiguous policy, which it is in respect to the United Nations, but it springs from an unambiguous ambition: to remain politically autonomous in critical questions of war and peace.

The United Nations initially faltered in its effort to define itself as the center of the new world order that was put on the agenda following Iraq's August 1990 invasion of Kuwait and the Gulf War in early 1991. This war was uncontroversial in the sense that it was a classic case of self-defense, with Kuwait responding to the Iraqi invasion of August 1990 in collective defense and with the aid of a large U.S.–led coalition. In two respects it was not, however.

The war was not fought by the U.N. book if read literally. The United Nations can mandate the use of force to restore peace and security (U.N. Charter Chapter VII, Article 42), but the use of force must happen via national forces made "available" to the Security Council in special written agreements (Article 43) and with "strategic direction" coming into the hands of a U.N. Military Staff Committee (Article 47). None of this took place in the Gulf War. The United Nations authorized the war but made no reference to these articles. The lead could thus fall into the hands of the United States, which set up the coalition that fought the war and which remained in command throughout. Motivated by realpolitik and the limits to its influence, the United Nations adopted a light approach to its own charter. Boutros-Ghali's desire to promote subcontracting as a model was an effort to reverse this situation, but that came later.

In the Gulf, the United Nations also hesitated to draw the implications of the plight of the Kurd and Shiite groups that were prosecuted subsequent to the Gulf War and thus needed outside protection. The United Nations at first reacted strongly to the humanitarian situation by invoking its original resolution authorizing the war (Resolution 678) and adopting a new Resolution (688 of April 5, 1991) to "condemn" Iraq's behavior and "insist" on humanitarian access to the beleaguered people. However, then nothing happened—the humanitarian crisis continued, and the United Nations did not go into action. Resolution 688 did not foresee any action because it made no reference the charter's punitive Chapter VII. It criticized but did not deter. A vacuum had opened, and the leading Western powers—the United States, Britain, and France—stepped in to fill it. They decided to set up "no-fly zones" in Iraq's north and south (Operation Provide Comfort), and they enforced them with their national air forces.

Where the United States earlier had taken the lead in enforcing U.N. resolutions, the three Western powers now took the lead in enforcing the liberal values inherent also in the U.N. Charter. They had no explicit Security Council authorization to do so, and, knowing they would not obtain it, they did not ask. They hesitated because Iraq's sovereignty was uncontested, even in the Gulf War settlement, and because the breach of sovereignty would set a precedent: "All states, it was argued [in the U.N.], had reason to fear the effect of that precedent."[16] The Western powers thus left Saddam Hussein's regime in place but nonetheless intervened and bent Iraq's sovereignty. This was new: The Western powers wanted to do right and follow international law but were also willing to seek justice, and justice now meant conditional sovereignty even in cases not sanctioned by the Security Council. In time, it led to an enhanced emphasis on liberal principles of good governance and a step-by-step reform of international law and practice, and it was not the United Nations that was in the lead.

The United Nations did try to move into the lead, but Bosnia wrecked the attempt. As we saw earlier, U.N. Secretary General Boutros Boutros-Ghali and his 1992 *Agenda for Peace* sought to have the United Nations subcontract security work to regional organizations such as NATO. At first, through 1992 when the U.N. Protection Force (UNPROFOR) was set up, NATO hesitated to respond and get involved. NATO did not want to find itself defined as a U.N. "regional security arrangement"—which it had avoided in 1949 but which the

U.N. secretary general now pushed for. Therefore, as UNPROFOR was set up in February 1992 and reinforced in its mandate in August 1992, NATO watched from the sidelines and let the EU, along with the OSCE, seek a diplomatic solution. But, as the Bosnian house caught on fire for good, NATO got drawn into the game.

A diplomatic drama opened. NATO had the means to act, but the allies were divided, with the United States seeking a bombing campaign that European allies along with Canada opposed on the grounds that it would endanger their UNPROFOR troops (the United States did not contribute to UNPROFOR). Boutros-Ghali vented his fury with Western states that had the means to act but did not.[17] Inevitably, the UNPROFOR command-and-control chain got bungled. It was already a complicated affair: NATO air forces were from 1993 (Operation Deny Flight) designated as backup forces to UNPROFOR peacekeepers that had a particular responsibility to protect a number of designated safe havens. In line with the subcontracting idea, the U.N. representative Yasushi Akashi and NATO's allied commander General Joulwan shared command of NATO's air forces in a dual-key arrangement. Though NATO acted tough in February 1994 and shot down four Serb planes violating the no-fly zones, the command arrangement was overall an ineffective affair that nourished conflicting ambitions. NATO concluded that it needed greater autonomy, and its secretary general, Willy Claes, emerged as a strong advocate of a rupture with the U.N. model of subcontracting.[18] Boutros-Ghali regretted this view, holding Claes's predecessor Manfred Woerner in higher esteem, and countered by treating NATO de facto as a U.N. subcontractor.[19] In May 1995 he centralized the dual-key system by removing the authority of the UNPROFOR commander to request air strikes and placed it in his own hands—in New York.

Kofi Annan, who was responsible for U.N. peacekeeping operations, played a key role over the summer of 1995 in bringing about change. Serb attacks on the Srebrenica safe haven and Sarajevo, with the first involving an outright massacre of the civilian population, drove Annan to rework the dual-key command system and enable decisive action by NATO, with Boutros-Ghali agreeing to this new arrangement only on NATO's explicit recognition of the dual-key arrangement and thus confirmation that authority ultimately remained vested in him.[20] NATO granted the recognition and then launched a determined air campaign (Operation Deliberate Force) that drove the Serbs

to the negotiation table in Dayton, Ohio. With peace in place, UNPROFOR
ceased to exist, and a new NATO-led force took over (an Implementation Force
[IFOR] that in a year's time transformed into a Stabilization Force [SFOR]).
Thus began a new era of "robust" peacekeeping—and NATO was in the lead.
The force (IFOR/SFOR) was mandated by the United Nations, but it operated
"under the authority and subject to the direction and political control of the
North Atlantic Council and through the NATO chain of command," as stated
in the Dayton peace agreement of 1995. In short, the mission depended on
NATO.[21]

This leads to some general observations. Above all, there were always formidable obstacles to a U.N. challenge to NATO—to the prospect of pulling
NATO in as a regional security arrangement under the charter. Three NATO
allies are permanent members of the U.N. Security Council and thus in an
ideal position to arrest radical change. This helps explain why the United Nations in the context of the 1991 Gulf War failed to challenge the principle of
U.S. as opposed to U.N. command and control. It also helps explain why the
subsequent U.N. effort to have nations step up to the plate of peacekeeping
referred to subcontracting and the spirit of Article 43 but without directly
mentioning it. Finally, it helps explain why the United Nations, when authorizing the passage from UNPROFOR to IFOR in December 1995, simply acted
with reference to Chapter VII in its charter and disregarded Chapter VIII.[22] In
some ways, the United Nations "made things easy for NATO."[23]

Another observation concerns NATO's willingness to change. It is possible to look back at the Balkan civil wars and other crises, the steam the
liberal vision was gaining in the international community writ large,[24] and
the attempt made by Boutros-Ghali to spur global change, and to conclude
that NATO did not do enough.[25] NATO remained focused on territorial defense and considered out-of-area missions only on a strict case-by-case basis,
which went a long way to preserve NATO's Cold War procedures, doctrines,
and decision-making norms. However, this critique is made with the benefit of hindsight and downplays the important point, which is this: NATO
and the United Nations were not only in the business of solving problems in
failed states; they were also engaged in a struggle to define a political order.
Had they been mere problem solvers, they would easily have recognized that
cooperation on the ground made sense. NATO shared the liberal vision that
was in vogue but also wanted to preserve its own privileged position, which
was a realist ambition par excellence. The U.N. Secretariat learned through

the 1990s that it was not in a position to challenge NATO. By 1999, its secretary general implicitly endorsed NATO's humanitarian war in Kosovo even as the U.N. Security Council refused to authorize it, the U.N. role in running Kosovo subsequently was made possible by NATO, and NATO continued to provide for the region's security outside any reference to the issue of "regional security arrangements."

Adam Roberts observed in 1993 that "Humanitarian war is an oxymoron which may yet become a reality."[26] It was an apt depiction of the mood of the times but not of NATO. There was no oxymoron for NATO because it embodied a match between the *progressive* liberal vision and a *conservative* view of power, and humanitarian war became NATO's reality: wars intended to *advance* the liberal vision and *cement* the Western alliance's political leadership.

WHO'S THE FAIREST LIBERAL OF THEM ALL?

There are distinct views regarding the Franco–American rivalry that marked the 1990s and that pulled the EU and NATO into its orbit. Through this decade some observers saw the end of alliance.[27] Others saw a traditional diplomatic struggle to refashion common institutions that remained just that: common.[28] Hindsight is advantageous when sorting out this debate. The skeptics rightly emphasize the weight of the United States and its ability to make NATO prevail by virtue of its diplomatic and military clout, especially in light of France's early ambition to favor the EU, which partly involved NATO's precursor, the WEU (Western European Union). This French effort failed.[29] It turns out that NATO's success was not merely a case of U.S. arm-twisting; The wider European preference for a transatlantic security guarantee proved both durable and strong. What mattered was the ability to define a European option that somehow built on instead of rejected this transatlantic foundation. The option at first worked at odds with NATO and failed; it then moved inside NATO, only to move back outside at the turn of the decade, though this time in an alleged complementary version, which is the Common Security and Defense Policy (CSDP—formerly ESDP) of the EU.[30] The saga continues, therefore, but by 2001 NATO's preeminence was secure. The ongoing NATO–EU debate concerned the organization of complementary options within the transatlantic framework.

The critical case to consider is the ESDP, which emerged in the run-up to the Kosovo war, in late 1998, when President Chirac of France and Britain's newly elected Prime Minister Blair agreed to a meeting of minds. Their

December 1998 communiqué stated that "the European Union needs to be in a position to play its full role on the international stage" and that "this includes the responsibility of the European Council to decide on the progressive framing of a common defence policy in the framework of CFSP."[31] The meeting took most allies by surprise, partly because Franco–British differences on this issue were long-standing, partly because the consensus following the Bosnian Dayton peace accord in 1995 was that the European option was best located inside NATO. By a fit of Franco–British engineering, it now moved back out. The other EU members, and Germany in particular, sought to catch up with the initiative, and, prompted by the heat of the Kosovo war, the outcome became a whole new framework, the EU's European Security and Defense Policy (ESDP), adopted in June 1999. It was an important dynamic that NATO recognized at its fiftieth anniversary summit in April 1999.[32]

The ESDP reflected French ambitions in important ways. France had always worked for a more pluralist alliance.[33] France initially opposed NATO's enlargement in favor of NATO–Russian dialogue and at one point suggested that the (coming) air war over Kosovo should be controlled by the Contact Group (including Russia) rather than the North Atlantic Council.[34] Bringing Russia into NATO diplomacy, referring matters to the Security Council where France has a permanent seat, and enhancing the role of the EU, which naturally has no American participation, all contribute to enlarging the scope for French diplomacy.

President Mitterrand—France's socialist head of state for fourteen years (1981–1995)—was a Gaullist convert who pushed this policy to a point where it hurt French interests. Though caught off guard by the liberal ideas sweeping the continent, he helped bring the EU into being, which was a considerable diplomatic achievement. It renewed the Franco–German commitment to European cooperation and sealed the debate on German power, which now had the potential to unhinge the European balance. However, Mitterrand lost his balance in respect to continuity and change. He did entertain the idea of a possible *right* to intervene (*droit d'ingérence*)—and did sanction the no-fly zones to protect the Kurds and Shias in Iraq—but did not follow his activist health minister and founder of Doctors Without Borders Bernard Kouchner who sought a *duty* to intervene, and Mitterrand ended up supporting existing states and regimes, be it in the Soviet Union, Eastern Europe, Iraq, or Yugoslavia. Mitterrand's conservatism became acute in defense affairs. He refused to consider military reform at home (that is, professionalization and capacity building for expeditionary warfare) or the reform of French NATO policy (notably regarding France's withdrawal from the integrated command).

The French footprint on U.N. affairs was likewise notable. When Boutros Boutros-Ghali in 1996 stood for reelection as U.N. secretary general, the United States opposed the candidacy, but France favored it. The cards seemed to be stacked in France's favor as the United States lost the first vote in the Security Council fourteen to one, having to cast a veto to prevent Boutros-Ghali's reelection. Madeleine Albright, the U.S. ambassador to the United Nations, sought to promote an alternative candidate, but at this point of the affair diplomacy had lost its flexibility. It was a test case of the reach of U.S. power. In ensuing straw polls the United States consistently vetoed Boutros-Ghali, whom France favored, while France consistently vetoed Kofi Annan, whom the United States promoted as the alternative candidate. Boutros-Ghali writes that "French–US antagonism was at a peak." Madeleine Albright claims to have foreseen the confrontation but must have been surprised by its intensity, nonetheless.[35] U.S. power prevailed but with concessions to France: While the United States could see its candidate move to the U.N. helm, France gained a greater French language footprint inside the United Nations—and it offered Boutros-Ghali a retreat as head of La Francophonie, a French-language league based in Paris.[36]

Yet insistence on pluralism and French interests is not the end of the story on Franco–American relations within a NATO context. France could be pragmatic, first of all. Elected in mid-1995, President Chirac used the organization of a French–British–Dutch reaction force to make a push for change that undermined the caution of both Boutros-Ghali and President Clinton. NATO's Operation Deliberate Force followed.[37] Chirac also recognized the paucity of the EU alternative to NATO and agreed to Europeanization *within* NATO.[38] He then sought to bring France back into NATO's integrated military command, a move that would break with three decades of Gaullist orthodoxy. The fact that this move failed and helped bring the Socialist opposition into government should not obscure that Chirac's policy was markedly more realistic, seeking to break orthodoxy to gain influence.[39]

Pragmatism as a French policy principle was put to the test in 1998–1999— and it prevailed. For a while it looked as if it would turn out differently. The new socialist government cohabiting with right-wing President Chirac had put the reform of French NATO policy in cold storage and generally opposed U.S. policy for a more global and activist NATO. Hubert Védrine, the foreign minister of Jospin's cabinet from 1997 on, argued in late 1998 that NATO actions must be placed under the authority of the Security Council.[40] However, soon thereafter Védrine, Jospin, Chirac, and the rest of the French leadership ignored this policy and supported NATO's war in Kosovo. The specter of ethnic cleansing trumped principle and motivated France to support NATO once again. In the course of the air war, in mid-May, President Chirac went to Moscow for a summit and naturally looked to express understanding for the Russian position, which was to oppose NATO's war. Still, Chirac explained his support for the war with reference to liberal principles—Serbia's pursuit of "ethnic cleansing" affronted all those who "base their policies on the principles of democracy and the respect for human rights."[41] This liberal standard and the pragmatics of upholding it aligned fully with the policies of the key allies, which amounted to a kind of Western-led humanitarian internationalism under Western leadership, and it put Chirac's France squarely in the Western camp.[42]

Kosovo did not efface the principles that caused France to search for international reform. Madeleine Albright would later write—in a preface to a book by Hubert Védrine—that going to war outside a U.N. mandate "ran contrary to some of Védrine's strongest instincts," which concerned the role of the United Nations and the need for balanced leadership within the Alliance:[43]

> So why did Védrine support intervention in Kosovo? The answer, quite simply, is that it was the right thing to do. Neither the United States, nor France, nor our other allies were prepared to stand by and watch as thousands of innocent people were killed or made homeless in the heart of Europe. NATO's action served the cause of justice, saved many lives, and presaged an end to Milošević's disastrous political reign.

Hubert Védrine is not particularly happy, looking back. In his view, NATO had become a "mini–United Nations" under U.S. control and with popular European support made possible by the widespread "belief in the West's democratization mission."[44] The rancor aside, Védrine really depicts NATO as the kind of benevolent alliance emphasized in this book. It was one France contributed to, though it was sometimes reluctant to do so. The Franco–American rivalry, much noted, is of a kind that is endemic to alliances: a rivalry for influence within a common framework of security. It may break an alliance, but it did not break NATO. Instead, it pushed NATO in new directions and imbued it with new political meaning suited to a new geopolitical environment.

CONCLUSION: A BENEVOLENT ALLIANCE

NATO traversed the 1990s with no shortage of rival designs for Europe's order. Still, the events and negotiations that brought NATO past the Kosovo intervention in 1999 and into a new millennium infused the Alliance with new meaning, the essence of which is captured by the ideal-type of "benevolent alliance." NATO thought of itself as both—benevolent and an alliance—and this combination accounts for NATO's durability beyond the Cold War.

It was benevolent because, at the end of the day, the allies agreed that liberalism was the right thing to pursue. The allies could not agree to an alliance based on "interests"—be they oil, territory, or simply power in the abstract; it had to be an alliance of ideas and principles that made for a progressive order. This was the spirit of the founding treaty, it informed the allied efforts through the Cold War, and it was now renewed for a post–Cold War world. The allies wanted a greater good for a greater number but outside major conflagrations. The new and potentially revolutionary policy was that rogue states that systematically and brutally transgressed liberal boundaries should not be able to hide behind the curtain of sovereignty but be punished and eventually brought into the liberal fold.

NATO remained an alliance, though. Its liberal vision targeted external and illiberal states. It conferred superiority to NATO. As such, it involved an unmistakable measure of power politics. It was also applied in the traditional manner of power politics where vital national interests prevail over humanitarian interests. The sum of NATO allies' national interests was an agreement that NATO should seek to govern security relations with U.N. support but not at the world body's mercy. Russia and China sought to deny the Alliance legitimacy, but Kofi Annan sought to be pragmatic and establish a working relationship that accommodated the Alliance. NATO invited the compromise as well, seeking a short "humanitarian war" as well as a quick handover to the United Nations. NATO leaders could point to international consensus, but at bottom they labored in favor of a particular relationship they had sought to promote since the Gulf War of 1991. Coalitions of the willing were not submitted to the United Nations, nor was NATO, whose Balkan activities otherwise invited its express agreement to become a formal regional organization under the U.N. Charter's Chapter VIII. Putting operational keys in U.N. hands proved bad enough from NATO's perspective, and by the time of the Dayton agreement and the deployment of a Bosnian peacekeeping force, NATO was alone in the driver's seat. IFOR and SFOR were NATO operations; NATO was not a Chapter VIII organization; and the one who had pushed for such reform, Boutros Boutros-Ghali, was pushed off center stage.

National interests could be debilitating for collective action, naturally. In Bosnia, James Gow observed the "triumph of the lack of will."[45] Beyond Bosnia, the experience was similar. Operation Restore Hope in Somalia turned sour when the humanitarian mission became bloody. National interests were not there to motivate a continued engagement. They were not there at all when Rwanda in 1994 descended into hell on earth and up to one million people got brutally slaughtered in a civil war. National interests also account for the pluralism that France has sought and that has fed the NATO–EU and NATO–UN rivalry. These regional conflicts and disputes over institutional architecture remind us that national interests are paramount and that NATO in important ways is a geopolitical amalgamation of national experiences and outlook.

Yet this plurality should be placed in context. NATO is more than the sum of its parts. Its collective sense of purpose is visible in the liberal purpose infused into post–Cold War operations and in the reservations the allies shared vis-à-vis the United Nations. The allies continued to experience principled disagreements because of the underlying logic of geopolitical diversity, but they also articulated a Western point of view that was distinctively liberal and that they upheld in military operations as well as diplomatic negotiations. It was never a perfectly coherent West, but it was visible and important. By the turn of the decade, the Atlantic Alliance had thus become a benevolent alliance promoting progressive reform while cementing its leadership.

3 NATO AND AFGHANISTAN

AFGHANISTAN, ONCE A ROGUE REGIME led by the Taliban, was put on track for a new future in late 2001 following a brief war and a diplomatic conference to commence the rebuilding of the country. Discounting the large sums of development money the international community seemed willing to disburse, the effort of assisting the new government was meant to be fairly painless. Things turned out differently. In late 2011 Western forces had been in Afghanistan for a decade, and the stress and difficulties experienced by the Atlantic Alliance easily surpassed those of earlier allied experiences. This chapter provides an overview. It is designed to set up the analysis that follows and will therefore focus on NATO's involvement, how it happened, and how it divides into distinct phases. The chapter begins with a brief outline of the 2001 Bonn agreement and the Afghan government it gave birth to. It is, after all, this government that NATO is assisting. The chapter then moves on to three phases in NATO's involvement: how NATO got into Afghanistan and in the process defined a potentially very comprehensive role for itself that was unexpected but that flowed with the currents inherent in the benevolent alliance; how NATO was severely challenged once it fanned out into all of Afghanistan and yet managed to define a comprehensive response corresponding to the role it had set for itself; and how it has struggled to have this comprehensive response evolve and transition into a strategy for detachment. We begin in Bonn, Germany.

THE NEW AFGHANISTAN

The blueprint for a new Afghanistan emerged in Bonn, Germany, between November 27 and December 5, 2001, at a diplomatic conference held under

U.N. auspices. The Taliban regime, which the U.S.–led Operation Enduring Freedom had begun a war against on October 7, was coming apart. At the time of the opening of the conference, the Taliban forces had receded to their geographical center of gravity, Kandahar in southern Afghanistan, where they stood their ground until two days after the Bonn conference. With the fall of Kandahar and the Taliban defeat, the Afghan ground was seemingly cleared for the new government defined in Bonn.

Bonn was an appropriate town in which to negotiate Afghanistan's future. Western Germany's small-town capital through the Cold War, Bonn crystallized the intricate web of hostility, hope, anxiety, and suspicion that was the Cold War and that John le Carré captured in his 1968 novel, *A Small Town in Germany*.[1] Some thirty years later, Bonn became host to yet another intricate web, only this time it was Afghanistan's web of political, ethnic, and tribal intrigue. However, where John le Carré's improbable 1968 hero, Leo Harting, symbolically operated from the doldrums of the British embassy's cellar, the 2001 peace conference was lifted to the heights of the Petersberg Mountain across the Rhine and the fashionable Petersberg Hotel on top of it. The site portended a brighter future for Afghanistan, but the intricate and troubled relations that in a way had become the trademark of the town of Bonn remained.

The Bonn Agreement essentially provided a road map for rebuilding the Afghan state that should be understood literally: The focus was on state institutions, and the agreement foresaw a process through which they were to fall into place.[2] The key enabler in the realization of the blueprint was the type of grand assembly of community leaders known from Afghanistan's history, a *loya jirga*. According to the script agreed to in Bonn, *loya jirgas* would be the engine of the new Afghanistan.

The Bonn conference was de facto a first such *loya jirga*. The Bonn negotiations took place principally among Afghan parties and under the auspices of the U.N. special representative, Lakhdar Brahimi, an Algerian with extensive experience in the business of peace mediation and conflict resolution. Brahimi had made his first steps in this business in Lebanon, from 1989 to 1991, where he as an Arab League envoy successfully mediated an end to civil war; later in 1997 through 1999 and now as a U.N. envoy, he moved on to mediate—unsuccessfully, as it turned out—another peace in Afghanistan. Brahimi later led a U.N. review of peacekeeping operations before the terrorist attacks of September 2001, and the Afghan war once again directed his attention to Kabul—though via Bonn. At the Petersberg Hotel in Bonn external parties such as the United States and other countries were present but not allowed into the principal chamber of negotiation. The principal negotiators were Afghans, divided into four delegations representing the principal interests in the country, save for the Taliban who were still fighting at the time of the conference.[3] At this Bonn *loya jirga* the delegations agreed to establish an Interim Authority in lieu of a government and invest its leadership in Hamid Karzai, a Pashtun who had sought to rally Pashtuns against the Taliban in the midst of Operation Enduring Freedom in the fall of 2001. Annex IV of the Bonn Agreement appoints him as such and names a set of ministers to serve under him. Hamid Karzai was sworn in as interim head of state on December 22, 2001.

An "emergency" *loya jirga* (foreseen in the Bonn Agreement) in June 2002 led to establishment of a Transitional Authority, again headed by Karzai, and also of a Constitutional Committee. A third and this time "constitutional" *loya jirga* followed in December 2003 through January 2004 and resulted in the adoption of a new constitution for the Islamic Republic of Afghanistan. It also resulted in a road map for presidential and parliamentary elections. These were meant to take place simultaneously, but events caused them to take place about a year apart: Presidential elections were held on October 9, 2004, with Hamid Karzai winning; and parliamentary as well as provincial elections followed on September 18, 2005.

With these events, the state institutions were established, and the Bonn process came to an end. The new Afghanistan is a centralized state in which the president has considerable power: The president appoints ministers (who must be approved by parliament, though) and presides over the government; local assemblies of the principal territorial units (provinces, of which there are thirty-four) are elected but merely consultative; and power is delegated from the president downward, which is to say the president appoints provincial governors in the spirit of "centralism."[4] Keeping in mind Afghanistan's intricate webs of friendship and hostility nourished by the approximately twenty-five years of war that preceded the Bonn Agreement, the Bonn delegations really argued that Afghanistan faced a choice between a strong center and continued war—and thus they opted for a strong center.

The international community was involved from the outset in the new Afghanistan. The Bonn Agreement invites this involvement along the lines of security (Annex I), governance (Annex II), and development (Annex III). Annex I calls for an "international security force" to operate in "Kabul and its surrounding areas" in support of the Interim Authority. "Such a force could, as appropriate, be progressively expanded to other urban centres and other areas," the Annex continues, but the original U.N. mandate for the force, from December 20, 2001, limited the force to Kabul and the surrounding areas. Extension of the force—which in the meantime had come to be labeled the "international security assistance force" (ISAF)—thus required renewed international agreement.[5] Annex II invited the United Nations to assist in the implementation of the Bonn Agreement, and Annex III requested the United Nations and the international community writ large to assist in the country's development.

The international community responded in parts by organizing and deploying an ISAF force, which will be discussed shortly. It moreover organized an aid and development program. For the duration of the Bonn process, from January 2002 through December 2005, and as defined at a Tokyo donors' conference in January 2002, the program was organized thematically in five pillars and with a lead nation assigned to each pillar: The United States took the lead in rebuilding the Afghan National Army; German the lead in rebuilding the Afghan National Police; Italy in reconstructing a judicial system; Britain in setting up a counternarcotics program; and Japan in disarming, demobilizing, and reintegrating war lords' militias. In parallel, and beginning in March 2002, the U.N. assistance mission in Afghanistan (UNAMA) coordinated the work of multiple U.N. agencies in the country. In early 2006 it was time for change because the Bonn process had come to an end and the Afghan state had been stood up. The result was a new "Afghan Compact" that was de facto an equal partnership between Afghanistan and the international community.[6] It focused on three "critical and interdependent" pillars of security, governance, and development, and it was translated into an Afghanistan National Development Strategy (ANDS), an interim version of which was ready in 2006 but which was finalized in 2008.[7] Such was the theory of Afghan government and international assistance.

GETTING INVOLVED (SEPTEMBER 2001–DECEMBER 2005)

NATO became the official lead organization behind ISAF on August 11, 2003, slightly less than two years after the onset of U.S.-led operation Enduring Freedom. "A greater role for NATO simply makes sense," is how NATO's deputy Secretary General Alessandro Minuto Rizzo phrased it at the ISAF assumption of command ceremony in Kabul.[8] It made sense, he argued, because NATO had already been involved in supporting ISAF and because ISAF nations had primarily also been NATO members (ISAF lead nations had to this point been Britain, Turkey, and then Germany and the Netherlands in unison).[9] With this commonsense approach, NATO stepped out of the OEF shadows and into the Afghan spotlight, de facto acquiring a direct stake in the management of the Afghan conflict where it had previously been involved merely as background support.

NATO had invited this direct involvement in the immediate wake of the September 11, 2001, terrorist attacks with its unprecedented Article V declaration. The "appalling attacks perpetrated yesterday against the United States" were henceforth to be considered an attack against all allies, though only if the attack could be determined to have been directed from abroad.[10] Following visits to NATO by Deputy Secretary of State Richard Armitage and Deputy Secretary of Defense Paul Wolfowitz, on September 20 and 26, respectively, U.S. Ambassador at Large and Department of State Coordinator for Counterterrorism Frank Taylor briefed the North Atlantic Council (NAC) on October 2 and cleared away any lingering doubts. "The facts are clear and compelling. The information presented points conclusively to an Al-Qaida role in the 11 September attacks," concluded NATO Secretary General Robertson, and Article V was therefore conclusively activated.[11] Within two days, NATO was ready to define the first and concrete measures with which it would participate in the new fight against terror. Six of these measures were individual in nature, two were collective:[12]

- Enhanced intelligence sharing and cooperation;
- Assistance to allies and other states under terrorist threat as a result of this campaign;
- Increased security for U.S. and allied facilities on national territory;
- Backfill of selected assets in NATO's area of responsibility to support operations against terrorism;
- Provision of blanket overflight clearances for U.S. and allied aircraft in operations against terrorism;
- Provision of port and airfield access to U.S. and allied forces in operations against terrorism;
- Readiness to deploy NATO's Standing Naval Forces to the Eastern Mediterranean;
- Readiness to deploy the NATO Airborne Early Warning and Control Force System (AWACS).

Within about five days of this declaration, NATO deployed its Standing Naval Forces Mediterranean (STANAVFORMED) and also its AWACS aircraft: It was the first time that NATO had deployed assets in support of an Article V operation.

The war in Afghanistan had begun in the meantime, however, on October 7, and it was undertaken not by NATO but the broad coalition organized by the United States under the banner of Operation Enduring Freedom (OEF). NATO was supporting OEF but not participating in it. NATO's decision-making body, the NAC, had no say in the campaign, nor had NATO's military command. The shots were called by the White House and the Pentagon's Central Command (CENTCOM) headquartered in Florida. An OEF village of containers housing coalition partners grew up next to CENTCOM, and many partners were also NATO allies, but this was not NATO. NATO's AWACS did not head toward Afghanistan: They deployed to the United States (Operation Eagle Assist) to backfill for U.S. assets heading to Afghanistan (Operation Enduring Freedom).[13]

In early December 2001 NATO's foreign ministers meeting in the NAC could therefore only make small moves. One was to continue NATO's support for OEF: "We will continue our support to the United States for the US-led operation against these terrorists until it has reached its objectives." Another was to begin work on adapting NATO to the new world of counterterrorism and operations beyond the Euro-Atlantic area, which implied work on "capacities" and "partnerships" and an ambition to define a reform program for the November 2002 Prague summit.[14] "All dressed up and nowhere to go" may have been an appropriate view of NATO at this time, but NATO was about to discover that it did have places to go; the question was whether NATO was truly ready.

If we were to identify a single point in time to illustrate NATO's growing involvement in ISAF, it would be April 16, 2003, when NATO decided to become ISAF lead by August. NATO's decision involved three measures that all related to the challenge of providing a more solid and continuous command and control structure for ISAF:[15]

- The deployment of a composite headquarter to Kabul;
- The appointment of local commanders by NATO's top military commander, SACEUR;
- And the exercise of strategic coordination, command, and control by SACEUR and his headquarters, SHAPE (Supreme Headquarters Allied Powers Europe).

To these three points, emphasized by NATO's spokesman, we might add a fourth, namely political direction by the NAC, which is the political authority guiding SACEUR. The NAC thus also became a key interlocutor of the U.N. Security Council, which had mandated ISAF and would continue to do so.

ISAF at this point comprised around 4,000 troops and was confined to the city of Kabul, and it would therefore not be outrageous to downplay the significance of the April 2003 decision. "The keyword here is continuity," as NATO's spokesman emphasized, with reference to ISAF's mandate and operations. Yet the decision portended great change.

This was so first of all because NATO became the architect of operations whose design had begun outside the Alliance. ISAF was not defined by NATO, nor did it fully control its implementation by virtue of the continuous operational involvement of non-NATO nations in ISAF, the political involvement of the mandating body, the UNSC, and the continuous political leadership granted to the Afghan government that ISAF was mandated to "assist." Diego Ruiz Palmer of NATO's International Staff saw in this a significant new way to conceive of NATO's relationship to the wider international community: "as an architect in the planning, organisation, generation and sustainment of complex multinational peace-support operations, combining forces from NATO, Partner and other non-NATO nations."[16] The decision to take on this role as "architect" of complex peace-support operations dated back to reactions to the terrorist attacks of 2001 and more specifically to the desire to maintain NATO as a relevant security organization in spite of its sidelining by the U.S.–led OEF in Afghanistan. NATO laid the groundwork for its architect role in the course of 2002 first in October when it agreed to assist ISAF and then when it agreed at the Prague summit on November 21 to its own "transformation."[17] ISAF assistance followed a German–Dutch request for assistance in setting up their ISAF lead, which resulted in NATO's principled decision to help ISAF nations generate forces, share intelligence, and coordinate airlift. In reality, therefore, there had only been two ISAF rotations without NATO assistance (Britain and Turkey, December 2001 through January 2003), and from ISAF assistance to ISAF lead there was only a comparatively small step.

This leads us to the second major change portended by the April 2003 decision: that of NATO's involvement in Afghanistan's nationwide struggle to rescue the political regime that had been erected by the 2001 Bonn agreement and subsequently challenged by a growing insurgency. In the spring of 2003 it may have been hard to predict the scale and severity of the insurgency that would erupt in subsequent years, but it was not hard to predict that ISAF would expand beyond Kabul. The Bonn agreement foresaw this possibility, as we have seen. Moreover, NATO had not done its own mission analysis between the April decision and the August takeover. It had simply taken over the old ISAF mission and put NATO labels on it. It had been convenient to do so because time had been short, decision makers feared to an extent the kind of demands a new mission analysis might come up with, and NATO's operational command (Joint Forces Command in Brunssum, or JFCBS) had never been put to a real test.[18] It was clear that NATO would have to do its own mission analysis at some point, therefore, and more than likely that this requirement would merge into the debate on ISAF expansion.

Around one month after taking the ISAF lead, on September 18, 2003, the NAC tasked NATO's military authorities to assess options for ISAF expansion beyond Kabul and required their receipt within eight days. The buck therefore soon came back to the NAC, which needed to decide on the big issues: Who would actually do the hard work of expansion, and according to what game plan? For a brief moment it seemed that NATO would get bogged down in this issue. The problem was that NATO had taken the ISAF lead at a time when ISAF by its U.N. mandate was limited to Kabul: NATO's operational plan (OPLAN)—SACEUR's plan of August 11, 2003 (OPLAN 10149)—was therefore a Kabul-only plan. Changing this plan could be done in one of two ways, either ad hoc in the shape of revised OPLANs or more thoroughly by devising first a type of strategic concept for the entire operation, which would have to come out of the NAC. In NATO such strategic concepts are known as "concepts of operations" or CONOPS.

When Germany on October 6 announced its readiness to take over the American Provincial Reconstruction Team (PRT) in Kunduz in northern Afghanistan it provided an answer to the "who, where, and when" question of ISAF expansion but not to the question of "how" NATO should plan for it. The end result reached in mid-October was a split decision: NATO agreed to revise its OPLAN to allow for the German expansion of ISAF and simultaneously begin work on new a CONOPS for the entire mission. The ISAF expansion train could thus start running. NATO asked the United Nations to amend ISAF's mandate accordingly, which it did one week later on October 13, 2003, with Security Council Resolution (UNSCR) 1510. NATO de facto assumed control of the German PRT on December 31, 2003. The North Atlantic Council meanwhile, in mid-December, received a drafted CONOPS from NATO military authorities, and it approved it early in January 2004. With the Kunduz PRT as well as its CONOPS in place, NATO could turn in earnest to the task laid out in UNSCR 1510: to plan its support to Afghanistan's government "in the maintenance of security in areas of Afghanistan outside of Kabul and its environs."[19]

The German force deployed north of Kabul was small, around 250 troops, but it was bigger than the previous American Kunduz contingent and moreover a first of several expansive steps. The provision of political guidance—a CONOPS—was difficult, as the December 2003 NAC conclusions illustrate. It was clear that NATO would work primarily with PRTs but in a "progressive" deployment that on the one hand would be "limited in size and duration" but whose "scope" on the other hand would have to be addressed continuously.[20] The virtue of the PRTs was their character as forward-operating bases housing both military troops and civilians and therefore offering an integrated package of security, development, and reconstruction for a given province. The basic idea was to spread a network of PRTs across Afghanistan with the help of lead nations. The CONOPS of early 2004 thus had PRTs as its centerpiece and foresaw a counterclockwise PRT-led expansion that began in the north and proceeded to the west before encountering the south and east (Table 3.1).

Two comments should be attached to Table 3.1. First, the table may convey the impression that expansion happened smoothly and according to plan. It did not. It was a slow and tortuous process marked by political debate and division that illustrated how difficult the realization of the "architect" ambition could be. NATO decided in December 2003 that it wanted to expand ISAF but only stepped up to the plate six months later in Istanbul. The decision to move west was made in February 2005 when planning for a move south and east also began, but it was only in December 2005 that NATO approved the revised operational plan for these two latter moves. In practice, ISAF expansion involved a difficult debate on burden sharing, alliance commitment, and adaptation to a new kind of war for which the Alliance was unprepared.

Second, ISAF is more than just a headquarters in Kabul and then PRTs; it has a significant military infrastructure to support the PRTs—the so-called leading edge. This infrastructure consists notably of (brigade) task forces assigned to support PRTs in the local area and since 2006 of (divisional) regional command headquarters to run regional efforts. Outside of Kabul there were originally four regional headquarters located in Mazar-e-Sharif (RC/N), Herat (RC/W), Kandahar (RC/S), and Bagram (RC/E); these multiplied into

Table 3.1. ISAF's counterclockwise expansion.

Region	Date	PRTs	Location and framework nation
North (ISAF Regional Command North, RC/N)	First PRT decided in December 2003; an additional four in June 2004 at Istanbul summit	5	Kunduz (Germany), Kunduz province Mazar-e-Sharif (Sweden), Balkh province Feyzabad (Germany), Badakhshan province Pol-e-Khomri (Hungary), Baghlan province Meymaneh (Norway), Faryab province
West (RC/W)	Decision in February 2005; PRTs set up in May–September	4	Herat (Italy), Herat province Farah (United States), Farah province Qala-e-Naw (Spain), Badghis province Chaghcharan (Lithuania), Ghowr province
South (RC/S)	Decision in December 2005; ISAF command July 2006	4	Kandahar (Canada), Kandahar province Lashkar-Gah (United Kingdom), Helmand province Tarin Kowt (The Netherlands), Uruzgan province Qalat (United States), Zabul province
East (RC/E)	Decision in December 2005; ISAF command October 2006	13	Bamyan (New Zealand), Bamyan province Bagram (United States), Parwan province Nurestan (United States), Nurestan province Panjshir (United States), Panjshir province Gardez (United States), Paktika province Ghazni (United States), Ghazni province Khowst (United States), Khowst province Sharan (United States), Paktika province Jalalabad (United States), Nangarhar province Asadabad (United States), Kunar province Mihtarlam (United States), Laghman province Wardak (Turkey), Wardak province Logar (Czech Republic), Logar province

SOURCE: Retrieved in January 2010 from www.nato.int/isaf/topics/prt/index.html. This table provides an overview of the original ISAF PRT and regional command structure, which has since been revised.

five when in the summer of 2010 RC/S divided into two new commands (with a reduced RC/S still headquartered in Kandahar and a new southwestern command, RC/SW, based in neighboring Helmand and headquartered northwest of the capital of Laskar Gah in Camp Leatherneck, lying adjacent to British Camp Bastion).

Each regional command involves a number of task forces to support the PRT and conduct operations, and each task force has its own elaborate infrastructure of bases and support elements. These structures continually evolve: They have been built up and are now being drawn down. Consider the regional command south, RC/S:

- The original RC/S was headquartered at the airfield outside Kandahar and covered six provinces but with only four PRTs. The United States ran one PRT (in Zabul province), but RC/S command rotated among the three NATO allies who had delivered the other three PRTs: Britain, Canada, and the Netherlands (Helmand, Kandahar, and Ouruzgan, respectively). Each PRT had a task force assigned to it, and each task force was multinational. U.S.–led Task Force Stryker comprised notably Romania; British-led Task Force Helmand, Denmark and Estonia; Dutch-led Task Force Oruzgan, Australia; and Canadian-led Task Force Kandahar, a number of U.S. battalions.[21] Each of these came under RC/S command but had its proper force headquarters and base infrastructure.

- The British-led Helmand Task Force, for instance, was finally headquartered in Helmand's capital of Lashkar Gah following initial deployments to Kandahar air base and then Camp Bastion. The British-led PRT that the task force supported was also located in Lashkar Gah, with Camp Bastion serving as a logistical hub for all British operations. The prize of Helmand has been the green zone, the cultivated land stretching north of Gereskh, the other main urban center in Helmand, and along the Helmand River. To control it or to stem the insurgency in favor of the PRT activities, the task force relied on a Main Operating Base (MOB), Camp Price, right outside of Gereskh, and a number of Forward Operating Bases (FOBs) such as Sandford, Keenan, Armadillo (later Budwan), and Musa Qala inside the green zone.

- In 2010 RC/S was split into two (RC/S and RC/SW) given the need for ISAF to align with Afghan force structures in light of the new emphasis on transitioning to Afghan lead; the decisions of Canada and the Netherlands to drawn down their contributions; and the U.S. decision to surge in Afghanistan, which has notably brought an influx of U.S. troops to the old RC/S.

- RC/S continued to be headquartered in Kandahar but with responsibility for four instead of six provinces (Kandahar, Oruzgan, Zabul, and Dai Kundi) under British lead. The British-led Helmand Task Force has remained in Helmand, however, and has now come under U.S. command in RC/SW, based at Camp Leatherneck next to Camp Bastion. The U.S. Task Force Leatherneck operates in Helmand's north and south, leaving central Helmand to the British-led task force, and has pushed from Helmand into neighboring Nimroz where ISAF previously had no presence. In northern Helmand a British Battle Group along with the Musa Qala FOB has come under Task Force Leatherneck, but British and American forces tend to operate in parallel and under overall U.S. regional command.

One could probably regress indefinitely into the details of ISAF command but, the basic points are that ISAF covered most provinces; that provinces were engaged via PRTs; that PRTs were supported by task forces gathered in regional commands; and that the task forces varied significantly in size and composition, with the heavy and large forces engaged in RC/S and RC/E. Finally, it was all run from ISAF (corps) headquarters in Kabul, where the central regional command or RC/C (divisional) headquarters also was. This was the ISAF footprint—and in early 2012 it still was, though the structure will evolve significantly as transition progresses.

It would be appropriate to define December 2005 as the end point of NATO's entry phase. NATO had taken the ISAF lead in Kabul and extended it to the north and the west and in December 2005 finalized its revised Operational Plan for moving south and east. NATO knew that conditions would be more difficult in these other two regions, but it remained within the planning framework of security assistance. "Provincial Reconstruction Teams are at the leading edge of NATO's effort, supported by military forces capable of addressing security threats where ISAF operates, and reinforced by flexible, robust reserve forces, whenever the situation on the ground so requires," is how NATO chose to describe its approach.[22] The need for "robust" forces would soon become apparent.

STUNNED BUT NOT SHATTERED (JANUARY 2006–APRIL 2008)

In going into Afghanistan's south and east, NATO exposed itself to the full thrust of the insurgency it is still seeking to come to terms with. NATO officials and decision makers foresaw that things could get heated but not the extent of it. By late 2006 the insurgency had erupted, and NATO looked stunned and shaken through 2007. Yet by April 2008 it managed to put together a response—a comprehensive strategy—that at least represented the Alliance's ability to recover and articulate a response to a situation that could have proven mortal for the Alliance.

The expansion to the south and east was gradual and involved in parts the deployment of new troops from Europe and Canada, largely to the southern command RC/S, and the inclusion of American OEF troops under the ISAF umbrella, largely in the eastern command RC/E run from the air base Bagram north of Kabul. This expansion to the south and east formally took place in July and October of 2006, which is to say that this is when ISAF's command began. As is practice, though, NATO forces began moving in quite soon after the approval of the revised operational plan in December 2005. In an anticipatory move, Canadian personnel had already deployed to Kandahar prior to this date, though the bulk of Canadian forces—from Kabul as well as Canada—moved in only during the spring of 2006. Britain deployed to the south in parallel, with British Special Forces (Royal Marines Commandos) moving to Helmand in mid-February to enable the buildup and with the British 16 Air Assault Brigade taking over the security of Helmand from American forces by May. The 16 Air Assault Brigade then became the nucleus of Task Force Helmand. By August, and thus once ISAF's command was in place, Dutch forces moved in to Oruzgan, north of Kandahar, to form Task Force Oruzgan. In short, the transition began in mid-2005, a full year before ISAF's formal command.

Table 3.2 illustrates the dramatic rise in allied casualties and how big an impact RC/S and RC/E had. OEF continued, but it is fair to view 2005 through 2006 as the decisive turning point in the OEF-ISAF balance: Beginning in 2006, the level of casualties was mainly an ISAF concern. OEF continued to have casualties that thus fell outside ISAF, and this distinction is not made in Table 3.2. With this caveat in mind, Table 3.2 illustrates the trend in violence and the stress to which NATO was submitted.

Table 3.2 also illustrates that the insurgency slowly began in 2002–2003 and that the U.S.–led OEF forces were submitted to the brunt of it because they dominated the eastern region up to 2006. ISAF forces were submitted to violence in 2005, particularly in RC/West where they suffered twenty-one fatalities. Still, the ISAF total for 2005 and 2006 contrast significantly: thirty in 2005 and 154 in 2006. From this point on, the upward trend continued,

Table 3.2. Allied casualties by year and region.

Region	2001	2002	2003	2004	2005	2006	2007	2008	2009	Total
North	1	0	**0**	**0**	5	**1**	8	5	12	32
West	0	0	0	**0**	21	**1**	8	20	31	81
South	3	9	6	13	32	**85**	107	144	175	574
East	0	5	26	26	60	57	62	85	120	441
Central	0	**15**	**8**	**10**	4	**10**	**13**	**19**	**21**	100
Total	4	29	40	49	122	154	198	273	359	1228

SOURCE: Compiled from data available at iCasualties, http://icasualties.org/OEF/ByProvince.aspx. Figures boldfaced in this table indicate ISAF command of the regions (North, West, South, and East). The Central region is Kabul, ISAF's original area of operation, which prior to 2006 was not a regional command but referred to as Multinational Brigade Kabul. The total figure in this table deviates slightly from the total figure provided by iCasualties, which is due to the omission here of fatalities whose location could not be attributed.

and it grew particularly worrisome in RC/S, which in some respect was the Alliance's main new challenge, with the United States continuing its efforts in RC/E while mostly changing hats from OEF to ISAF.

NATO's method for dealing with such an operation consists in part of Concepts of Operations (CONOPS) and Operational Plans (OPLAN). The CONOPS concern the political framework; the OPLAN the military campaign. There are many OPLANs for any given mission—moving from the strategic OPLAN of the SHAPE headquarters to the operational OPLAN (in Afghanistan's case written by the Joint Forces Command Brunssum, JFCBS) and then to the ISAF commander's plan made in Kabul, which again trickles down into operational plans for ISAF regional commands and individual military units. NATO can adjust these as the campaign evolves, and this will happen within a broader and phased view of the campaign that begins with assessment and preparation, followed by engagement and stabilization, and concluding with transition and withdrawal or redeployment (see Table 3.3).

NATO's Afghan difficulties have appeared mainly in the phase of stabilization, which has necessitated a clear conception of what "stabilization" is in the Afghan context and how NATO might achieve it. The challenge was on the agenda at the NATO summit in Riga, Latvia, in late November 2006, at which point NATO had completed its geographic expansion and now needed to confront the reality of the campaign. The response was timid, however, as NATO stuck to the Bonn provision that all ISAF was there to do was to support the Afghan authorities.[23]

Table 3.3. ISAF phases.

Phase	Focus	Timing*
1	Assessment and preparation	Initiated in September and completed by December 2003
2	Geographical expansion	Initiated in December 2003 and completed by October 2006
3	Stabilization	Ongoing
4	Transition to Afghan lead	In preparation since October 2009,** with first transfer of security leadership taking place in early 2011 and with full transfer of nationwide Afghan leadership completed by mid-2013
5	Redeployment	Completed by end of 2014

SOURCE: Compiled by author.

* There are overlaps between the phases, for instance between expansion and stabilization where stabilization began before expansion was completed, just as transition will take place in parallel to stabilization.

** NATO approved a Strategic Concept for this phase in October 2009.

The timidity of the Riga declaration turned out to be real and a sign of strategic and political hesitation on the Afghan issue. The summit was dominated by another issue that deflected attention—the issue of missile defense—which in and of itself is a noteworthy point: At a moment when its soldiers were severely stretched at the foot of the Hindu Kush, NATO became engulfed in a debate on Europe's nuclear architecture that recalled the days of the Cold War. To the extent that the allies did address Afghanistan, and they did, they grappled with two issues and provided no real solutions. One was how to pull together a greater civil–military effort to provide sustainable solutions to Afghanistan's problems; another was the question of burden sharing because, as always, burdens were not distributed evenly in the Alliance.

The elasticity and complexity of civil–military cooperation and of simultaneously providing for security, development, and governance help explain the timidity of NATO but also served as a convenient foil for inaction. NATO noted that Afghanistan now had its own national development plan that originated with the conclusion of the Bonn process and the renewed contract between Afghanistan and the international community—the Afghan Compact and the ANDS. NATO was thus guided by the principle of "local ownership," which put the onus on the Afghan government. If this government experienced problems of capacity or skill, it was also up to other organizations to step in and help it out: "NATO will play its full role, but cannot assume the entire burden."[24] As it turned out, the Afghan government lacked both capacity and skill, and thus emerged the Afghan Gordian knot of security, development, and governance.

NATO was at this point failing to comprehend, much less to address, the full implications of the Taliban insurgency. NATO, the key agent of security provision, needed to step in and devise a strategy that addressed the nature of the insurgency and devised ways and means for dealing with it. True, NATO was in a supporting role and not responsible for development and governance, but security was critical across the board, and NATO faced a determined and expanding adversary. This required a strategic approach that indicated in which ways security, development, and governance could be made to evolve simultaneously, and it required political leadership vis-à-vis other parties involved, from the insurgents to the Afghan government and U.N. agencies. The insurgency had very quickly in 2006 relegated "the Compact to the history books," as Ahmed Rashid writes,[25] and the question for NATO was what it could put in its place and hope to achieve.

General James Jones knew well the predicament of NATO because as SACEUR between January 2003 and December 2006, interacting with NATO political authorities and directing the military strategic work of the Alliance, he oversaw NATO's descent into the desolation of Afghan insurgent warfare. Jones, who would later become President Obama's assistant for National Security Affairs, issued a dire warning in early 2008: "Make no mistake, the international community is not winning in Afghanistan." This warning was issued as part of a larger offensive in which think tanks and prominent experts highlighted NATO and the wider international community's predicament and offered advice for improvement.[26] The common thread running through these reports and assessments was the observation that the international community lacked a strategy and that any strategy needed to be comprehensive and to address all three lines of operations—security, development, and governance. The advice dovetailed with NATO thinking on the issue, which goes back to the civil–military debate of the Riga summit and even further back, as we shall see, but now the call for moving beyond thinking to action was gaining steam. Remarkably, action followed. The NATO heads of state and government who met in Bucharest in early April 2008 agreed to a blueprint for comprehensive action that in fact would become NATO's recipe for relief.

NATO's Bucharest summit was a comprehensive summit resulting in a comprehensive strategy for Afghanistan. It was a comprehensive summit because NATO had invited the full ISAF family, including ISAF partners such as the United Nations, the World Bank, the World Food Program, and the High Representative for External Relations of the EU Council, as well as the president of the European Commission and other organizations and countries. And the outcome was comprehensive because NATO took the lead in writing an ISAF Strategic Vision that was issued at the summit and in parallel wrote its own and confidential plan for realizing this vision, the Comprehensive Strategic Political-Military Plan (CSPMP), which remains in place to this day. The summit communiqué dealt briefly with Afghanistan and mostly referred to the parallel Strategic Vision, but it did take note of the ISAF mission as NATO's "top priority" and highlighted the need for long-term and comprehensive engagement.[27] The Strategic Vision set out four themes that crystallized the lessons learned from the past six to seven years of conflict:[28]

- The commitment to Afghan must be long term and include the provision of adequate troop levels and flexible and unconstrained command options.
- Afghan leadership must be encouraged and implemented, and ISAF should therefore increasingly focus on the training and mentoring of Afghan national security forces.
- Coordination within the international community must be enhanced, which concerns notably NATO and U.N. agencies. PRTs are maintained as a key enabler of reconstruction and development.
- The regional dimension must be addressed more systemically, which notably means Pakistan and the Afghanistan–Pakistan border area. No other country is mentioned by name in the Vision.

The underlying and more substantial CSPMP fleshed out these themes and defined them as a range of "desirable outcomes" (seventeen in all). It did not matter if the outcome related to security, development, or governance—NATO dealt with it, comprehensively. In matters of security NATO foresaw its own lead, while in matters of development and governance it wanted merely to act in support of other organizations. It was thus comprehensive and cooperative.

At this point NATO had come some way toward defining its leadership role, therefore. It had continued the emphasis on the simultaneous development along all three lines of operation and now tied them together in a

comprehensive strategy. It had thus not substituted itself for the Afghan government or the United Nations, but it had taken the lead in devising the strategy, which was in fact anchored inside NATO where the short and generic
vision was published as ISAF's. It prodded the ensemble of the extended ISAF
family to do more—the Karzai government in Kabul, the United Nations, and
individual partners in addition to its own allies—as it developed this strategic
approach.

This we knew by April 2008, then: NATO had managed to respond to the
insurgency that exploded in its hands once it completed its counterclockwise
expansion to all of Afghanistan; the response consisted of a comprehensive
strategy that placed NATO within a network of security, governance, and development actors; and NATO had taken the lead, using its ISAF hat, in organizing the comprehensive strategy.

COPING AND PREPARING FOR TRANSITION
(MAY 2008–MARCH 2012)

NATO now had a blueprint for addressing how it would contribute to the successful implementation of security, development, and governance. The risks
remained obvious: Coordination and implementation needed to happen; the
Taliban remained an impressive adversary; and NATO still needed to devise
a security strategy to simultaneously counter the Taliban and underpin the
comprehensive strategy. If progress could be made, however, NATO could begin to move its mission from phase 3 (stabilization) to phase 4 (transition) and
let the Afghan government take control to a much greater extent. The CSPMP
is classified, but sources reveal that it contains seventeen desired outcomes
(revised upward from an original fifteen outcomes) that run across the three
lines of operations (security, development, and governance), and for each desired outcome the CSPMP specifies a number of intermediate goals and notably also NATO's role. The CSPMP is a framework document because NATO is
supposed to prioritize issues within it that will then drive the overall process.
It is in addition evolutionary because this prioritization will change with time.
The CSPMP is regularly reviewed in the so-called Policy Coordination Group
under NATO's Division of Operations and fully updated once a year, with the
first update taking place in late 2008 and another following in late 2009. Three
issues stand out.

One is the question of regional diplomacy and the role of Afghanistan's
neighbors, notably Pakistan, in stabilizing or destabilizing Afghanistan's gov-

ernment. Pakistan generally climbed up on the Western agenda in 2008, and we saw how regional diplomacy and Pakistan were emphasized in the Bucharest Strategic Vision. It is also through 2008 that U.S. drone attacks in the Pakistan border area picked up, though the increase was to become much more pronounced from 2009 on, and it was in July 2008 that President Bush secretly approved of new and permissive rules for Special Forces ground assaults inside Pakistan.[29] NATO's role in this regional affair is limited because ISAF is strictly confined to the Afghan territory, but NATO still seeks to promote greater use of the ISAF–Afghan–Pakistan Tripartite Commission, including a Joint Intelligence Operations Center, that has lingered on to address border cooperation, just as NATO has sought to establish the presence of a Pakistani military representation in Kabul and has promoted a range of political and military contacts, ranging from visits to Pakistan by NATO's secretary general and to NATO by Pakistan's president, to visits by Pakistani military officers to NATO's school in Oberammergau, Germany, in what NATO hopes will be Pakistan's inclusion in its Partnership Cooperation Menu (PCM).

Another issue has been the presidential elections in Afghanistan scheduled for August 2009. Being focused on security, NATO prepared for the elections with enhanced security measures, including additional force contributions announced at the sixtieth anniversary summit in Strasbourg-Kehl in April 2009. NATO managed to muster an additional 5,000 troops for the elections, although this was counting some troops already in Afghanistan whose deployment was prolonged. Around 3,000 of the new troops were scheduled to go home following the elections, but at this point the Obama strategy review was reaching its conclusion and pushed the allies to revise plans and contribute more forces.[30]

A third and final key CSPMP issue was the training of Afghan national security forces—armed forces as well as police—that was a sine qua non of moving to stage 4 and Afghan leadership. Hitherto most training had fallen under the U.S. lead in the framework of its coalition operation (OEF), where its Combined Security Transitions Command-Afghanistan (CSTC-A) ran the training of the armed forces as well as most police forces (the EU had from the summer of 2007 taken over the police academy training in a European Union Police, or EUPOL, mission). However, the OEF label did not square with an enhanced NATO effort in this area, and the debate therefore turned on whether the training effort could be moved under NATO's command. This was another issue solved at the Strasbourg–Kehl summit, which saw agreement to the establishment of a NATO Training Mission–Afghanistan (NTM-A).[31] The NTM-A took over from CSTC-A on November 21, 2009. These decisions—concerning Pakistan, Afghan elections, and the training mission—were outcomes of the evolving CSPMP, which is not to say that the initiatives would not have happened in its absence but that the CSPMP facilitated strategic thinking and initiatives in distinct but related domains.

NATO's work happened in parallel to U.S. strategy, which, like NATO's, continued to evolve. The year 2008 was the final stretch of the Bush presidency, and President Bush had put in motion a number of strategy reviews that came to a conclusion in December 2008 and fed into the reviews that had begun on the election (in November 2008) of President Barack Obama. President Obama announced a first set of reforms, as it turned out, in March 2009, a few days prior to NATO's sixtieth anniversary summit. Unsurprisingly, the allies endorsed the American strategy that consisted of a triple surge in terms of troops (21,000 troops), civilian personnel, and regional diplomatic effort. President Obama decided on a second strategic review in the fall of 2009, which this time resulted in an additional troop surge of 30,000 U.S. soldiers, greater efforts to protect major population centers (a more stringent population-centric counterinsurgency strategy), as well as greater efforts to eliminate the hard core of insurgent and terrorist leaders (a renewed counterterrorist strategy) and a determination to draw down troop levels beginning in the summer of 2011. President Obama outlined the results of this second review on December 1, 2009; NATO and its ISAF partners welcomed it three days later following the regular NAC meeting and also added more forces to the mission.[32] The NATO increase did not match the American increase in terms of numbers—NATO in December 2009 committed an additional 7,000 troops, although only around 5,500 of these were new troops; the other 1,500 were already in Afghanistan but hitherto temporarily—but it did signal NATO's commitment to the new strategy.[33]

NATO's CSPMP was broad and flexible enough to dovetail with the Obama administration's refinements of U.S. strategy, and the summit and regular NAC declarations of support did therefore not require strategic reassessments on behalf of NATO. NATO needed to provide troops and funds, but this was not new. The cause for strategic concern came from Afghanistan, where the presidential elections of August 2009 turned into a farce of fraud and incompetence. The incumbent Hamid Karzai won the elections but with such a degree of taint that the result was canceled by the electoral commission and a runoff prepared between Karzai and his principal opponent, Abdullah Abdullah. When the latter withdrew his candidacy on November 1, and the electoral commission then canceled the runoff elections, the incumbent Karzai was able to continue but as a besmirched and weakened president. Parliament, sensing an opportunity to leave its mark within Afghanistan's centralized political system, in two turns refused to approve of Hamid Karzai's list of ministerial appointees.

ISAF's commander (COMISAF) had in some ways foreseen this situation insofar as he had placed a corrupt government on par with the insurgency in his August 2009 assessment of the security situation. General Stanley McChrystal, who took over command from General McKiernan as COMISAF in June 2009, wrote over the summer a "Commander's Initial Assessment" that was finalized in August and, while confidential, leaked and appeared in the *Washington Post*. COMISAF wrote that ISAF faced two threats and that a failure to address both of them would lead to mission failure:[34]

- "The first threat is the existence of organized and determined insurgent groups working to expel international forces, separate the Afghan people from GIRoA [the government of the Islamic Republic of Afghanistan], and gain control of the population.
- The second threat, of a very different kind, is the crisis of popular confidence that springs from the weakness of GIRoA institutions, the unpunished abuse of power by corrupt officials and power-brokers, a widespread sense of political disenfranchisement, and a longstanding lack of economic opportunity."

COMISAF General McChrystal in consequence wanted to pursue a stringent policy of counterinsurgency (COIN) that would protect the population from both insurgents and corrupt government officials, a demanding task requiring considerable troop numbers, development skills, and patience. It was the formulation of force requests subsequent to the Commander's Initial Assessment that set off Obama's second review process in the fall of 2009, even though the assessment flowed from the principles inherent in Obama's first review of March 2009. McChrystal wore two hats: He was the commander of U.S. forces in Afghanistan and thus part of the U.S. chain of command, and he was the ISAF commander that forms part of NATO's chain of command. His political masters were the U.S. government and NATO as a whole.

This put NATO in a delicate position through 2009, although the dual command structure goes back further than that and has been a consistent problem for the allies. We shall delve more into this issue later, but 2009 was different because NATO now had a comprehensive "strategy"—the CSPMP—that the local commander could refer to, and he did. This was a first such connection because prior commanders simply did not have a NATO strategy to refer to: They had political guidance and concepts for the operation but nothing resembling a theater strategy. General McChrystal astutely made reference to the CSPMP as well as Obama's review in the opening paragraph of his document. It begins as follows: "The stakes in Afghanistan are high. NATO's Comprehensive Strategic Political-Military Plan and President Obama's strategy to disrupt, dismantle, and eventually defeat Al Qaeda and prevent their return to Afghanistan have laid out a clear path of what we must do."

This "clear path" is then what he set out to, if not define, then operationalize in the guise of a COIN campaign plan. It was astute, of course, because he argued that the military strategy followed logically from the political strategies. Political objections to his preferred course of action would thus be both difficult to raise and controversial. President Obama's second review in the fall of 2009 was certainly controversial, and we shall have more to say about this process later. NATO did not enter into such controversy. In fact, NATO approved of McChystral's assessment before the U.S. government did, albeit it happened at the level of defense ministers—at an informal meeting in Bratislava, Slovakia, on October 23, 2009. U.S. Secretary of Defense Robert Gates understandably adopted a low profile at the meeting—"I am here mainly in listening mode," he said—but NATO Secretary General Anders Fogh Rasmussen noted "broad support from all ministers of this overall counterinsurgency approach."[35]

This was a remarkable turn of events because NATO had hitherto been split on the nature of the mission and had resisted COIN terminology. Now, at Bratislava, the Alliance endorsed COMISAF's COIN strategy and, as a logical follow-on, tasked NATO military authorities to work out a NATO COIN doctrine because NATO, in Afghanistan for five years, simply did not have one. Moreover, the Alliance endorsed a strategic concept for moving to Phase 4 planning (see Table 3.3, p. 55). With the military strategy shaping up, NATO needed then to work at the political strategy—or on specific initiatives that would move the political process in Afghanistan forward within the CSPMP framework. The allies have sought to do so along three tracks.

The first has been to work out a plan for the transfer of lead to Afghan authorities and forces. The transfer will happen gradually and province by province, based on certain conditions that must be in place first—which is to say a competent local police force, the presence of durable government service, and signs of reconciliation with Taliban. At a large international conference held in Kabul July 20–21, 2010—the first such conference to be held inside Afghanistan—President Karzai outlined his vision that this transfer should be completed in full by the year 2014. It was the culmination of a process that began in the fall of 2009 and in preparation of a London conference on January 28, 2010, which was focused on "phase 4"—transition, that is.[36] NATO endorsed the Kabul transition road map at an informal foreign ministers' meeting in Estonia on April 22–23, 2010, and put it in motion at their Lisbon summit on November 16, 2010.[37] President Obama renewed his commitment to the surge in a review of December 2010 but also stuck to the logic of drawing it down sooner rather than later, and in June 2011 he thus announced that 10,000 U.S. troops would come home by December 2011 and that the remaining surge force of 23,000 would come home by September 2012.[38] In the meantime, on March 11, 2011, a first tranche of Afghan areas was set to transition to Afghan security leadership, with a second tranche announced on November 27, 2011. With these two tranches, approximately half the Afghan population moved under Afghan security leadership. An Istanbul summit on November 2, 2011, was engineered by Turkey in an effort to bring notably both Pakistan and India on board for regional stability, and the mere fact that these countries could agree to meet was seen as promising. This summit was followed in early December 2011 by a grand rerun of the 2001 Bonn summit, though the "Bonn 2.0" label was not endearing to diplomats who struggled to make a new contribution to the peace effort. They made little progress on the issue of Afghan reconciliation but some headway on defining the long-term, post-2014 international engagement in Afghanistan. Political reactions to the casualties of war made the work of diplomats all the harder. Pakistan refused to go to "Bonn 2.0" because of a border incident in late November 2011 in which ISAF forces by mistake killed twenty-six Pakistani troops; and President Karzai, reacting to US troops' accidental burning of several copies of the Koran in February 2012 and also a massacre on civilians inflicted by a disturbed U.S. sergeant in March 2012, has asked ISAF not only to end night raids by special forces—a long-standing demand of his—but to pull back troops to major bases by 2013 in what would significantly advance security transition to Afghan leadership.[39]

The one sure thing about these diplomatic ups and downs is their testimony to the reality of an end game with high stakes. The international community and NATO seek to frame their efforts to put phase 4 on track with continuing international summits: in 2010 in London, Tallinn, Kabul, Lisbon, and Washington, in 2011 in Kabul, Washington, Istanbul, and Bonn, in 2012 in Chicago, and more are to come. In this fight for transition, the underlying tension remains: The combined desire to do things right (condition-based) and to see the end of the engagement (calendar-based).

The other and closely related track is reconciliation and reintegration, by which is meant an Afghan government–insurgent dialogue to engineer peace. The idea is to incite the insurgency's political core to negotiate with the Kabul regime (reconciliation) and to lure low-rank insurgents—the accidental guerrillas—away from the fight with prospects of improved living conditions (reintegration). The Afghan lead has been visible in this respect, notably with the Karzai-led Consultative Peace *Jirga* of June 2–4, 2010, which took place in Kabul and gathered 1,600 Afghan delegates. NATO's official policy is to insist that all this must be Afghan-led and done in respect of the constitution that came out of the Bonn process, but NATO then distinguishes between reintegration, which it will support, and reconciliation, to which it is ready to contribute. Put differently, NATO as a whole is more engaged in drawing in the accidental guerrilla than in making deals with the hard core of the insurgency.[40] Individual allies contribute to the reconciliation effort, but it is all very discrete and also very difficult, as we can gather from the murder of Burhanuddin Rabbani, president of the Peace Council, on September 20, 2011, and the subtle change in the December 2011 Bonn conference's agenda from reconciliation to long-term international strategy.[41] Shortly into 2012, the Taliban announced the opening of a political office in Qatar, which raised hopes for a negotiated settlement, but both the Afghan and Pakistan governments jostle to gain influence on what is mostly a U.S.–Taliban dialogue. The widespread perception is that the Taliban must struggle to cohere on the issue of whether to talk and on what terms, but so, for sure, must the international community.

Finally, the allies have with limited success sought various ways to prop up the Karzai regime and President Karzai himself following the disastrous presidential elections of the fall of 2009. In the spring of 2010, relations were at a low as President Obama revoked an invitation for a Karzai state visit to Washington; as President Karzai responded by inviting the bête noire of the

West, Iran's president Ahmadinejad, to Kabul for an official visit; and as President Obama then jetted into Kabul for a quick nighttime rendezvous with President Karzai to remind him of his duties to clean up government, with President Karzai subsequently accusing the West of instigating the election fraud. Ahmed Rashid, who has good access to President Karzai, has argued that President Obama's alleged decision to seek confrontation rather than partnership equals a missed opportunity.[42] In contrast, almost every diplomat interviewed for this book has emphasized how difficult President Karzai is to work with, confirming his reputation as a difficult and temperamental figure, with some diplomats going so far as to pinpoint President Karzai as Afghanistan's key obstacle to progress. At issue is the question of whether Karzai is a nuisance with whom we to an extent can do business or rather an integral and critical part of a predatory (corrupt) Afghan state that feeds the insurgency and which therefore must be fundamentally changed. Western allies waver, hoping to build up the administrative capacity of the state—notably at the local level where so-called Village Stability Programs (VSP) sometimes combined with local security in the shape of Afghan Local Police (ALP) have gained traction since 2009–2010—while fencing them off from central spoilers. Not coincidentally, President Karzai has only with reluctance endorsed the VSP and ALP. The international hope seems to be that they can draw in enough stakeholders in villages and provinces and build up enough ministerial capacity in Kabul to leave behind a system that will be imperfect but functioning. If President Karzai can deliver on reconciliation with the Taliban, so much the better, the idea seems to be, but in the meantime ISAF must anchor Afghan stability and phase 4 in other parts of Afghanistan's complex physical and social geography.

CONCLUSION

This chapter has reviewed the trajectory of NATO's Afghan mission to identify the mission's key phases and the nature of turning points. The chapter has not sought to scrutinize and much less criticize NATO decisions but to present a certain pattern based on the facts of the matter—the nature of the new Afghan political system, the Bonn agreement, NATO decisions as communicated by the Alliance, and NATO actions in Afghanistan. The pattern consists of three phases and a troubled ambition to become the architect of complex multinational peacekeeping operations. Table 3.4 presents an overview. Summit agendas are rich, of course, and the overview is therefore to be treated as

Table 3.4. NATO summits and Afghanistan.

Phase	Key events	Summits
Going in, December 2001–December 2005	ISAF support and then lead Control of Kabul Expansion to North and West	Rome, May 28, 2002: No Afghan agenda/focus on Russia Prague, November 21–22, 2002: Transformation of purpose, partners, and means Istanbul, June 28-29, 2004: Support for northern ISAF expansion Brussels, February 22, 2005: Affirmation of ISAF expansion to West and beyond
Stunned, January 2006–April 2008	Expansion to South and East Insurgency and war Review of mission and adoption of comprehensive strategy	Riga, November 28–29, 2006: Burden sharing and measures to counter-insurgency, comprehensive strategy in principle Bucharest, April 2–4, 2008: ISAF Strategic Vision and comprehensive strategy (CSPMP)
Coping, May 2008–December 2010	Implementation of strategy Adaptation to COIN and new U.S. strategy Review of NATO's purpose	Strasbourg-Kehl, April 3-4, 2009: Maintain Vision, enhance Afghan lead Lisbon, November 18, 2010: Endorsement of *Inteqal* plan for transition to Afghan lead and new NATO Strategic Concept Chicago, May 20–21, 2012: Irreversibility of transition, financing of ANSF, partnership beyond 2014

SOURCE: Compiled by author.

such, a mere overview. Moreover, as this chapter has highlighted, several key NATO decisions were made during foreign ministers' NAC meetings that do not qualify as summits but that can be of great consequence nonetheless.

The first phase runs from the Bonn agreement in late 2001 to mid- to late 2005, and this is where NATO defines its ambition to become relevant to the new world of globalized terror threats and new security missions and where it gradually becomes the ISAF lead organization. It would be both possible and reasonable to distinguish between the two periods of 2001–2003 and 2003–2005, between the sidelining of NATO in favor of OEF and the inclusion of NATO into the Afghan game, because the politics of this shift in 2003 matter enormously to the way in which NATO's mission was defined. However, and while the politics of this shift will be analyzed in detail in the next chapter, it is ultimately of greater consequence that NATO continuously saw an opportunity to continue its Balkan experience—to come into a troubled country and support if not a peace agreement between belligerents then the peace offered by the central government. The modalities differed, to be sure, and NATO knew this well, but the framework of thinking and planning was one of peace-support operations. The extension of ISAF into Afghanistan's north and west embedded rather than challenged this framework, not least because it happened in parallel to the realization of the Bonn blueprint for a new Afghan government.

It follows that the second phase is the period of NATO's rude awakening. Moving into Afghanistan's south and east, NATO encountered a stubborn, brutal, and growing insurgency for which it was unprepared. It was a kind of war. Counterinsurgency (COIN) is how most observers today label it, but NATO was not in the counterinsurgency business back then. It was simply not an articulated task for the Alliance. NATO was stretched militarily and threatened politically at this point—in 2006–2007—insofar as it was failing in its mission. NATO did manage to step back from the brink of the abyss, as we saw, and the outcome of this reversal was the adoption of the comprehensive strategic political–military plan—the CSPMP—in Bucharest in April 2008.

The third phase runs from the Bucharest summit in 2008 to the present and is defined by NATO's effort to maintain its strategic focus while adapting to the evolving war and dysfunctional government in Afghanistan. NATO has used the CSPMP as a framework within which it can prioritize certain issues, such as regional diplomacy and training of Afghan forces as designated engines in the larger effort. We know from the record of events that NATO has found this strategic approach appropriate and valuable: It has been maintained while the United States, quite clearly the number-one international player in Afghanistan, has undertaken a number of important reviews of its Afghan policy; it has incorporated the ISAF commander's request for a COIN approach that previously was anathema to NATO; and it sustains NATO's engagement in the string of international conferences that began in London in January 2010 and that open the end game of transition to Afghan lead and thus, by 2014, the "redeployment" of NATO and ISAF forces. What this implies for NATO's sense of rationale and political purpose is what this book is about to account for in earnest.

ANALYSIS

Section II

4 ORIGINAL SINS

A Benevolent Alliance Goes to War, 2001–2005

THERE WAS NEVER ANY DOUBT that the Atlantic Alliance felt a need to confront and defeat the perpetrators of the September 2001 terrorist attacks. The NATO allies, more than any other group of countries, saw themselves as threatened by Al Qaeda's strike against liberal institutions and values and offered that same month to go to Afghanistan. The outrage was global, but the West moved into action—except that the West no longer easily identified with NATO. The U.S.–led OEF coalition looked Western, but it was not NATO.

NATO's march to Kabul, Kunduz, Herat, and Kandahar was a double attempt to confront and defeat terrorists, though by way of assisting a new Afghan government, on the one hand, and to salvage the transatlantic alliance on the other. All allies knew well that ISAF in Afghanistan was different from past missions—the history, geography, culture, and politics of the country made it obvious. They knew that they had to bring new equipment and skills to the table, and they knew that this truly out-of-area operation would stretch their lines of command and supply. Yet they opted to resurrect the Alliance they knew in terms of politics, purpose, and organization. NATO's recent history provided a track record of success and comfort and made the choice obvious. But the choice was made also in opposition to the coalition design of the Bush administration and the War on Terror, which saddled the United States with war in Iraq. As in the past, NATO encountered obstacles; only this time the obstacle had moved inside the Alliance. The war for the West had begun.

The Atlantic Alliance's move into Afghanistan built on both political imagination and blindness. The imagination—perhaps indeed vision—was that the Alliance remained the good and benevolent option in a complex and sometimes wicked world. NATO's principles and values were uncontested, and the Alliance operated as a collective whole along multilateral and deliberative tracks. NATO was the wise and balanced option, in other words. The blindness refers to the real state of political affairs because this image of NATO was ephemeral. It was what the U.S. allies wanted, and the United States was willing to let them have it—in the shape of the ISAF mission—because it was useful, not because it was particularly reflective of political reality. The United States remained focused on Iraq, and those European allies who were in disagreement on the War on Terror, Iraq, and the U.S. operation in Afghanistan (Operation Enduring Freedom) fell back on what they could agree to—the benevolent alliance of the Balkans.

The combined effect of imagination and blindness was a benevolent alliance that did not function as such: It was certainly of a benevolent mind, but it did not act as an alliance. ISAF was a high-stakes bet that post–9/11 Afghanistan would allow for a smooth ISAF campaign. How the allies backed the Atlantic Alliance into this situation is laid out in this chapter. It contains four sections, of which two discard common explanations for NATO's ills and two pinpoint the original sins of the engagement. The first section assesses the immediate reactions to the September 11, 2001, attacks and the argument that the United States should have done more to work through the Alliance already at this point. The argument is off target, though not entirely. The real problem in the early phase lay in the "light footprint" for the Afghan engagement and notably the underlying lack of patience in regards to Afghan reconstruction. The second section assesses this footprint and its numerous sources. The third section turns to the Provincial Reconstruction Teams (PRTs) that became ISAF's "leading edge" and that have been criticized for being fragmented and inadequate for the task. This criticism is off target as well because there was considerable scope for learning from the OEF campaign that had invented the PRT concept and integrating the PRTs into a holistic campaign plan. This integration did not happen, though, which was another original sin. Section four investigates the politics behind it and exposes how allied fissions over the War on Terror allowed deep-seated national perspectives to mark Alliance policy. In failing to provide for a functioning operational policy, the allies invited the type of near philosophical discord that is a sure cause of Alliance misfortune.

Two perspectives developed in the wake of the 2001 terrorist attacks: that allied discord reflected the diminished value and relevance of the "liberal Western order" and that its "diplomatic mistakes, personality clashes, unfortunate timing, faulty analysis, and bad luck" may reflect poorly on some decision makers but not necessarily the fundamentals of the Alliance.[1] Events in Afghanistan did bring into question the fundamentals of the Alliance, and poor political management helps explain why.

INVOKING ARTICLE V: A MISSED OPPORTUNITY?

Much has been made of the fact that NATO invoked Article V on September 12 but then was marginalized by the Bush administration's Operation Enduring Freedom (OEF). NATO had put its most valuable commitment on the table only to find it ignored, presumably because the neoconservative streak in the Bush administration made for a knee-jerk reaction against NATO and in favor of informal coalitions. Though it contains a kernel of truth, the interpretation is exaggerated.

Rapid Reaction Innovation

NATO had never activated its precious mutual defense clause prior to September 12, 2001. There was thus no precedent to rely on. The procedure for invoking it did not attract much attention during the Cold War when the threat was abundantly clear. Nor had the procedure been on people's mind through the 1990s when non–Article V missions dominated and the treaty's security guarantee was a bit like nuclear weapons: nice to have but hardly relevant to ongoing security concerns.

The idea of invoking Article V came from inside the NATO headquarters in Brussels. Early reports indicated that it was Secretary of State Colin Powell who on the day of September 11 urged his allies to recognize the terrorist attacks as "a declaration of war against democracy"—and in NATO such a declaration of war is tantamount to an Article V declaration.[2] In fact, Powell was asked to authorize a draft statement that had been prepared inside NATO headquarters in the context of the first emergency meeting of NATO ambassadors, which took place in the secretary general's office following the evacuation of nonessential personnel. The source of the idea of invoking the article was the dean of the NATO ambassadors, Canadian David Wright, who— sources indicate—first brought up the idea in a phone conversation with U.S. Ambassador Nicholas Burns, then at the first emergency meeting held among the ambassadors at the secretary general's office.[3] A group of NATO officials, some of whom had overheard the exchange in the office, then drafted a statement for Secretary General Lord Robertson so that he could guide North

Atlantic Council deliberations. Lord Robertson approved of the draft and asked his U.S. deputy director, Damon Wilson, to gain his government's approval for the idea. Late that evening—in the late afternoon U.S. time—Ambassador Burns was in touch with National Security Advisor Rice and also the State Department and was told that the United States "would welcome the action."[4] At this point—"late at night on 11 September," recalls Ambassador Burns—the North Atlantic Council was ready to formally consider the activation of Article V.

There were two critical issues involved in the allied debate at this point—in the hours immediately following the attacks. One concerned the source of the attacks, which might have been domestic (as was the Oklahoma City bombing of 1995) and thus outside NATO's purview. NATO's treaty concerns only *international* peace and security, and its defense commitment concerns allied territories in the North Atlantic area and therefore attacks on these territories from the outside. It would not be long before the world knew that the culprits were Al Qaeda, but in the evening of September 11 the allies did not know this. They naturally hesitated to enounce a policy that in principle could commit NATO to a fight against domestic terrorists in, say, Northern Ireland, the Basque country, or Corsica. The Article V declaration therefore hedged NATO's commitment, referring to NATO's assistance only if "it is determined that this attack was directed from abroad against the United States."

The other critical issue concerned the nature of the attack because the treaty applies only to "armed attacks." This is clear in the Treaty's Article III, referring to defense capacities, Article V, which is the mutual defense clause, and Article VI, which outlines the area to which Article V applies. On September 11, 2001, the United States was attacked not by traditional military means but civilian airplanes in the hands of terrorists. NATO would indeed be irrelevant if such civilian terrorism could not be classified as an armed attack. However, and apart from the underlying political desire to activate the Alliance at this critical juncture, two arguments spoke in favor of a positive reply: that the allies had included terrorism as a threat in their 1999 Strategic Concept and that on September 11 the civilian aircraft had served as the equivalent of missiles.[5] Thus was made an in-house consensus that the treaty applied. This left the Alliance with a public relations challenge because NATO could not afford to be seen to stretch its treaty commitments beyond its original confines. Lord Robertson, who was very active in promoting the Article V declaration once the idea was brought to the table, made a distinct difference here. He repeatedly stressed the similarity of the attack to that of an armed assault. The civilian aircraft had ceased to be civilian when taken over by terrorists and had become "flying bombs" that were "mightier than practically any bomb Nato has in its armour."[6]

With the decision late in the evening of September 11 to designate the attack an armed attack but qualify its implications, the NAC cleared the way for national consultations on September 12. In the early morning Secretary General Robertson had conversations with both U.S. Secretary of State Powell and National Security Advisor Rice and apparently had to massage the concern that one or several allies might object to the Article V declaration. Robertson continues: "Five and a half hours of consideration in 19 capitals followed. I had fraught, nerve-racking telephone conversations with Prime Ministers, Foreign Ministers and in one case, through the Foreign Minister's mobile phone, with a whole Cabinet meeting."[7] At the end of the day, though, Ambassador Burns could call National Security Advisor Condoleezza Rice to "let her know that the European allies would stand with us."[8] NATO was henceforth engaged in the War on Terror.

However, and given the compressed timeframe and the nature of the debate, NATO was not ready for action. Naturally, no plan for NATO military action had been considered by the North Atlantic Council, and no plan had been prepared by the organization. Moreover, by virtue of the treaty it was up to each ally to decide for itself how it would contribute to this war, and the hedge built into the Article V declaration ensured that the North Atlantic Council would have to consult again before committing NATO to any particular path of action. The Article V declaration was not a "drive" putting NATO in motion for military action; it merely "teed up" the Alliance for possible action once the terrorists behind the attacks had been identified, as Secretary of State Powell underscored.[9] On September 12, 2001, when the declaration fell into place, the initiative moved into U.S. hands, as NATO's Secretary General Lord Robertson drew attention to: "At the moment this is an act of solidarity," and "The country that is attacked has got to make the decision and has got to be the one that asks for help."[10] Only then would each ally and in accordance with the treaty's Article V take "such action as it deems necessary, including the use of armed force," to restore security.

From Article V to Coalitions

U.S. Deputy Secretary of Defense Wolfowitz's visit to NATO headquarters on September 26 would later become a focal point in the debate on the U.S. policy on coalitions as opposed to multilateral institutions. To the collective group of NATO defense ministers Wolfowitz stated, "If we need collective action, we'll ask for it. We don't anticipate that at the moment." They were instead asked to get ready for a very broad and lengthy but poorly defined campaign against international terrorism that had numerous fronts, including the possession of weapons of mass destruction by illicit states. Wolfowitz did bring along specific requests for military action in respect to the Taliban and Al Qaeda in Afghanistan but handled these in a number of bilateral meetings because, as Wolfowitz declared, the Article V declaration gave the United States "a very powerful basis for a variety of individual requests to individual countries."[11] Vice President Cheney argued from the outset within the administration that "it was important . . . that we not allow our mission to be determined by others," and Secretary of Defense Rumsfeld wrote a memo to President Bush on September 22 suggesting that "the mission must determine the coalition."[12] This was alliance diplomacy à la carte. In reference to Wolfowitz's NATO visit and coalition policy, Edgard Buckley, who helped draft the Article V declaration, remarked, "This was, in my opinion, a fundamental misjudgment about the nature of the Alliance that devalued the importance of strategic solidarity."[13] Condoleezza Rice would later write, "I've always felt that we left the Alliance dressed up with nowhere to go. I wish we'd done better."[14]

However, we now know that it would have been difficult for the United States to run the campaign through NATO, even if it had wanted to. Afghanistan was a tough nut to crack. The Soviet Union had tried and failed. Moreover, the United States had no real plan for an armed attack on Afghanistan, save for a reinforced air strike option dating back to 1998. President Bush was "determined" to counter the impression that the United States was weak and could be forced to run, but he was in need of a military plan.[15] Hugh Shelton, chairman of the Joint Chiefs of Staff, suggested the reinforcement of this plan with a ground force component at a war cabinet meeting at Camp David on September 15–16.[16] However, the Shelton plan elicited the following comment from Secretary of Defense Rumsfeld: "The shock of 9/11 had not provoked much originality or imagination from the Chairman or his staff"—and there were more questions than answers left after this Camp David meeting.[17] On September 25 President Bush asked Secretary of Defense Rumsfeld about international participation in the first phase of the operation and was informed that this was difficult because "we're not able to define a special operations role for our own forces." Moreover, on September 26 the idea that the United States could work both the northern and southern front in Afghanistan fell apart. U.S. officials had hoped to challenge the Taliban regime hosting Al Qaeda not only from the north—via the pocket around the Panshjir valley where the Northern Alliance remained in power—but also from its own backyard in the south. To do so required U.S. sources on the ground and reliable local allies, and officials discovered that they had neither. The United States could thus not fragment the Taliban from within; it would have to confront it from without, via the Northern Alliance. Such was the state of U.S. strategy on the eve of Wolfowitz's NATO visit.

The working strategy ended up relying partly on CIA teams liaising with the Northern Alliance and partly on Special Forces (SOF)—A-teams—that could make U.S. (and allied) air power work in support of Northern Alliance ground forces. The first CIA team moved into Afghanistan's Panshjir valley on September 26 (Operation Jawbreaker), and Special Forces arrived in mid-October. The numbers of U.S. forces on the ground were small—in total the United States deployed 110 CIA officers and 316 A-team forces—but the airpower applied was significant—the U.S. air force flew between 29,000 and 38,000 sorties and delivered 22,000 bombs.[18] Bringing in these special operatives, connecting them to local forces with limited capacity, organizing the alliance and bringing it to bear in a military operation, while working out a political agreement to underpin the alliance; the sum total was a daunting task that required innovative thinking and organizational agility. It did not validate the optimistic claim that U.S. technology (notably airpower) had reached such an advanced state that it could bring down just about any government, akin to a revolution in military affairs; it rather reinforced the point of expeditionary warfare that you need to exploit the opponents' weaknesses (the Taliban was unpopular at home, had no air defense, and few regular troops) in a coordinated air–ground campaign.[19]

If the NATO allies lacked the expeditionary capabilities to participate, they had political and diplomatic skills that could be brought to the table. Yet here again the degree of improvisation under the duress of war undercut collective diplomacy, though things did improve through the fall. On October 4—the day that NATO approved its contributions to OEF—President Bush asked his closest advisers in the White House who would run Afghanistan after the war, and they had no answer. "There was silence," recalls President Bush, and National Security Advisor Condoleezza Rice was allegedly thinking, "We should have addressed that."[20] Through the month of October various ideas were put on the table, including the idea of having the advancing Northern Alliance contour the capital of Kabul to leave the city open and under U.N. supervision as a gesture to facilitate a local peace agreement. Moreover, U.S. officials foresaw a decentralized Afghanistan given the fragmented nature of the Northern Alliance as such and Afghanistan writ large. In late October, as the U.N. special envoy to Afghanistan, Lakhdar Brahimi, was preparing the rendezvous that became the Bonn conference, Secretary of State Powell appointed a U.S. special envoy to participate in these preparations as well as the conference itself and informed this person, James Dobbins, that the government had no clear idea of what to put in the place of the Taliban.[21] Then, in mid-November, the Northern Alliance decided not to contour Kabul but to occupy it and make it the seat of its new government, a move that was certain to worry Afghanistan's neighbor and traditional backer of the Taliban, Pakistan.

The move to the United Nations did improve the conditions for collective diplomacy, but the problem from an Alliance perspective remained that the Alliance leader, the United States, had been thrown into an Afghan campaign for which it was ill prepared. It had turned its back on Afghanistan in the early 1990s when the end of the Cold War seemingly justified (mistakenly, as it turned out) its abandonment of Afghan affairs. Since the Afghan civil war and the coming to power of the Taliban, it had at times developed plans for countering Al Qaeda and its head, Osama bin Laden, who had moved to Afghanistan from Sudan in 1996, but these efforts remained anchored inside the intelligence community and never developed into full-blown national strategies.[22] Now, in September and October 2001, the U.S. government had to invent one while simultaneously fighting a new kind of war.

Action and Vision

There is thus reason to conclude that NATO was not ready to move into action in the fall of 2001. The U.S. government was not ready, either, but it had the capacity to get ready and to develop strategies while aligning forces to support them. Three days prior to the war, Operation Enduring Freedom, NATO approved a set of measures in support of it. These measures were important because they confirmed in action NATO's Article V declaration of September 12 and because they signaled NATO's involvement in the Afghan campaign, however indirect. NATO was an enabler, and it was the realistic option. No ally pleaded for a collective NATO operation in Afghanistan or for placing NATO ties on the OEF campaign that was gearing up, nor was this implied in the Article V declaration. When queried as to whether he experienced some effort in this direction, Ambassador Burns answered in the negative: "There was no inclination to make Afghanistan a NATO mission at that time. There was no formal proposal to make it a NATO mission, and over the next two to three months all allies became involved in supporting OEF along the lines agreed to in one form or another."[23]

If OEF was not inimical to NATO, the role of the Alliance in the War on Terror remained to be defined. In this respect the Bush administration's lack of vision for the Alliance became a liability. It did not see NATO as a ready strategic partner. It was rather a cumbersome alliance that had complicated matters in the Kosovo war and now, through 2001, exercised a kind of veto over U.S. troop withdrawals from Balkan countries according to the principle, "in together, out together." Moreover, prior to the terrorist attacks, allied relations had bogged down over the issue of missile defense, which the Bush administration gave priority but which most allies saw as an impossible vision whose only certain effect would be to antagonize Russia. The ideological undercurrent of the Bush administration that became known as neoconservatism, though it was never clear if any of the principals were actually neoconservatives, likewise spoke against NATO as a multilateral institution sure to serve as a break on U.S. policy. U.S. power was better served by bold initiatives carried out by U.S.–led coalitions of the willing.

Stringent neoconservatism did not prevail, though, because NATO was asked to renew itself. NATO needed to "transform" to become a strategic partner. Through the fall of 2001, therefore, NATO began defining the agenda that would become the 2002 Prague summit, officially heralded as NATO's "transformation summit." It exposed the underlying lack of vision, as a matter of fact. Transformation is like change except that it does not imply change from A to B but a constant process of adaptation. There is no end state, just adaptation. A number of events and issues justified an engagement with this process of "transformation," beginning with terrorism and Afghanistan and the need to be able to undertake expeditionary warfare with the support of partners beyond North Atlantic borders. But neither events and issues nor continued adaptation amount to vision. Transformation soon boiled down to the ability to do certain things (like expeditionary warfare) and to renew this ability. It failed to address the geopolitical rationale of transformation: Why the *Atlantic* Alliance? NATO embodied the marriage between global (liberal) values and Western interests; the Bush administration emphasized the same values but then a mix of either global or national interests. The regional dimension had gone missing. The administration asked NATO to transform because NATO was there and might as well be put to use, not because it had a vision for the West.

NATO MOVES INTO A LIGHT FOOTPRINT

The initial ISAF force was small and confined to Kabul, as we saw in Chapter 2. NATO had no stake in it before October 2002, when it agreed to assist in generating forces for ISAF III, which led to the April 2003 decision to take over ISAF command by August 2003. Later that year, it was decided to expand ISAF via Provincial Reconstruction Teams (PRTs), which then became big ISAF. In this section we shall assess the origins of the initial "light footprint" that conditioned NATO's early engagement in Afghanistan. It is noteworthy for two reasons. The engagement was made without NATO's involvement, but NATO inherited it. Moreover, it was designed to assist the new Afghan regime that had come into being in Bonn in 2001 but that needed to come of age in a process that would take years to unfold as the transitional regime matured into a permanent one based on a new constitution. The footprint was light, but it therefore needed to be dynamic and long term. These conditions were not fulfilled, however, and this became an original sin by the terms of this book.

Key Architects

The light footprint was built into the Bonn process of 2001. The architect of the footprint is sometimes said to be Secretary of Defense Rumsfeld because he resisted a sustained and broad military engagement in Afghanistan and played to President Bush's inclination to eschew nation building.[24] The apparently successful strategy of backing indigenous forces with U.S. air power and Special Forces favored the U.S. objective of tracking down and eliminating terrorist groups while outsourcing the job of governance to local Afghan power brokers.

Some of these power brokers eagerly supported this approach. The three most important players in the Northern Alliance at this point were Mohammad Qanooni, Abdullah Abdullah, and Mohammed Fahim. All of them had served under the reputed leader, Ahmad Massoud, the "lion of the Panshjir Valley" who withstood the Soviet Union and the Taliban but who succumbed to a suicide bomber on September 9, 2001, and they now had to put the Bonn agreement into practice. To be sure, Hamid Karzai was the transitional head of state and was widely connected in Afghan society, but he had no boots on the ground (no militia) and needed to work with the power brokers of the Northern Alliance. Qanooni thus became interior minister; Abdullah, foreign minister; and Fahim, defense minister and also vice president. It was they who decided to take Kabul in November 2001. They participated in the Bonn nego-tiations and thus signed the deal that foresaw a neutralized capital city (only ISAF in Kabul), and then they refused to honor it. ISAF therefore had to agree to the presence of Northern Alliance forces in Kabul. They—Qanooni, Abdul-lah, and Fahim—were not opposed to ISAF as such, not even to an expanded ISAF, but they predominantly foresaw its expansion into areas under the con-trol of their allies cum potential rivals—notably Adbul Dostum to the north and Ismail Khan to the west (the "lion of Herat")—and also the Pashtun areas to the south. They did not foresee a strong ISAF working with Karzai and to the disadvantage of the core of the victorious Northern Alliance (that is, themselves), and they could not, therefore, support Karzai's calls for a stron-ger ISAF moving beyond Kabul. Inevitably, their alliance with Karzai came to an end. Abdullah survived the presidential elections of October 2004 that Karzai won, remaining in office for another six months, but Qanooni, angered by Karzai's eviction of Fahim as vice presidential candidate in the summer of 2004, ran against Karzai but lost. Qanooni moved on to become speaker of the house instead, while Abdullah reemerged as presidential challenger in 2009.

The complexity of Afghan politics and the power realities on the ground made it easier for an administration already biased against "nation building" to argue in favor of an Afghan-led solution. The U.S. priority was going after Al Qaeda. However, in practice the strategy failed on notable accounts. Above all, the Al Qaeda leadership was not eliminated but escaped. In mid-December 2001 the United States had pinned down Osama bin Laden and his leader-ship group and forces in the Tora Bora mountains. Feeling trapped, the Al Qaeda leader wrote his testament on December 14, 2001, and expected to die in an American assault. Still, he got away, and the light footprint explains how. Only around 100 U.S. Special Forces participated in the Tora Bora assault: The other forces were Afghan militias, some of which the Al Qaeda forces bought off to give passage of safety.[25] Beyond Tora Bora and beyond 2001, the policy of favoring weak modernizers in the shape of President Karzai and a cohort of other exiles returning to manage the new state while de facto hav-ing to rely on powerful militia leaders for managing Afghan society proved contradictory.[26] President Bush's memoirs reflect the contradiction, with the president observing that 9/11 "changed my mind" on the appropriateness of nation building but also that through 2002 he settled for a small U.S. presence in Afghanistan. It was a policy built on the "false comfort" of quick results, he notes.[27] James Dobbins, U.S. special envoy to Afghanistan, sees not comfort but policy driven by political inclinations: "The fact that security was not extended beyond Kabul was largely driven by the disinclination of the U.S. administration to get involved in Afghan peacekeeping."[28] Secretary of State Powell tried to push the issue but found his suggestions shot down by Secretary of Defense Rumsfeld, and U.S. policy deliberation on the issue simply ceased in February 2002.[29] In retrospect, former U.S. ambassadors to Afghanistan as well as key observers agree that the policy of advocating big change with small means—the Bonn blueprint via warlords and a light footprint—was a mistake.[30]

Lakhdar Brahimi was another important architect of the light footprint. Brahimi was the U.N.'s special representative to Afghanistan and main architect of the Bonn conference. He had previously been the U.N.'s special envoy to Afghanistan in 1997–1999 and was experienced in the ways of U.N. peacekeeping, which by the turn of the century had flourished into vast nation-building endeavors. In 1998 Brahimi had said of Afghanistan that it was "a failed state which looks like an infected wound. You don't even know where to start cleaning it."[31] He tried but gave up in 1999 because of Taliban intransigence and neighboring intrigue. Now, in October 2001, he was asked to start anew, and he brought with him the conviction that Afghan peace had to be generated locally. By implication, peace needed to be negotiated among Afghan parties absent overt outside interference, and peace's implementation needed to be done largely by Afghans themselves. This led to a compromise whereby outside powers—Afghanistan's six neighboring states along with the United States and Russia (the 6+2 format)—endorsed the upcoming U.N.-led conference among local Afghan groups and then left them to do the negotiation under Brahimi's chairmanship. The initial U.S. policy preference was for greater outside involvement, but the United States ended up deferring to the U.N.'s special representative.[32] Moreover, it led Brahimi to urge a light post-Bonn footprint. Afghanistan "has no future" if the Afghans do not "feel ownership," he said.[33] The liberated country would naturally need a security force, and of three options on the table, Brahimi, in a briefing to the U.N. Security Council, cast his lot with that of an all-Afghan force.[34]

This option proved illusory, though, and, as no one pushed for a traditional U.N. "blue helmet" force, the third option, that of a multinational force, came into play. This force became ISAF. It soon became an issue of dispute. Some, including Secretary of State Powell and officials from his State Department and also Brahimi and the designated Afghan president, Hamid Karzai, urged the deployment of an international force to at least all major Afghan cities. They lost the debate to the other camp led by the Pentagon and notably Secretary of Defense Rumsfeld and CENTCOM commander General Tommy Franks, and also the Northern Alliance leaders previously mentioned. Reticence about extensive security commitments had already caused this camp to insist on inserting "assistance" into the ISF (International Security Force) foreseen by the Bonn agreement, which then became ISAF.

Early in 2002 Brahimi emerged as an advocate of an expanded ISAF, which would seem to indicate a reversal of his "light footprint" approach. In February 2002 he "urgently" asked the Security Council to consider ISAF's expansion, and he was now head of the U.N. Assistance Mission in Afghanistan (UNAMA), whose task was to coordinate political, human rights, relief, and recovery and reconstruction activities in all of Afghanistan. It was a vast task of which Brahimi remained in charge for most of three years (until December 31, 2004), and, while it led him to call for enhanced efforts, it did not lead him to question the light footprint as a whole. We need a "light expatriate footprint," Brahimi argued in 2002, which would build Afghan as opposed to U.N. capacities for governance.[35] An expanded ISAF was supposed to enable the indigenous capacity, not overwhelm it. Unsurprisingly, therefore, Brahimi favored the inclusion of previous strongmen—or warlords—in the political process, including in the Constitutional *Loya Jirga* and the preparation for it in 2003, which entailed a large and elaborate consultative process through which strongmen and political networks operated. Some saw in this a unique diplomatic skill in getting an unprecedented political process off the ground in Afghanistan; others a bow to power politics in the shape of warlords and a U.S. preference for a centralized regime (of assistance in the War on Terror).[36] What seems fair to say is that Brahimi followed the logic of the light footprint and aimed for an inclusive political process that would substitute for a substantial international presence.

The Role of NATO Allies

NATO allies may not have been at the heart of the light footprint, but they contributed to it. Foremost among them was Great Britain. Britain was the only NATO ally that played a significant role in the war against the Taliban, and Britain signed up to run the first ISAF deployment in mid-December in

the wake of the Bonn conference.[37] The decision followed from the firm alignment of the Blair government with the United States and the status of the British armed forces as the most capable of the allied forces.

British Major-General John McColl, who as first ISAF commander had
negotiated a military technical agreement with Mohammed Fahim, gained
a firsthand experience of the intransigencies of local Afghan politics. McColl
tried to obtain the withdrawal of Northern Alliance forces from the capital
but failed and had to settle for a compromise whereby these militia forces
stayed mostly on base and promised not to interfere with ISAF activities. This
happened not merely because Northern Alliance leaders were eager to keep
their new national leader, Hamid Karzai, on a leash; they distrusted the British forces. In mid-November 2001, as U.S. and other leaders wanted Kabul to
remain an "open" city and watched with concern the approach of Northern
Alliance troops, British Special Forces flew into Bagram airport just north
of Kabul in blacked-out planes. The British government claimed the forces
were simply the advance party of a larger force meant to protect the British
presence in Kabul and participate in the campaign against the Taliban and
Al Qaeda, but Northern Alliance leaders felt differently concerned about this
sudden intervention in their drive toward the capital. The advance party of
100 British marines thus "came within an ace" of being shot at by Northern
Alliance forces, and Abdullah Abdullah was reportedly "extremely angry"
with the British for intervening. Given their history in the country, Abdullah
argued with reference to the British empire of the nineteenth century, they
should not be coming back.[38]

The British advance party and a follow-on force of up to 1,000 troops had
been in preparation since mid-October when the war was in its very early
phase and when it was not clear that the Taliban regime and forces would be
routed as quickly as it turned out to be possible. In line with its credentials
as a battle-hardened ally, Britain was ready for a fight. In November and as
the fortunes of war changed, the debate turned on the coming peace. Britain
maintained the plan for flying into Bagram airfield but now as a strategy for
assisting a Turkish-led security assistance force. French Special Forces were
ready to fly into Mazar-e Sharif to secure the airfield there and enable the
logistics of the relief effort that was to follow the war. Turkey was the designated lead because it was both a NATO ally and a Muslim country: Its lead,
bolstered by other Muslim nations such as Bangladesh, Jordan, and Indonesia
but notably NATO partners such as Georgia, Azerbaijan, and Kazakhstan,

would sooth "local sensibilities."[39] It was in effect another version of the light footprint.

The Turkish lead evaporated in late November and early December, however, for multiple reasons that are not easy to disentangle. It seems certain that the U.S. reluctance to consider a peacekeeping force for Afghanistan contributed to Turkey's hesitancy, combined with Turkey's need to rely on U.S. support for the mission: Turkey may boast a large army but one that historically has been deployed at home to guard borders and the regime against domestic insurrection (that is, Kurdish uprising). Moreover, Turkey had undergone a severe financial crisis in early 2001 and was still reeling from its impact. Money was short, and so was the experience of acting as out-of-area lead nation.

It befell to other nations experienced in the ways of expeditionary warfare (even if for the purpose of security assistance) to respond to the agreement that came about at Bonn—namely to set up a Kabul force with a potential for expansion. The Bonn conference ended on December 5, 2001, and nine days later, in London, leading allies met to organize the force. It was at this meeting that the British lead was agreed to. Britain had consistently been more forward leaning on the peacekeeping issue than the United States, both prior to the Bonn conference and during it when its representative, Robert Cooper, pushed the issue. Moreover, Britain was simply the most capable ally. By mid-December, it had become the natural choice as ISAF lead. However, Britain was not all enthused. Tony Blair wanted an initial three-month lead, which was a very short one.[40] It suited the British forces, which had a limited capacity for a sustained ground presence in Afghanistan and which did not wish to become entangled in the vicissitudes of Afghan politics. In the end, Britain had to agree to a six-month lead, but it was clear that Britain moved into Afghanistan to prepare to move out again. Moreover, and while all agreements— from the Bonn agreement over the UNSC Resolution authorizing the force (UNSCR 1386) to the Military Technical Agreement entered by McColl— emphasized the autonomy of ISAF, British officials were in no doubt that ISAF de facto depended on the U.S. Central Command for air cover and evacuation facilities in emergencies. CENTCOM was in "overall command" even if invisibly so from an official ISAF point of view.[41]

It thus became British policy to reinforce the "light footprint" underlying the ISAF agreement from Bonn. It would have been difficult to challenge, for sure, given the alignment of political forces, but a challenge was not impossible: Hamid Karzai wanted it, and soon Lakhdar Brahimi did as well. Britain would have none of it, however. The next in line for ISAF lead toed the same line. Turkey had hesitated to become the first ISAF lead and was now lined up to take over from Britain. Uncertainties persisted, though, and surfaced as the April handover approached (in the end Turkey took command on June 20). The coalition government of Bülent Ecevit continued to operate in the narrow straits defined by the financial crisis, and the United States had increasingly visible designs for change in Saddam Hussein's neighboring Iraq.[42] Toppling Saddam Hussein was a U.S. ambition but a Turkish worry given the extensive freedom of action it would grant the Kurdish groups operating in the border area. Prime Minister Ecevit was adamant that the ISAF mission should not interfere with these more vital interests, therefore. James Dobbins, who along with Assistant Secretary of Defense for International Security Affairs Peter Rodman negotiated with Turkey on the ISAF issue, recalls, "Turkey was completely against ISAF expansion: They simply weren't ready to take on a large commitment. . . . They wanted U.S. assurances that the U.S. would help them get out if necessary."[43]

Matters hardly improved while Turkey was at ISAF's helm. The Ecevit government collapsed under the strain of domestic reform in the early fall of 2002, provoking general elections that the conservative Justice and Development Party (JDP) of Recep Erdogan won. The JDP was an untested and controversial political force given its alignment with political Islam, and the election therefore hardly improved Turkey's ability to focus on Afghanistan.[44] Nor did the Iraq dossier, with Turkey coming into the line of fire (as we shall see later)—at first provoking turmoil in NATO with its request for security consultations, then provoking resentment in the United States when it—due to a parliamentary vote—declined to let U.S. ground forces invade northern Iraq from Turkish territory. As Turkey's ISAF lead advanced toward its end, toward February 2003, therefore, ISAF plummeted to the bottom of the Turkish political agenda.

The next in line for ISAF lead, Germany and the Netherlands, were differently geared for change. They wanted to prioritize ISAF, and they wanted to draw NATO into it. NATO was not only a political cover: Its assistance was necessary because the two countries wanted to deploy their NATO-assigned multinational corps headquarters, which was a bigger and more complex affair than deploying a national divisional headquarters, which is what Britain and Turkey had done. Unless NATO stepped in, force generation and coordination, logistics, and operational command would all fall on the two host nations. They thus asked for NATO's help. It was a move with a potential to bring substance to the light ISAF footprint—had not politics intervened. Germany, the Netherlands, and also Canada wanted NATO involved to bolster their ISAF contributions but more importantly to anchor the entire mission in a fixed multilateral framework (NATO) that contrasted with the Bush administration's coalition approach (OEF). This policy—which we shall assess in greater depth in the following pages—in the end brought NATO into ISAF but also maintained a light ISAF because it was so clearly distinguished from OEF: There could be no question of considering CENTCOM to be in "overall command," however informally, now that the collective alliance was involved.

In the end, therefore, the blame for the light footprint must be distributed widely. The key players in the early phase of the new Afghanistan—the United States, the Northern Alliance, and the United Nations—all wanted it. Hamid Karzai, the new head of state lacking a militia of his own or a national army, wanted instead a strong ISAF, but he found no support among the NATO allies that contributed to and ran ISAF. ISAF thus was part of the light footprint. It might be tempting to jump from this conclusion to another conclusion that ISAF's method of expansion—the PRTs—was simply another version of the light footprint (à la "expansion light"), but this would be mistaken. In the next section we shall see that the PRT concept was promising because it grew out of the OEF force's innovative response to a dynamic and troubled security situation. It was the right idea but insufficiently developed and in need of political support. This is where the Alliance committed another original sin: It took over the PRTs but, in a fit of wishful thinking, failed to understand the kind of conflict they portended.

FUSION: ISAF STEPS INTO OEF FOOTPRINTS

The high pitch of Alliance controversy took place in February 2003 and involved a notable French–American clash, with France aligning with Germany and Belgium in opposition to Turkey's Article IV request—encouraged by the United States—for NATO's aid at a point in time when the Iraq debate in the U.N. Security Council was raging. It was a "near-death" experience for the Alliance, as the U.S. Ambassador to NATO Nicholas Burns stated and analyst Elizabeth Pond later concluded.[45] Press reports (confirmed by several anonymous interviews for this book) revealed at the time that the French and American ambassadors to NATO—Benoît d'Aboville and Nicholas Burns—had unusually frank and critical exchanges inside the NAC. One observer who sat in on the meetings described it as a "terrible fight."[46] The affair was in the end solved by the innovative application of NATO Secretary General Robertson's rulebook: France got sidetracked by the decision to move the NATO debate from the NAC to the Defense Planning Committee (DPC), which France did not partake in, leaving Belgium—the remaining dissenter—faced with the message that aid to Turkey was going ahead either by way of a hitherto over-looked practice of letting NATO's military commander deploy military assets in a crisis or by way of Belgian assent. Belgium caved in, and NATO initiated Operation Display Deterrence in aid of Turkey. NATO consensus prevailed but at a high cost.[47]

Was there a negative spillover from this inflamed Iraq debate to the debate on ISAF and Afghanistan? There was not, and the effect of Iraq was instead to rally support for the Afghan mission. Ambassador Burns recalls that February 2003 was "the most divisive time I remember at NATO," but "the heated issues on Iraq did not spill over into Afghanistan. We were not arguing about Afghanistan in the North Atlantic Council. The fact that we were divided on Iraq encouraged countries to be more engaged in Afghanistan."[48] His recollection is supported by the fact that NATO collectively decided in April 2003—two months following the pitched confrontation over Turkey's Article IV request and one month following the breakdown of U.N. diplomacy and the actual Iraq war—to take full command of ISAF. All allies supported this opportunity to move beyond the Iraq dispute and focus on common issues. The April 16 press briefing of NATO spokesperson Yves Brodeur was a case in point: At the meeting where the NAC decided to terminate the Article IV–related Operation Display Deterrence regarding Iraq it also decided to enhance the Alliance's support to ISAF.[49]

NATO now took overall political-strategic command of ISAF and provided for operational and tactical command of the force. NATO's strategic commander (SACEUR) henceforth appointed the theater commander, COMISAF, and SACEUR's organization ran the conferences that generated forces for ISAF rotations. This much was clear. What was less clear was ISAF's role beyond Kabul. By its U.N. mandate and agreement with the Kabul regime it had no such role, but pressure was building for it to acquire one because the Bonn process was grinding along. Afghanistan had gained a Transitional Authority in mid-2002 and was gearing up for a constitutional assembly of December 2003–January 2004 that would decide on permanent political institutions for the country, and presidential and parliamentary elections were scheduled to follow in 2004. The allies knew that an additional effort on their part was required because the security situation remained unsettled and tense. NATO was therefore fairly quick off the bat in the fall of 2003 moving outside of Kabul, though initially only to Kunduz, as we saw in Chapter 2. A trickle of NATO decisions had by late 2005 committed the Alliance to security assistance throughout Afghanistan.

But NATO had no history of moving by small and light steps into unsettled regions to assist a transitional and shaky regime. NATO knew from the Balkans how to move massively into out-of-area territories to enforce peace, but Afghanistan was different. NATO needed a template, and OEF had one on offer: the PRT structure. This was one of two structures that had developed within the OEF as a result of the unforeseen consequences of the campaign. The PRT structure resulted from the need not least to provide safe retreats for the troops going out on combat missions in remote mountain passes but also to assist the Bonn process and the Karzai regime. The other structure concerned Afghan governance capacity and specifically the new Afghan national army (ANA) that the United States was in charge of helping to develop.

Nation Building I: The Afghan National Army
In November 2001 Secretary of State Rumsfeld had wanted the OEF to "bulk up" at Bagram airport outside Kabul and "go after Al Qaeda to the East," and President Bush had agreed.[50] Later in 2002, as the G8 nations divided up the Afghan portfolio, they accepted that the United States should be the international lead on the Afghan National Army's (ANA) development. This caused a major if largely unintended shift of emphasis within the OEF.

The ANA challenge was immense. Major General Karl Eikenberry, who in October 2002 took command of the Office of Military Cooperation-Afghanistan (OMC-A) working on the ANA dossier, was astounded by the enormity of the task once on the ground. "It was just an extraordinary set of challenges. I have been in the service for 33 plus years and I have never seen a set of infrastructure challenges, leadership challenges, and organizational challenges as we were facing in Afghanistan in October 2002."[51] Power was de facto in the hands of militia strongmen of the Northern Alliance, which itself was a loose congregation of strongmen who had brought civil war to the country once the Soviet Union collapsed and ended its support of the central regime, who thus had nourished the ground for the Taliban's successful grab for power in 1996, and who since united in opposition to the Taliban while jealously guarding their regional influence and wealth. The Afghan constitution of 2004 makes for a strong and centralized state, but this was a vision, not reality. There was a blueprint for building the state, though. The United States would take the lead in building an ANA based on reformed militia men who had first been vetted by the Japanese-funded but U.N.-led program for disarmament, demobilization, and reintegration (DDR).[52] Unsurprisingly, the militias proved resilient. Some of them—led by Marshal Fahim—moved into the Defense Ministry and took control of it; others operated in their regions, and following a classical patron–client script they de facto managed the DDR process, selecting the units that were to be "demobilized" and integrated into the ministry's ANA payroll (alternatively into the police force under the Interior Ministry, which was exempt from the DDR program) while maintaining levers of political power in their network. While the DDR program thus did achieve a degree of warlord disarmament, its effects were strictly limited because it presupposed the ability of the international community to override the fragmented power structure of Afghanistan, which it could not.[53]

By the time Karl Eikenberry arrived in Kabul, it had dawned on the United States that a pure bottom-up approach was unlikely to work. The militias were formally subjected to ministerial control as part of the Afghan Military Force (AMF), but de facto they were not. U.S. forces on the ground hunting for Al Qaeda groups were naturally not concerned with ministerial authority in Kabul and made use of militias in their hunt, and when the AMF was abolished in 2002–2003 they continued using small indigenous groups now known as Afghan Security Forces (ASF). The ASF were completely funded and run by U.S. forces under OEF, and until their disbandment in 2006 they symbolized the ambivalence of U.S. policy: supporting the Bonn process and Afghan state building on the one hand, chasing terrorist groups with all necessary means on the other. There were many obvious problems with this policy, but one of them was that the ASF in fact were unreliable in combat. A stronger and capable ANA might therefore serve both U.S. purposes. This at least was the conclusion that U.S. officials were reaching in mid- to late 2002, and Eikenberry's job was therefore to do state building.

State building meant abolishing the AMF and building a truly national army, the ANA. It took some time to get this off the ground, but by September 2003 the United States opted for a "tabula rasa" approach of tearing down all existing structures and rebuilding everything from the Ministry to the ground units from scratch.[54] The aim was a lean and capable ANA force of 60,000 soldiers in total, run by a capable ministry under civilian control. It contrasted with the design put forth by Marshal Fahim of a large and almost Soviet-style army of 250,000 soldiers: It would have been able to host most former militia forces, but it would have been neither capable nor under civilian control.[55] The lean and capable force, in contrast, had a clear operational mission that dovetailed with that of OEF: to be an agile counterinsurgency (COIN) force. Its organizational backbone therefore was planned as light infantry units and to an extent motorized units; armored units were kept at a minimum, and training would focus on how to handle a civilian population as opposed to antitank or antiaircraft operations. The U.S. interest in promoting this kind of ANA was obvious: They wanted a capable ANA for counterterrorist missions but also an ANA too light to upset neighboring Pakistan.

The United States—the OMC-A—had to convince the strongmen of the Northern Alliance that a central state was in their interest. And not just any central state but a state focused *not* on countering the Pashtun tribes from which the Taliban had sprung and that crossed into Pakistan but on national needs and national governance—the antithesis to any insurgency. It was a tough nut to crack. The United States eventually found a capable leader— Minister of Defense Adbul Rahim Wardak, appointed by President Karzai in December 2004 and still minister at the time of writing—but Tajik (Northern Alliance) groups continue to dominate the officer corps, just as patron–client relations remain under the varnish of ANA unity. Moreover, the ANA, by virtue of its light infantry focus, was really trained to become an "auxiliary force" to U.S. or other international forces providing command, logistics, and air support.[56] This emphasis may have been necessary, considering the afore- mentioned concerns of the United States, but it also ensured a lengthy U.S. engagement in the ANA buildup.

In time, and by the time Eikenberry became U.S. ambassador to Af- ghanistan, in 2009, the entire training mission was transferred from the U.S. command (which had become CSTC-A) to a new NATO training command (NTM-A). ANA buildup is now a heavy footprint, which the allies readily ac- knowledge. In 2002–2003, however, this acknowledgment was some time off. The ANA nonetheless served as an engine of transformation in the U.S. en- gagement, drawing it from search-and-destroy missions into the task of build- ing public authority in Kabul to achieve the same mission—the elimination of Al Qaeda. Back in 2002–2004, when NATO got involved in ISAF, the ANA mission thus provided for a common "security sector reform" focus among the allies at a time when issues of dispute were in abundant supply (Iraq but also the stovepiped G8 effort [lead-nations] and the political mythology attached to ISAF and OEF missions). The ANA's effect on OEF–ISAF relations was ultimately indirect even if important; the OEF vehicle for handling what turned out as an insurgency, the PRT, would more directly invite OEF-ISAF cooperation.

Nation Building II: A Safe Operating Environment

Following standard practice, the coalition forces that entered Afghanistan in October–December 2001 brought military civil-affairs teams that could undertake so-called Quick Impact Projects to create local support for the forces. In the course of 2002–2003, these teams grew into an OEF PRT structure, which got on track in early to mid-2003, and which NATO then took over as it gradually expanded ISAF.

OEF opened its first PRT in January 2003 in the town of Gardez, Paktia province, close to the Tora Bora Mountains where Osama bin Laden had slipped away a year earlier. A second PRT went up in March 2003 in Bamyan, capital of the centrally located Bamyan province, and a third in April 2003 in Kunduz, capital of the northern Kunduz province. The fourth and first non-American PRT was the British-led PRT in Mazar-e Sharif in the Balkh province, also up north. The basic American idea—and it was American—was to create an interagency process that brought together the whole gamut of security, development, and governance agencies that could deliver the effects of good governance—schools, jobs, medical facilities—that would cause local leaders and communities to support the new regime. In short, the PRTs were a means to "galvanize" the state.[57] This was hardly an original OEF mission objective, but it developed into one.

It had begun to dawn on the U.S. military chain of command in the early spring of 2002 that the antiterrorist operation would involve significant force, and the large military offensive in the Shahi-Kot valley in March 2002 (Operation Anaconda) drove home the point. It involved a surprising level of resistance, and the Al Qaeda leadership is believed to have slipped away once again. It was now clear that the OEF forces needed to do more to win local support and isolate the opponent, and for this it needed greater strategic weight as well as development capacities.[58] Strategic weight was granted with the deployment of Lieutenant General Dan McNeill and his XVIII Airborne Corps headquarters, which took command on May 31, 2002. McNeill was three-star where his predecessor Major General Hagenbeck was two-star, and his OEF force (known as CJTF 180) would by the end of 2002 comprise 10,000 troops, having begun the year with a mere 2,500.

Development capacities were built into this force but modestly so. OEF had a designated task force to run a number of "coalition humanitarian liaison cells" (CHLC), which were really units to provide the aforementioned Quick Impact Projects—wells, schools, periodical medical clinics.[59] The CHLC structure was an ad hoc concept invented during the campaign preparations in late 2001,[60] and it could not deliver large or sustained projects. It had one advantage as a military structure, though, which was its ability to move into hostile and dangerous environs, especially in Afghanistan's eastern region, and this it was increasingly ordered to do in late 2002. It also sought to change its focus from logistics to "doing things," but it remained a weak structure hampered by complex lines of command and conflicting mission goals.[61] In consequence, in mid-2002 planners began developing a new idea of Joint Regional Teams—the precursor to the PRTs. They put forth the JRT concept to President Karzai, who appreciated its potential positive impact on governance but resented the "regional" heading, which could be taken to indicate regional autonomy.[62] Hence, the concept gained a green light wrapped as PRT.

The purpose was to "galvanize" the state, but this was merely the vision. The reality on the ground was that the PRT compounds were small, isolated, and military dominated. They conjured up images of the Wild West. Robert Kaplan, journalist and defense expert, visited the Gardez PRT in southeastern Afghanistan—the first PRT of them all—in the fall of 2003 and found only one civilian in the compound besides himself: "a rugged leathery-skinned official from the US Department of Agriculture" who reminded Kaplan of a *Jurassic Park* dinosaur hunter. A State Department official was supposed to be on site but was in Kabul at the time, and that left Kaplan, the dinosaur hunter, and an army civil affairs battalion with military escort and interpreters as the PRT staff. The PRT concept was "the brainchild" of the U.S. force command in Afghanistan, the Gardez troops confirmed to Kaplan, and the ultimate goal was to "civilianize the PRTs by embedding reps from the State Department and USAID."[63] Given the difficult and dangerous area inhospitable to civilian efforts in which the American PRTs operated, it was no small challenge to get this transition off the ground. Civilian government agencies struggled to get out there, and nongovernmental aid organizations (NGOs) generally wanted to keep the PRTs at arm's length so as not to get caught in a fight. The initiative remained in military hands, therefore, and the military understandably continued to focus on Quick Impact Projects that would provide relief and offer force protection there and then.

The PRTs that fell into ISAF hands and that ISAF developed turned out differently. They had a markedly stronger civilian component and could afford by virtue of the more benevolent operating environment to direct more attention to long-term institution building in their province—providing for a functioning judiciary and police force, for instance—as opposed to mere Quick Impact Projects. Peter Marsden, coordinator of the British Aid Agencies Afghanistan Group from 1989 to 2005, thus saw a qualitative difference between the "hearts and minds" civilian-oriented military programs of the U.S. PRTs and the security sector reform work of the ISAF PRTs.[64] This is a fair point because it captures the difference between OEF and ISAF: They simply operated under very different conditions. Yet it is noteworthy that the allies were driven to think along the same lines. At first the OEF–ISAF difference was neat, but ISAF expansion erased it to a great extent because ISAF moved into insurgency country and faced the same difficulties as OEF forces in the east. Moreover, ISAF did get the concept from the OEF. What we witness is therefore a PRT-focused process of convergence, and, though the OEF reformed earlier than ISAF, there was definitely potential for cooperation.

Some may object that the OEF invented the PRT as a measure to fight an insurgency, that this was not ISAF's mission, and that the two remained worlds apart. The historical record tells a different story. Today, NATO and ISAF fully accept the COIN logic, and OEF has by and large been folded into ISAF. This potential for cooperation was also there in 2002–2003, and the PRT is a case in point. The OEF was at this time a type of nation-building force: It sought to build a capacity for central governance (the ANA); it promoted local development (PRTs); and it fought the enemies of the state (the insurgency and Al Qaeda). It was not recognized as such back in Washington, and campaign strategy developed bottom up in ad hoc fashion, none of which was ideal. But the trend toward nation building was unmistakable. Remarkably, NATO missed it. The Alliance took over the PRT but imagined that this was a sole and useful instrument that could be lifted from an otherwise tainted campaign of hit-and-run counterterrorism. The reality was different, but NATO politics sustained this perception, ultimately erecting a barrier between OEF and ISAF.

FISSION: ISAF–OEF PULLED APART

It may be that the NAC managed to keep Iraq and Afghanistan separated, as we saw, insulating ISAF from the Iraq controversy and generating support for a collective ISAF effort, but the terms on which this investment was made undermined the overall effort. Germany drove the effort to define a transatlantic compromise but in such a way that it would be difficult for the United States to support the effort wholeheartedly. France, going along, reinforced the tortured compromise. This made it easy for U.S. officials to uphold the cover of Alliance unity while choosing to relegate the Afghan operation—be it ISAF or OEF—to a secondary effort. The appearance of Atlantic Alliance unity in ISAF was thus deceptive.

German Terms of Endearment

Germany was an unlikely candidate for the role as transatlantic mediator on the Afghan issue: For political reasons it had a very limited experience in matters of force projection, though a decade of Balkan conflict resolution had brought change; its defense forces were almost wholly organized for territorial defense; and it was politically opposed to any ties between ISAF and OEF, however informal, a position that was made clear as Britain committed to the first ISAF lead.[65] In the course of 2002–2004 Germany sought to revise the two first and national legacies to embed the latter distinction (ISAF–OEF) and make it the foundation for NATO's commitment to ISAF. Germany's government, led by Chancellor Schröeder, had good domestic reasons for making this political choice, but it almost ensured all on its own that the United States would not be able to commit in earnest to the NATO–ISAF campaign. The gambit succeeded insofar as Germany helped engineer NATO's entry into Afghanistan, but Germany's leadership failed the test of statesmanship—to secure broad support for its conception of international order.

German Foreign Minister Joschka Fischer famously demanded more allied consultations from U.S. Secretary of Defense Rumsfeld at the annual Munich security conference in February 2003. Pounding his hand on the table and looking directly at Rumsfeld, Fischer impassionedly argued, "My generation learned you must make a case, and excuse me, I am not convinced."[66] To Fischer, NATO should be akin to a strategic parliament where strategy was under deliberation until a majority agreed to it and the talking ceased. This was not Rumsfeld's vision of an ideal NATO, but Fischer was willing to confront him on the issue.

Fischer was not alone in defining German policy, though, and particularly German Defense Minister Peter Struck sought a closer alignment between his government and the Bush administration. Struck soon discarded traditional German reticence about NATO's operational boundaries—the question "became irrelevant on September 11, 2001," as he said—and initiated a set of defense reforms that focused the German forces on expeditionary warfare (both combat and stabilization). The reforms were outlined in 2003, and, though their operational impact was minimal in the short run, the conceptual switch mattered.[67] Struck was thus also more ready than his foreign minister counterpart, Joschka Fischer, to embrace the expeditionary warfare force introduced in NATO by the United States at the November 2002 Prague summit—the NATO Response Force—because, as he stated in an interview, the defense of Germany began in the Hindu Kush.[68] Struck's position was at first marginalized, though, because the government was heading for a general election in September 2002, and Chancellor Schröeder bolstered his flailing opinion poll numbers with criticism of the U.S. approach to the War on Terror and the coming war in Iraq. Schröeder's course of criticism allowed him to regain the chancellorship and reinforce the relationship to his principal coalition partner in government, Joschka Fischer, but also gained him the hostility of President Bush.

To back out of this precarious position, which culminated in the Article IV debacle inside NATO in February 2003, Germany needed an offensive Afghanistan policy. It also needed a policy that rested on an implicit transatlantic division of labor. The United States would run OEF, NATO would run ISAF, and never the twain should meet. This became the overriding rationale for Germany, which consistently pursued a light and civilian footprint in line with the division of labor but which did not put much strategic thinking into it otherwise. It sought out safe areas from which to operate—Kunduz in 2003 and Feyzabad in 2004—and it provided for combined civilian–military command of its PRTs (which was unique at the time) in line with its stabilization focus. However, its guiding strategy—a so-called Afghan Concept from 2003 that was only officially published in 2007—was short and vague. It asked the German PRTs to increase the population's "feeling of security through visibility" and to "radiate" into the environment to achieve stability.[69] German forces and civilian agencies would have to learn by doing, in other words, and what was clear in the high politics of the Alliance was the German desire to energize ISAF around a new, if vague, concept of Afghan stabilization.

Germany did participate in the otherwise controversial OEF operation, it should be noted, and this was in fact Germany's first military operation outside Europe since 1945. It participated in naval operations off the Horn of Africa and in the Mediterranean, it had air personnel and support in Turkey assisting U.S. air operations, and a small number of its Special Forces went into Afghanistan. These contributions were put on the table in the wake of September 2001, however; the course of events in 2002 brought Germany and the United States on a collision course, and Germany's OEF contribution dwindled down to naval operations. To bounce back and overcome the misgivings created by the electoral rhetoric in Germany and the Iraq diplomacy, Germany needed a fresh start, and Foreign Minister Fischer and Defense Minister Struck worked in tandem from mid-2003 to create it.

They were to an extent pushing an open door. The United States encouraged a greater NATO footprint in Afghanistan and an ISAF lead that would free up U.S. resources for Iraq. The challenge for Germany was to maintain a degree of U.S. interest in the Afghanistan mission, on the one hand, and convince the remaining allies that NATO's control of ISAF and ISAF expansion was viable, on the other. The more the United States emphasized Iraq, the less viable ISAF expansion appeared because it would lack U.S. attention and support. It was therefore convenient to emphasize ISAF as a stabilization mission. This would not require great amounts of U.S. assistance (and the United States could run OEF counterterrorist operations in parallel if they wanted to), and it would fit the European bill in terms of know-how and capability. Peter Struck lobbied for this position among defense colleagues both within the EU and NATO; Joshcka Fischer also did so among foreign ministers and also in a visit to Washington in July 2003, the first bilateral visit following the diplomatic crisis over Iraq. The two officials were well aware that an economy of effort could be devastating to NATO's ISAF mission, and particularly Foreign Minister Fischer repeatedly stressed the need for allies to not let Iraq divert their attention from the Afghan dossier.[70]

In the fall of 2003 it was decision time, however, and NATO—in charge of ISAF since August—needed to come up with a design for a bigger ISAF that could help stabilize the country ahead of the critical presidential and parliamentary elections in 2004 (though the latter were later postponed to 2005). Germany now staked its bet fully on the PRT track. Germany's Lieutenant General Goetz Gliemeroth, who was the first theater commander of NATO's ISAF, saw PRTs as an "ideal" tool for expanding ISAF beyond Kabul and found that the "time is now right" to do it.[71] Gliemeroth and others provided ammunition for the campaign, which now had Foreign Minister Fischer in a clear lead. In Brussels, where NATO was vacillating on the expansion issue, Fischer pushed for a commitment and offered to have Germany take the first step in Kunduz. As we saw in Chapter 2, Germany thus solved NATO's problem of defining who should take the expansion lead, and SHAPE duly began revising its Operational Plan (OPLAN) of August to fit the Kunduz development. But the revised OPLAN was a stopgap measure. What NATO needed was a new overarching strategy for ISAF's full expansion, which in NATO-speak is a Concept of Operations (CONOPS). The Alliance was hesitating along the CONOPS track, but Germany was using the Kunduz OPLAN to ram through change—to commit the Alliance to big ISAF. Ahmed Rashid, an expert on the region, was in the early fall of 2003 invited to NATO to brief the ambassadors on the Afghan situation, and Rashid writes in his book, "Some of the NATO ambassadors were clearly disinterested in or nervous about an increased deployment or they did not take the Taliban resurgence seriously. Privately some criticized Fischer, whom they blamed for steamrolling NATO into Afghanistan when NATO was unprepared to go there."[72]

Germany was thus critical in engineering big ISAF and NATO's commitment to it. Germany's Kunduz investment provided a lead for NATO to follow, and Germany's desire for strategic deliberations within NATO was laudable. However, the diplomatic offensive came with a price tag. The United States was not brought on board because it was politically inclined to prioritize Iraq but also because Germany's deliberate choice of presenting ISAF as a kind of division of labor reinforced U.S. instincts. "Civilian power" ISAF did not evoke enthusiasm from the remaining allies, either, but they were in need of a platform for Alliance renewal and in the end committed to it. Thus big ISAF based on PRT expansion was born. The PRT concept contained all necessary ingredients for a concerted civil–military campaign; the politics of ISAF did not.

The French Exception

Among the allies concerned with the solidity of the ISAF blueprint was Canada, which was slated for ISAF command in February 2004 and which in the fall of 2003 occupied the post as deputy commander to Gliemeroth. Canada worried that the mission was insufficiently resourced, but still it committed around 2,000 soldiers to its ISAF command, with General Rick Hillier becoming COMISAF, and it later committed to running one of the most challenging PRTs—the one in Kandahar. France was perhaps the most prominent of the skeptics. It committed troops and invested in a lead mission, but it remained inherently skeptical of ISAF's civil–military mission and the PRT concept. This was the cornerstone of the approach promoted by Germany and adopted by the Alliance. Germany knew that the OEF–ISAF divide was real but sought to provide substance to ISAF via the PRT. France, Germany's privileged partner in European affairs, declined to follow Germany's lead and did not support the PRTs. It was a clear but troubling position because it further eroded the foundation for the big ISAF that was coming into being.

France was ready to let the Alliance move ahead because it too needed to mend fences following the Iraq debacle. Having thus refused during the month of February 2003 to consider a NATO takeover of ISAF, France the following month agreed to it.[73] And France did not merely offer rhetorical support. It invested forces in ISAF, an investment that culminated in the latter half of 2004 when, from August 2004 to February 2005, France with its European partners (Germany, Spain, Belgium, and Luxembourg) in the multinational Eurocorps took command of ISAF—under COMISAF General Jean-Louis Py—and simultaneously provided forces for the Franco–German brigade to run the ISAF force for Kabul. Security in Kabul was assured by a multinational brigade, and France and Germany were leading it; the entire ISAF effort, including Kabul and PRTs, was command by France and its partners. France and Germany had charted this path in February 2004 at their bilateral summit and thus at a critical time for the Alliance. The new CONOPS was there, but the political commitment was uncertain, and the new secretary general of the Alliance, Jaap de Hoop Scheffer, had made Afghanistan the Alliance's top priority.[74] In short, France invested and provided momentum.

But it was a charged momentum running counter to both American and German policy, and as such it failed to galvanize the Alliance's commitment. Sean Maloney, a Canadian defense expert, observed in the wake of the double French lead in Afghanistan (overall ISAF as well as Kabul) that the whole affair had been "very dysfunctional."[75] The allies were in political disagreement, and the ISAF mission was hostage to it. France shared Germany's concern that the mission was being insufficiently funded. There has to be a means-end symmetry, Defense Minister Michèle Ailliot-Marie made clear in the run-up to the Franco–German summit of February 2004. This was partly a comment on the desire of the United States to prioritize Iraq, having commenced the effort in Afghanistan, and partly a comment on the reluctance of allies in general to invest resources in ISAF. ISAF might have to scale back its commitments to fit the capabilities, she was saying. Unsurprisingly, Jaap de Hoop Scheffer thought the relationship should be inversed: Capabilities should be augmented to fit the commitment.[76]

The underlying motive of French policy was to counter OEF, strengthen the European defense option, and keep NATO boxed into a military role. Providing military forces for ISAF lead missions fitted the bill; counterterrorism did not, nor did investments in PRTs. Thus, as France invested quite significant military force in ISAF through 2004, it refused to invest in a French PRT and erected a firewall between ISAF and OEF. The French daily *Le Monde* was hopeful that this policy package would "reinforce the credibility of European defense," not least given "the French-German partnership" that brought the Eurocorps to Kabul.[77] It was not a credible scenario. The policy directly undermined the PRT track that was so important to German and NATO policy, and not only because France would not invest in a PRT on its own. Other allies could carry this burden, as turned out to be the case. More troubling was the civilian component of the PRTs, which naturally needed significant enhancement, both in the individual PRTs and centrally in Kabul where PRT efforts were in need of coordination. France effectively blocked NATO and EU initiatives in this direction. France feared that a PRT effort of this sort would bolster NATO's strategic role in civil–military affairs and thus turn the EU into NATO's handmaiden. In diplomatic-speak, France feared a "Berlin Plus in reverse"—a term coined in the course of 2005 but the implications of which had dawned on French officials earlier.[78] The outcome was institutional stalemate. NATO decided on the PRT policy in late 2003: It would take the EU another two years, until December 2005, to decide on its support for PRTs, and even then the EU offered to work purely through the PRT civilian components—a hands-off approach that virtually precluded effective civil–military integration.

French policy thus ultimately worked at odds with German policy. The two countries labored to reinforce ISAF, but where Germany sought an expanded ISAF based on PRTs that would bolster NATO's role in a transatlantic division of labor, France sought a purely military mission that would boost Europe's foreign policy credentials, not NATO. This was a fateful European split that made it easy for the United States to continue along the track laid out in late

2002 and early 2003: to move the War on Terror from the Hindu Kush to Mesopotamia.

The United States and Operation Iraqi Freedom

The United States had lost its ability to significantly influence these allied debates because of the Iraq war, which drained U.S. resources and turned Afghanistan into a sideshow. This did not mean that key U.S. officials were unaware of events in Afghanistan: Secretary of Defense Rumsfeld reportedly focused clearly on Afghan governance issues beginning in the fall of 2002; in September 2003 he went to Kabul and endorsed ISAF expansion; and in December 2003 at the NATO defense ministerial he urged NATO to take full control of the country.[79] But Iraq—Operation Iraqi Freedom—overwhelmed Rumsfeld and the Pentagon team and caused them to place force caps on the OEF force and withdraw key enablers from Afghanistan to Iraq. In October 2003 they created a new command for Afghanistan—the Combined Forces Command-Afghanistan (CFC-A)—which was in fact a means to sidetrack OEF in favor of OIF. CFC-A belonged to the CENTCOM chain of command, but, with CFC-A in place, CENTCOM turned its full attention to OIF and Iraq. Lieutenant General David Barno, CFC-A commander, had to spend "an immense amount of time, energy, and effort" over eighteen months merely to get the required 400 officers for his command staff.[80] In short, Barno "was not the primary supported commander in CENTCOM, and his theater became an economy-of-effort mission to operations in Iraq."[81]

A schism now developed within U.S. policy. On the one hand, Rumsfeld and other officials promoted ISAF as a kind of substitute for a U.S. presence and as a means to engage the stabilization of the country. On May 1, 2003, both President Bush and Secretary Rumsfeld—the former in Washington, the latter in Kabul—announced the end to combat operations in Afghanistan. A new phase of stabilization and reconstruction could begin. The new CFC-A command encountered a different reality, however, and developed a new rule book for the engagement based on counterinsurgency (COIN) operations. To facilitate interagency coordination, the CFC-A headquarters was moved from Bagram airbase to a location next door to the U.S. embassy in Kabul, and General Barno's office and personal staff were located within the embassy.[82] The result was a more coherent and stringent use of the Provincial Reconstruction Teams. Moreover, and to support the PRTs, individual CFC-A task forces were assigned Areas of Operation (AO). This amounted to "a dramatic change in the way US military units operated within the country," the U.S. Army later concluded.[83] Rather than operating from a few select bases and conducting search-and-destroy missions, the forces now had to live in their province or AO and build better relations with Afghan communities. The campaign thus gained a new center of gravity.[84]

In principle the Washington principals and Barno were in alignment because COIN is about stabilization and reconstruction rather than combat. In reality they were not because COIN demands massive resources, extensive interagency coordination, and patience in setting up a stable government that can out-govern local warlords and limit the damage inflicted by the narcotics trade. Beginning in the summer of 2004, the secretary of defense held weekly video teleconferences with CFC-A commander Barno. Barno and his chief of staff, Colonel Lamm, initially sought to focus these conferences on COIN intangibles such as government capacity and popular opinion but were soon pulled in the direction of providing figures for a "business model." The secretary of defense was looking for "very strict metrics" for measuring ANA training, Lamm later said, "so he could figure out when to pull out troops."[85] Rumsfeld, on the other hand, argued "that we should train as many Afghans as we could so they could begin to take over the security responsibilities for their country."[86] Rumsfeld was right that COIN demands local capacity and legitimacy but getting to that point was just an immense task, as the preceding discussion on Afghan army training demonstrated, and it takes patience and coordination to get there. The time frame of 2004–2005 was a thought-provoking moment in the campaign because the insurgency was manageable and training was the focal point. Had it worked, there would have been no need for the 2009–2011 surge to quell the insurgency and get the campaign back on the training track. However, Rumsfeld and the other principals were too hard pressed on the Iraqi dossier to focus stringently on the Afghan case. In the course of 2005 they in effect bungled the transition from the Khalilzad–Barno team—widely perceived as successful—to a new team. Khalilzad, a political heavyweight, was pulled to Iraq where the situation had greatly deteriorated and replaced with a career diplomat, Richard Neumann, who is reported to have had a poor relationship to Barno's replacement as COMCFC-A, General Karl Eikenberry. This is a rumor, but the fact behind it is that the interagency effort in Kabul in the course of 2005–2006 largely broke down. The conditions for continuing the incipient success of 2003–2004 were the coordination of political heavyweights in Kabul, Washington's continued engagement, and political patience. However, involvement and patience went to Iraq, and Afghanistan gradually became NATO's affair.

NATO's ISAF effort would, all else being equal, advance the date at which the United States could pull OEF troops into the OIF mission. The diplomacy of the Alliance was bedeviled by recurrent rumors of U.S. plans for Afghanistan withdrawals, which undoubtedly reflected Pentagon thinking but which was politically difficult to admit to because the allies were already worried that ISAF was insufficiently resourced. Shortly before the Afghan presidential elections in October 2004, ISAF meant to enlarge its footprint in western Afghanistan, close to Herat, but the effort nearly failed because Italy, providing a PRT and also Forward Support Base lead, lacked critical enablers at this base— helicopters, fighter jets, and emergency rescue and close air support—and no one volunteered to provide them.[87] U.S. withdrawal plans threatened to derail the extremely tedious effort of mobilizing allied capabilities piecemeal. At one point in 2005 such plans were described as a "bombshell" inside NATO, causing protests from Secretary General Scheffer, assurances from the Pentagon spokesperson that these were mere plans that had not yet been reviewed by the secretary of defense, and assurances also from CTC-A commander General Eikenberry that he certainly needed all U.S. troops currently in Afghanistan for the fight in the Afghan–Pakistan borderlands.[88]

Thus the allies moved into Afghanistan debating the details of force levels, national caveats, and command relationships, not really engaging the overall strategic issues of the day. Secretary of Defense Rumsfeld thought he had Afghanistan fixed, and key allies such as Germany and France were not about to challenge him for political reasons, while his own chain of command, the CFC-A, could not.

END GAME: BRIDGING THE ISAF–OEF DIVIDE
AND PREPARING FOR FULL EXPANSION

With the unified command and full ISAF–OEF fusion off the table, NATO had to make do with an ISAF–PRT fusion while concocting a complex relationship to OEF containing political firewalls and as good a command relationship as politics allowed. The political effect was unmistakable: In limiting its growing Afghan involvement to ISAF, NATO absolved itself from the wider political context of the conflict and from the need to think strategically about Afghan developments. NATO was about ISAF, and ISAF was about assisting a process defined in Bonn and sanctioned by the United Nations. The need to think outside the box, to adapt to Afghan developments on the ground, was obvious to most OEF observers. The OEF had become embroiled in state building even if the original campaign design was different, and it had espoused a new way of war defining the Afghan population as the center of gravity. The problem for the OEF was that U.S. policymakers were busy in Iraq and diverted resources away from Afghanistan, and its COIN campaign stood no chance of getting off the ground.

The problem for NATO and ISAF was conceptual. NATO allies did not fathom a conflict where tribal and ethnic fault lines, fragile governing institutions, and precarious political legitimacy would be of direct importance for NATO and their management a precondition for ISAF success. NATO therefore did not think strategically about Afghanistan. NATO did have a proper trail of paperwork, of course. It began with international agreements (the Bonn agreement and U.N. Resolutions) that the North Atlantic Council worked into political guidelines for a stabilizing mission and that were then written into a Concept of Operations (CONOPS) and subsequently into an Operations Plan (OPLAN), which is the overall military strategy. The chain continues. SACEUR James Jones, responsible for the overall or strategic OPLAN, directed his subordinates—the Joint Force commander (in Brunssum, Germany) and ISAF commander (in Kabul)—to develop follow-on operational and tactical Operational Plans. In this sense, NATO worked. Where NATO did not work was at the political-strategic level where the CONOPS and OPLAN find their origins and where the mission is conceptualized. It would take a severe and bloody encounter with the Taliban for NATO to learn this lesson.

The OPLAN

It is appropriate to take a look at the 2005 OPLAN (it has been revised since then) to see how political goals got layered into the military strategy. The OPLAN defines a "political end-state" for the operation and a corresponding "desired strategic military end-state." The former is "a self-sustaining, moderate and democratic Afghan government able to exercise its sovereign authority, independently, throughout Afghanistan" that comes out of the Bonn agreement and process. The latter is that "Afghan national security forces provide security and sustain stability in Afghanistan without NATO support."[89] The "main effort" to achieve these end states consists of supporting the new Afghan government, the G8 lead nations, and other international organizations, which translates into a "stabilization" effort on ISAF's part. Once stabilization has been achieved, ISAF must move on to the subsequent phases of "transition" and finally "redeployment."[90] Stabilization is therefore the critical effort, and PRTs "will be at the leading edge" of it.

In this inherently civil–military environment, SACEUR distinguishes between key military tasks and key supporting tasks, where the former involves "deterring and disrupting those who challenge the extension of government authority or prevent ISAF from operating freely" and also mentoring and supporting Afghan forces.[91] The latter involves a range of ISAF tasks in support of government and other actors. The coordination of these supporting tasks and the work of the "leading edges"—the PRTs—is naturally critically important, but here the OPLAN is ambivalent. The annex on PRTs states that "a 'one size fits all' PRT concept is neither appropriate nor possible," which is a clear reference both to the diversity within Afghanistan and the diversity among PRT lead nations in how they chose to organize and fund their efforts. However, the main text connects the "desired strategic impact" to *convergence* between PRT activities and *synchronized movement* toward common objectives, and it underscores ISAF's ability to help bring about "comprehensive awareness" of the situation on the ground across the country.[92] Somewhere between diversity and unity—between what was possible and desirable—a gap had opened, and this is where NATO ideally should have devoted political energy to anticipate adversity.

In fairness, the OPLAN did foresee a "robust" campaign given the "more challenging" security environment into which ISAF was now moving (the south and east).[93] It foresees a gradual buildup prior to ISAF command and also close coordination with existing OEF forces. This was not a naïve military strategy, but it had to make do with political constraints and a stabilizing mission that was hard to define. OEF had come to the conclusion that their mission could best be carried out with a COIN strategy, but NATO was not ready to define stabilization as something as confrontational as countering an insurgency.

Nor were NATO planners in the strategic headquarters of SHAPE ready to plan for a COIN campaign. They were trained to think along more conventional lines—and SHAPE as an institution encouraged them to do so. Classical thinking followed the principle that you needed a strategic reserve, and so this was written into the first version of the drafted OPLAN. Two-thirds of the forces would be put into the field; one-third would be located somewhere conveniently as a strategic reserve. This was the first military plan. It ran into political trouble because NATO's political masters did not see ISAF as a conventional or classical campaign in need of such heavy strategic reserves. The drafted OPLAN was therefore redrafted, and the strategic reserve was deployed into the field, which is to say that all forces would be deployed.[94] They would all go to provinces to work in support of PRTs—the "leading edge." With all forces in operation, the reserve—the insurance against contingencies—would have to come from forces in operation, of course. Plans were drawn up for pulling some PRT-related forces from province A, therefore, if trouble erupted in province B, and so on. It was not classical, but neither was the intention behind ISAF.

Making It Work

NATO remained stuck with stabilization instead of COIN, which at the time was conflated with counterterrorism. The need to shape and clear an area before holding it and rebuilding it was in some ways recognized because, as the OPLAN foresaw, moving south required an effort by individual allies and OEF forces. Someone had to tame Afghanistan's Wild West before ISAF could move in. The thing was that ISAF could not do it. ISAF was there to hold and build, not to fight to clear the ground. Though the distinction was hard to uphold in practice, the Alliance did try.

Refusing to merge ISAF and OEF was the most notable effort of the allies in this respect. The United States wanted the merger but found no support, and by the fall of 2005 the debate turned on maintaining the operations as distinct but also in synergy. ISAF resisted getting involved in Special Operations Forces (SOF), which therefore continued to run within OEF. ISAF likewise resisted counternarcotics but did concede that it would support the Afghan government's efforts in this direction. ISAF would not run its own prisoner and interrogation system, though it agreed to guidelines for dealing with prisoners. All this required distinct but coordinated lines of ISAF and OEF command, and SACEUR James Jones managed to work out a compromise in October 2005: The ISAF Commander would have three deputies—one for stabilization, one for air operations, and one for security—and the latter deputy would be a double-hatted American officer working both in the ISAF and OEF chains of command to "deconflict" missions. ISAF would then run security assistance while the OEF ran SOF, COIN, counternarcotics, and prisoners' interrogation.

This barrier was about to collapse early in February 2006, only two months following its elaborate erection in Brussels. A popular demonstration turning violent in Maymana, northwest Afghanistan, rattled the Norwegian PRT staffed by Norwegian but also Finnish, Swedish, and Latvian troops. Demonstrators managed to get into the PRT compound, set vehicles on fire, and occupy a building from where they reportedly both shot and threw hand grenades at the troops. Several troops got injured. They responded by firing rubber bullets, killing some demonstrators, and in the end managing to evict them all. For a short while it seemed that the PRT might fall, and this was a forceful reminder of how weak ISAF was if things went badly. ISAF had no "strategic reserve" because it was not meant to be necessary. When it turned out to be necessary nonetheless, the plan collapsed. The units deployed elsewhere that were designated as backup for the Maymana PRT were not ready. They were busy, were located far away, and lacked the logistics for quick relief actions. In the end NATO's reserve in Maymana consisted of two F-16s whose roars in the sky were loud but did little to evict the demonstrators.

The Maymana experience revealed the lack of cohesive thinking that had gone into the PRT setup that ISAF was now rolling out in Afghanistan. "NATO's rapid response capacity was then stretched to its limit, I can tell you," NATO's former Secretary General Jaap de Hoop Scheffer stated in an interview for this book. It was troubling not only for the Norwegian PRT but for the Alliance as a whole, as we can conclude from his observations. "The PRT concept was never discussed with any form of intensity within NATO because nations have their own approaches . . . It was discussed in NATO, but the PRT concept as such has never been an element in NATO decision making."[95] As secretary general, Jaap de Hoop Scheffer made a consistent and strong effort to focus NATO's attention, but the politics outlined in this chapter undermined him. Some would later say that Scheffer got the effort wrong, but the fact of the matter is that the allies had their mission wrong and willingly exhausted their secretary general.

NATO did do something to redress the situation in early 2006. With forces moving south, NATO agreed to toughen up its Rules of Engagement (ROE) that define the conditions under which soldiers can open fire. The new set of rules was more permissible (it allowed forces to shoot on the presumption of hostile intent) and the incoming ISAF commander, British General Richards, described the incursion into the southern region as a "combat mission," which was clearly a twist of ISAF's mission statement as defined by the U.N. mandate.[96] But ISAF's overall mission remained, as did its basic organization. ISAF gained neither greater reserves nor greater PRT integration, and the message to the troops heading south was effectively that they would have to prevail by their own force, only now with more permissive ROE in hand. Unsurprisingly, they soon found that they were in need of backup but that the reserve was tied down by a combination of logistics and political constraints (so-called caveats). Caveats are natural in allied missions, but the extent of these in ISAF was unusual and reflected Alliance disagreement regarding the mission's basics. At bottom, what the Alliance could agree that ISAF should be about was "hold and build." Excursions from this plan would have to be improvised.

CONCLUSION

Moving from Kabul down the Helmand and Arghandab rivers to the lowlands of Helmand and Kandahar provinces, NATO had come a long way since the 1990s when it contemplated out-of-area missions as an existential question, unsure of whether to do them at all and, if so, whether to do them as the handmaiden of the United Nations. NATO reached Afghanistan's southern cities of Tarin Kowt, Lashkar Gah, and Kandahar with its benevolent instincts intact: It was there to do good. The benevolent spirit that had become NATO's became the glue of the ISAF mission, just as it had been the glue of NATO's earlier out-of-area missions. However, its sense of cohesion had deteriorated in the intervening years. It entered Afghanistan, the reputed graveyard of empires, with second thoughts. NATO breached its "Euro-Atlantic" confines but was not ready to accept a global mission; it condemned terrorism and invoked its most precious treaty commitment, Article V, but was not ready to run counterterrorist operations in Afghanistan; it recognized terrorism as a threat transgressing borders but did not see Afghanistan in a regional perspective; it became the vital security crutch for a newborn and frail regime but was not ready to contemplate the politics of Afghan recovery, including NATO's role should the country reverse into war. NATO's intent may have been benevolent, but NATO did not work as an alliance.

Political hesitancy, controversy, and poorly managed projects of Alliance revival in effect turned the tables in the U.N.–NATO relationship. Where NATO had previously guided the United Nations, it now asked to be guided by it. NATO tied itself to the U.N. mandate underlying ISAF with such vigor that the mandate took on the appearance of a shelter behind which NATO allies could protect themselves and their alliance commitment from the storm raging on the diplomatic scene, caused by the September 2001 attacks and the War on Terror. By the time NATO entered Tarin Kowt, Lashkar Gah, and Kandahar, the lieu of the Taliban and some of NATO's heaviest fighting to come, NATO had to trust others to bail it out but found little support. The United Nations had a minimal footprint in the country and was hardly capable of coordinating the civilian reconstruction effort, much less providing relief to beleaguered PRTs. The Afghan government was supposed to provide national leadership but was young, inexperienced, and beleaguered in its own fight to extend its legitimacy outside government buildings in Kabul. The U.S. force in Afghanistan—the CFC-A—was never told by its political leadership focused on Iraq that it must support ISAF. CFC-A and ISAF headquarters therefore developed a type of rivalry, with CFC-A taking pride in the hard work it was carrying out in dangerous areas, as opposed to "I Saw Americans Fight" ISAF, and with ISAF believing it had its mission right where CFC-A had it wrong.

To an extent, NATO's ISAF lead was a small victory for the Alliance. It came in the wake of perhaps the most divisive diplomatic experience of the Alliance; the 1956 Suez crisis is comparable, but hardly any other crisis in the Alliance's history is. ISAF was not of NATO's making. It was a stabilization force created in the midst of war and diplomatic turmoil. Most stakeholders, including the United States and Britain, wanted ISAF to be limited in size and impact in line with a "light footprint." ISAF was tied down and difficult to dislodge, therefore, by the time NATO began engaging it in earnest in 2003. To dislodge it, NATO needed a political commitment to all of Afghanistan's stabilization as well as an operational blueprint for bringing the force into Afghanistan's provinces. It did manage, we should note. The political commitment was tortuous to craft, but by late 2005 it was there. NATO had decided on expansion in late 2003 and then spent about a year and a half on the details of its counterclockwise move out of Kabul. The operational blueprint was PRT centered. The civil–military structure of the PRT fitted the mission and the experience and inclination of most allies who did not see themselves as expeditionary warriors but rather expeditionary stabilizers. It invited cooperation between NATO and other stakeholders in Afghanistan, notably the range of international governmental and nongovernmental organizations working to promote governance and development. All this was an achievement that should not be belittled.

The PRT concept is the window through which we see the limits to the achievement, though. PRTs were an OEF invention and a component of an emerging COIN campaign. However, NATO was not ready to think COIN, much less pursue it. NATO discarded Special Forces operations, counter-narcotics, and prisoner interrogation and detention—all of which are part of the COIN package. NATO also was not ready to think broadly about civil–military cooperation, which is a COIN commandment. The United States was only then discovering COIN and mostly in Iraq; France would have none of it given its EU ambitions; and Germany pretended that COIN was unnecessary because it did not fit domestic political requirements. Thus, OEF continued developing COIN but lacked the resources and political backing to really develop the concept.

The liturgy of Afghanistan at this time involved competing characterizations for the mission—stabilization and counterterrorism come to mind—but the most apt one is probably the one suggested by an American officer in 2009: "kinetic COIN."[97] OEF and ISAF started from different premises but were pulled in the same direction—of considering the population as the campaign's center of gravity—and both were stretched thin in terms of personnel and resources. Firepower became a convenient substitute. As the officer continued, "kinetic COIN" is an oxymoron. It cannot work. Yet the allies tried. "Kinetic COIN" reflected the degree to which NATO was focused on the goodness of the mission but unable to settle questions of power. ISAF was an ideal—not only in terms of the benevolence it could bring to Afghanistan but also the collective and truly multilateral alliance it promised to reinstate in Brussels. In effect, the allies went to Afghanistan to save not so much the Afghans as their Alliance.

Thus began the war for the West. As local politics in Afghanistan veered off script, NATO was confronted with the paucity of its approach. The mission had enemies that NATO and ISAF needed to confront systematically and effectively. This realization—the crisis it provoked inside the Alliance and the Alliance's ability to step back from the brink of outright failure—is the topic of the next chapter. It shows that the Alliance did manage to focus on the essential problem—its ability to function as an alliance also in the field when challenged by enemies. By early 2008 it had an answer in hand that entailed a reduced or limited kind of alliance. It worked on the Afghan scene but then raised the question of whether NATO could still pretend to be a force for good—a benevolent alliance—or whether Afghanistan had turned it into something else entirely.

5 CRISIS AND COMEBACK

Confronting the Insurgency, 2006–2008

THE WESTERN ALLIES ENTERED THE DIFFICULT TERRAIN of southern and eastern Afghanistan at a moment when their Alliance identity was shaken. They were in need of success but instead got battered. The Atlantic Alliance experienced the stress of failing alliances: political dissent at home, poor coordination in theater, and initiative in the hands of the opponent. Still, NATO made a comeback. In around mid-2007 it jolted itself into action, focusing on the kind of comprehensive action that would be needed to turn things around. The key to this compromise was NATO's focus on enabling the actions of lead nations and the U.S. decision to increasingly assume this lead.

If NATO could stage a comeback of sorts it was because it was in trouble. NATO was not winning on the ground. The key ground for NATO in 2006 through 2008 was Afghanistan's south (RC/S) because the United States maintained the troops it moved under the ISAF umbrella out east (RC/E) while largely leaving the south to other ISAF forces. The United States faced a rough terrain and entrenched insurgent networks—notably the Haqqani and Hekmatyar networks—that had come into being in opposition to the Soviet occupation of Afghanistan and had been nurtured by the aid channeled to them by the United States itself and others through the 1980s. These networks operate across the Afghan–Pakistani border and harbor Al Qaeda forces, which is why the United States has retained its focus here. NATO's focus was in the south, where the regional capital of Kandahar is the birthplace and focal point of the Taliban movement that succeeded in gaining national power in 1996 through its war efforts. It is anchored in the Pashtun area that comprises not only Afghanistan's southern provinces but also Baluchistan of Pakistan, and it has proven a formidable foe of NATO and ISAF.

In this chapter we shall dissect the nature of a "benevolent alliance" in terms of its ability to confront a ruthless and able enemy and to devise ways and means in a strategy to prevail. More particularly, we shall see how NATO ran into dead ends and faced near defeat but nonetheless managed to zoom in on "enabling" lead nation action as its best option for coping. It was a step down from the ambition to act as a truly multilateral and coherent alliance but an improvement of the preceding years' wishful thinking. The first section of this chapter addresses the challenge of engagement, with military as well as political factors explaining why NATO was not a capable strategic actor. The second section turns to the high politics of the Alliance and the kind of international order it was capable of imagining and supporting. We know that NATO had a liberal inclination, and here we assess its ability to take a determined political lead in 2006–2007. With these two sections, we see why testing military operations on the ground—the tactical level—as well as political-strategic issues were troublesome to NATO. What was left was the middle ground, where in military parlance the operational strategy is normally defined and where, in the terms of this book, NATO's "enabling" role was carved out. But NATO needed to enable someone's lead, and this could only be a U.S. lead. Section three of this chapter therefore engages the process through which the U.S. role in Afghanistan was transformed from a limited one to a real lead. We should make no mistake: It was certainly not a wholesale transformation, and it did not happen without controversy. However, the transformation did get off the ground, and it gave NATO a lead to enable. By the time of the Bucharest summit in April 2008, the Alliance was ready to admit to this "enabling" role and had a blueprint in hand for realizing it.

THE AGONY OF STRATEGIC ENGAGEMENT
IN AFGHANISTAN

History shows that Afghanistan is a difficult theater of conflict and that outside forces—NATO or otherwise—will be hard pressed to prevail there, but history is in a sense mere context. NATO had freedom of maneuver to define its mission and carry it out. It did not always make the best use of this freedom. The ferocity of Afghan fighting was revealed through 2006 as NATO forces moved south, and a point of culmination came in September 2006 when Taliban forces challenged NATO to a fight. Happily for NATO, the Alliance prevailed. However, the complex and multifaceted conflict required a sophisticated and sustained intervention, and in this respect the Alliance did not prevail. The intervention has been sustained, for sure, but it lacked in sophistication because of the Balkanized structure of ISAF, civil–military tensions, and political divisions in the headquarters that resulted in the formation of a sort of in-house coalition of the willing.

A Phony Victory

Operation Medusa is the name of the pitched battle that NATO forces won in early September 2006 and that came on the heels of ISAF's new command, August 1. It flowed from a prolonged campaign to unsettle the Taliban in the region (Operation Mountain Thrust) that ran over the summer of 2006 and that had been planned for in the OPLAN. Medusa was ISAF's first real battle. It was a symbolically important in several ways. It was fought in the Panjwai district southwest of Kandahar city, the figurative birthplace of the Taliban movement and the literal birthplace of its leader, Mullah Omar. Moreover, its layout of irrigation ditches, dry canals, vineyards, and wheat fields favored the insurgents. The Taliban chose this battleground and sought a decisive engagement to strategically undermine the new security agent on the block— NATO/ISAF. The Taliban was thus committed and strategic. It is likely that the Taliban was amassing in preparation for an attack on the city of Kandahar itself, which they may not have been able to hold but whose fall would have undermined NATO's credibility akin to the Vietcong's Tet Offensive of 1968: militarily unsustainable but strategically decisive. But there was to be no Tet offensive because NATO forces won the battle of Panjwai. Symbolically, NATO then lost the peace. NATO forces could win because the Taliban force effectively tried to hold its ground, inviting the kind of territorial fight with which NATO forces, after all, were familiar. The Taliban did not give up holding patches of territory until toward the end of 2007, but by then they had become even more skilled in asymmetric warfare. Kandahar remained a center of gravity, with the Taliban seeking to encircle it and undermine ISAF and by extension the Afghan government's authority from within.

The ISAF operation in 2006 countering the Taliban offensive was led by Canadian forces under Brigadier-General Fraser and supported by forces from nine other nations, making for a combat force of around 1,400. These forces encircled the Panjwai district in late August and early September in an effort to surround and isolate the Taliban force, exhaust and diminish it with the use of fire power, and then defeat it with a ground attack from the south across the Arghandab River. It did not quite work out as planned. The southern attack was moved forward in time, which undercut the plan to batter the Taliban with firepower; Canadian forces ran into a heavy firefight and suffered casualties; and air cover was thin given the ongoing campaign in neighboring Helmand.[1] As the allies prepared to launch their attack anew the following day, a U.S. A-10 Warthog aircraft mistakenly attacked them, killing one Canadian soldier, wounding several others, and causing the interruption of the attack. The attack then moved to the northern front, where several days of firefights were followed by the decisive and successful NATO thrust into the heart of the Panjwai district on September 11. Mop-up operations began the following day.[2]

The operation was decisive because the Taliban had not succeeded in its gambit to overrun NATO and begin ISAF's unraveling. But the operation raised a number of questions. One regarded the Taliban's intent. There was no doubt that the Taliban in this case sought out a decisive confrontation that it thought it could win.[3] The question was whether the Taliban was following the Chinese insurgency doctrine, according to which such decisive confrontations are desirable only as the culmination of an extended campaign that initially relies on hit-and-run tactics while the insurgency gathers strength. There was evidence to support this. The Taliban had not suddenly begun its violent campaign in August as NATO's RC/S command began: The campaign had begun in late 2005 and early 2006 as NATO forces began preparing for command, and it was a typical asymmetric campaign of roadside bombing, assassination, and hit-and-run attacks. By February 2006, the *starting point* for the deployment of Canada's Task Force Orion into Kandahar (Operation Archer), no fewer than fourteen suicide bomb attacks had taken place over the winter, which was remarkable given that such attacks once were deemed unacceptable in Afghan culture.[4] Moreover, in the following six months in the run-up to the battle of Panjwai the level of violence increased by 600 percent, turning Kandahar into a "war zone."[5]

Although the Taliban alignment with Chinese insurgency theory and its desire to prepare for a final grand stand against NATO would have been good news given NATO's core competence, reality turned out to be more complex. The Taliban was an agile adversary who perceived a weakness in NATO's armor, acted to exploit it, and, when defeated, reverted back to other strategies for achieving their goals. These goals vary because the Taliban movement itself is varied. Part of it is locally anchored and seeks to redress local grievances and protect tribal areas against what is perceived as undue outside interference. Part of it fights a classical insurgency war that aims to overthrow the central government and thus install the kind of theocratic but also national regime that the Taliban represented in 1996–2001. Yet another part of it, the one most clearly linked to Al Qaeda, is transnational and motivated by jihadism, or ideas of religious war. That is why it has become customary among some analysts to talk of the neo-Taliban and not the Taliban, which would otherwise indicate the kind of coherent and unitary movement that we know from China, Vietnam, and elsewhere.[6]

The intent of the Taliban was dynamic, and it was improbable that the Taliban was operating in unison according to classic insurgency doctrine. Moreover, and adding to the complexity, evidence indicates that (perhaps former) Pakistani intelligence officials were active in organizing the kind of guerilla movement—in terms of organization, resources, and doctrine—that made the Panjwai confrontation possible and that the jihadist movement benefited from the transfer of ideas from the Iraq insurgency on how to conduct a campaign of violence and intimidation by terror.[7] The Panjwai battle was therefore not a precursor but a single point in the trajectory of a complex conflict. This then raised another question, namely whether NATO could be both smart and flexible—whether it could bring its battle skills to serve a larger political purpose in the fields and valleys of Afghanistan. The immediate evidence from Panjwai was that it was going to be difficult, at best.

The number of armed insurgents facing NATO forces in Panjwai varies according to estimates, but a rough figure puts their level of forces on par with NATO's—a one-to-one ratio with about 1,400 troops on each side. This was not a ratio that NATO was comfortable with, naturally. Reports from the district indicate that somewhere between 500 and 1,000 insurgents were killed, which still left a large number who could fight another day. These other fighters simply disappeared. They blended into the civilian population and basically got away. This was one worrying sign. Another was their ability to rely on local aid because of underlying tribal conflict. The months preceding the battle had seen local government and police forces drawn from the Achakzai tribe come into conflict with the Noorzai tribe. Both tribes are strong in the Panjwai area, but the insertion of official police forces drawn from just the Achakzai tribe ignited the conflict and apparently created fertile ground for a local alliance between the Noorzai tribe and Taliban forces seeking to confront

ISAF and government forces. The pattern of police behavior reportedly did not change much following the September battle, as the police continued to ransack homes and shops and extort people at checkpoints, all for the sake of private gain. Thus, Kandahar Governor Asadullah Khalid's declaration that the "enemy has been completely eliminated" was followed the same day by a suicide bomber killing a civilian and wounding several other civilians in addition to Canadian soldiers.[8] Asadullah Khalid, previously the governor of the Ghazni province, was forced to resign in mid-2008 amid rumors of his involvement in widespread corruption and the running of a narcotics syndicate—only to return to power in 2009 as minister of borders and tribal affairs.

The NATO forces moving into the south had no problem perceiving the complexity of the battlefield and understanding that there was more than traditional battle on the road to victory. After all, counterinsurgency theory "is not rocket science," as Gregg Mills, a senior civilian advisor to British ISAF Commander General Richards through 2006, writes.[9] If countering an insurgency is easy in theory, it is all the harder in practice, and the practice of understanding the opponent, locating him, shaping the battlefield, and engaging him was what turned out to be difficult in 2006. The U.S.–led Operation Mountain Thrust was the biggest operation to date in the region, and it was intended to flush out Taliban forces and prepare the region for the type of "security assistance" that supposedly differed from counterinsurgency and that was ISAF's business. British commander Brigadier Ed Butler of 16 Air Assault Brigade, which began deploying to Helmand west of Kandahar in April 2006 and played a key role in Operation Mountain Thrust, emphasized the preparatory nature of the mission and believed the mission was succeeding: "They have got fewer and fewer places to go and hide," he observed in mid-June.[10] Still, for all the optimism, Mountain Thrust required the assistance of Canadian forces, which proved of great frustration to Canadian commanders who were in charge of the Kandahar area that was not part of Mountain Thrust, and they knew well that the situation in Panjwai was dangerously deteriorating. The American command in overall charge became aware of the gravity of the Panjwai situation in early to mid-July, but by then the transition to ISAF command was only a couple of weeks away. It was thus at a moment of transitory command and in parallel to taxing operations elsewhere that Canadians forces finally were able to focus on the Panjwai. They had planned a large operation for October but, realizing that events on the ground were outpacing planning, brought the campaign forward, and this became Medusa.[11]

At this point it would be safe to say that ISAF may have grasped the complexity of Afghan warfare and that the versatility of the enemy and the need for a counterinsurgency approach should have dawned on the full chain of command. However, just as ISAF failed to foresee the scale of the battle of Panjwai, it failed to grasp the extent to which the Taliban intended to and was able to exploit a dynamic battlefield.

Controversial Military Leadership

As he prepared to leave Kabul and his ISAF command, British General Richards acknowledged that the complexity on the ground and the intensity of the fighting on occasion had come as a surprise, but he also maintained that he and his team had foreseen the nature of the campaign. If ISAF and NATO were in trouble, the root of the problem lay outside the country:[12]

> The problem is that of confusing and hugely politicised command and control. The risk, and sometimes the result, is an incoherent and "Balkanised" operation. Nations committing themselves to such operations must influence the campaign through influence at the strategic/political level—in the case of NATO through membership of the North Atlantic Council—and must then leave their commanders to get on and implement that direction in militarily sound ways, meeting the nations' agreed and combined intent.

General Richards was commander of ISAF—COMISAF—from May 4, 2006, to February 4, 2007, and he was thus responsible not only for seeing ISAF through the tests to which the Taliban put it in Kandahar and Helmand but also for ISAF's full range of activities. He developed an approach that was broad and inspired by tenets of classic counterinsurgency lessons. It is an approach that strongly resembles that NATO committed to in 2009, and it supposedly is the answer to situations like the one in Panjwai. To understand the rise, fall, and then renewed rise of this approach we must begin with Richard's design and the controversy it engendered.

General Richards's approach was comprehensive, classic as mentioned, and can be described along three lines:[13]

- First, to focus security, development, and governance efforts on restricted areas of relatively high population density. These areas are known as "ink spots" in the literature and became Afghan Development Zones (ADZ) in the Richards lexicon. Once security and development picked up inside the ADZs, the idea was to lash information operations around this progress—and thus to win the well-known hearts and minds that are at the center of gravity in counterinsurgency campaigns.

- Next, to make sure that there is input into the ADZs, which led to the creation of a Policy Action Group (PAG) in Kabul, headed by Afghan President Karzai and involving key ministries and the international community, ISAF included. General Richards portrayed the PAG as the equivalent of a "war cabinet"—a lever designed to achieve unity of effort. It was originally focused on southern Afghanistan (RC/S), but the intention was to broaden its gaze to all of Afghanistan.

- Finally, while the military campaign should look outside the ADZs as well, it did not mean that ISAF forces were free to conduct search-and-kill missions in the countryside. Military operations were integral to the "shaping" of an operational environment that came prior to the "clear, hold, build" logic of counterinsurgency. Shaping operations outside ADZs therefore involved a kind of military diplomacy whereby military forces should enable political alignment and reconciliation.

General Richards's situation was that of a newcomer treading on new ground, which was both advantageous and inconvenient. It was an advantage because he was free of past policy practice and tradition and could shape the campaign as he saw it fit. He was not operating in a vacuum, though. There was the U.N. mandate and NATO decisions to frame his actions, and the key NATO framework for his planning was NATO's OPLAN of December 2005. But it was an elastic framework because it was an untested document for an upcoming operation and because it was "neither strategic nor operationalized," as General Richards put it.[14] The OPLAN:

> contains lots of fine intent, phasing, and all that, but it is not an operationalized plan for ground forces in the provinces of Afghanistan. Leading on from that I began to see in January 2006—I assumed command May 4, 2006—in the context of our [preparatory] exercise in Norway, that there were big gaps between ground needs and the OPLAN. I wrote my own commander's intent based on OPLAN headlines, which we then exercised and put to the test.

And though careful to stress that "nothing that I developed was inimical to the OPLAN," General Richards also noted that "I had to develop in detail."

General Richards had the further advantage of bringing along his own headquarters for the command: the Allied Rapid Reaction Corps (ARRC) that he headed at the time. It had by then become a generally accepted view that NATO could fall back on the option of letting such headquarters from the force structure (NFS) deploy in operations and do a combination of tactical and operational tasks. NATO did have a command structure (NCS) with both fixed and mobile operational headquarters (the latter were known as Combined Joint Task Force [CJTF] command packages), and, while a fixed operational headquarters (in Brunssum) did intervene between Kabul and Brussels, it was the ARRC on the ground that called the shots during 2006. That changed in early 2007 when "big NATO" made its entry into the Kabul command scene. As General Richards and the ARRC wrapped up to go home, NATO was setting up a permanent Kabul HQ with a NATO (as opposed to a NFS HQ) infrastructure of command and communication systems and staffing according to complex rules of national quotas and rotations (as opposed to the fixed staff that comes with a force structure headquarter).

A new position, an elastic OPLAN, and his own headquarters—these were the factors explaining General Richards's scope for action. There was a downside to this, of course, and it concerned the lack of an agreed-to framework. The OPLAN rested on a political compromise, and efforts to push it in one or another direction would inevitably cause concern among some stakeholders. These stakeholders were the allied governments sitting in the North Atlantic Council (NAC), but concern and debate extended also to the operational environment. We see this in relation to each of the three components of General Richards's approach.

The first, the ADZ or ink spots, was controversial because it implied the presence of a dangerous environment and the need to mass forces to achieve reconstruction and development. This ran in opposition to the "light footprint" that characterized not only the early Bush approach to Afghanistan but also NATO's own thinking, according to which security assistance could be provided with PRTs dotted variously on the Afghan map and a minimal military presence. ISAF's footprint presumed a country ready for development. People knew that some areas were dangerous given the Taliban presence, of course, but the idea was then to launch operations prior to ISAF command in order to clear the area (like Operation Mountain Thrust in the south) and allow ISAF to get on with its security assistance business. This approach was reflected in the way that ISAF was organized on the ground: PRTs in distinct provinces and no strategic reserve of forces to reinforce any particular PRT or ISAF unit that could come under attack. Large attacks were simply not meant to happen. As we saw in the previous chapter, the OPLAN of December 2005 was initially drawn up with a classical strategic reserve of around one-third of the force, but, under the weight of the argument that this was not a classical military campaign, the reserve forces were simply assigned to PRTs.

The reality on the ground was different and deteriorating. By massing forces, General Richards was responding to these events but also in effect telling his political masters several uncomfortable things: First of all, that the protection of the Afghan population required a level of military force far superior to that of 2006; second, that protection involved traditional military art—the use of kinetic power to kill enemies; and, third, that in the absence of a real reserve the commander needed to be able to call in other forces, which was to say that NATO allies needed to be flexible about their military presence in the country. The need for more troops was clear because General Richards's ADZs were small in number and restricted to the limited population centers Afghanistan, a rural country, has, and yet this was more than ISAF could handle. Reflecting on this restrictive presence, General Richards remarked that "a lot of nations said silly things like we had to do development outside ADZs." These allies failed to see that "it's all about psychology and [that] you have to demonstrate progress. You must focus your effort."[15]

The key to succeeding was to substitute mass for kinetic power, which is also to say that limited force numbers push you to become more kinetic—a counterproductive approach to countering insurgencies. The ISAF campaign became more kinetic because NATO allies were not providing reserves and not allowing the flexible use of their forces, General Richards argued. He recalls asking, "Where are my reserves?":

> Never before in the history of warfare has a commander not had one, typically roughly one-quarter of the force. You need something, but I had no reserve except for one Portuguese company. And then there were the caveats: The ability to move forces was practically not there, only for the Americans. The Americans did help out though they needed their forces in RC(E).

The second component was the PAG set up in Kabul. It followed the logic of counterinsurgency experience because to prevail one must unify all efforts, military and civilian. But the PAG had not been foreseen by NATO, not to mention the OPLAN, which was a military document. Again, there was an assumption of how an integrated effort was to come about, and it was equally insufficient in the face of Afghan events. The assumed effort was the Bonn process, the new Afghan political system and leadership, and the international community's support of it. As we might recall, the Bonn process came to an end with the parliamentary elections in late 2005, but the international support was then framed in the Afghan Compact of January 2006, which foresaw a coordinated effort by all parties in terms of security, governance, and development, and which set up a mechanism for achieving this coordination—the Joint Coordination and Monitoring Board (JCMB). According to its terms of references, the JCMB was to "provide high-level oversight" of the compact's implementation, "provide direction" on significant issues, and "report on progress" to the Afghan government and the international community.[16]

General Richards's PAG—and the PAG was the fruit of his thinking—was tantamount to saying that the Compact/JCMB system was not working. By selling the PAG to President Karzai and putting him at the end of the table, General Richards was summoning the Afghan side to step up to the task of leadership. And by pushing the PAG through, General Richards was in effect telling the diplomatic community in Kabul that they had been failing up to now. In General Richards's view: "Soldiers' impact on policy is not particularly new, I'd argue, but I was stepping on a lot of people's toes. 'Richards is getting out of his lane,' they would say. But it was clearly the right thing to do."

The small Helmand town of Musa Qala became the focal point of some of the political–military tensions generated by General Richards's approach. According to this approach, military force should be applied for psychological and political effects, and if ISAF forces could sway a change of allegiance without engaging in a fight, so much the better. Pushed by President Karzai, General Richards had consented to deploying military forces into the Helmand district centers of Musa Qala, Sangin, Nowzad, and Kajaki but only reluctantly so. These small centers were not part of the ADZ plan, and deploying there would spread ISAF forces thin and make them magnets for Taliban hit-and-run attacks. In short, from COMISAF's perspective, the ISAF presence in these small places was counterproductive but politically necessary. In the course of September 2006, as Medusa unfolded, ISAF gained an opportunity to strike a deal with the Musa Qala elders, the town's leadership, and grabbed it. According to the deal, ISAF would withdraw its (British) forces to five kilometers from the town in exchange for Taliban doing the same, and the hitch was the local community's determination to keep the Taliban out and allow the Afghan government in. The local community as well as the Helmand governor, Muhammad Daud, underwrote the deal and, if it worked, it would turn Musa Qala into the small equivalent of an ADZ and perhaps provide a model for others to follow.

The deal was controversial from the outset because it de facto opened negotiations with the Taliban, albeit indirectly, and started a type of reconciliation with parts of that movement without knowing for sure where the political process would lead. The British approach was to encourage this process not only by endorsing it politically but by being actively involved in offering (monetary) incentives for tribal realignments and by establishing secret contacts to supposedly moderate Talibans. President Karzai was critical of the deal but ended up approving it, although with explicit "mixed feelings." The United States was likewise critical and remained so, likening it to a capitulation. While the British commander and forces were talking of exporting the model to Sangin or Nowzad, American diplomats therefore made clear that they did not see the deal as "a model in any way." The incoming COMISAF, U.S. General Dan K. McNeill, was a known critic of the deal, and British officers at this stage described U.S.–U.K. relations as "at an all-time low."[17]

The split was certainly real. The balance shifted in American favor in early February when Taliban forces first overran Musa Qala, killing government officials and terminating the deal of October, and when, just a couple of days later, General McNeill took over as COMISAF and launched several devastating air strikes against the Taliban leadership in the area. The shifting balance brought little relief, however. General McNeill's command—which ran until June 2008—would be mired in kinetic campaigns that sidetracked the ADZ focus of General Richards but that brought peace no closer (more about this later); the British continued favoring another approach and made covert attempts to negotiate with the Taliban's regional leadership and to buy a shift of allegiance; and the overall situation in the region kept deteriorating.[18]

In sum, where General Richards was blessed with a wide campaign framework that gave him considerable leeway, he was cursed by unresolved political tensions embedded in the Alliance. General Richards used his freedom of maneuver—sometimes deliberately pushing it to the limits—to define the comprehensive approach presented here: ADZ, PAG, and military diplomacy. Each dimension became controversial, and the fact that the Taliban overran Musa Qala just as he was leaving his command was bad news: The loss of this town became the focal point for all his critics, who now had "proof" of the need for change.

One should be careful to delimit the kind of impact General Richards could have had if the level of controversy had been greatly reduced. The structure of ISAF was debilitating, with NATO efforts divided into national PRT fiefdoms used by individual allies to showcase the magnificence of their national approach. All allies save for the United States lacked the capacity to provide a military infrastructure that was mobile and flexible: They struggled to implant a military footprint on the Afghan ground, and once there they became holding units. Moreover, General Richards defined his approach at a time when the RC/S nations—the Netherlands, Australia, Canada, Denmark, Estonia, and Romania in addition to Great Britain—were coping with the deployment to the region and the fact that they had to shoot to kill to survive. There was little capacity to think outside one's area of responsibility, therefore. The United States, mostly operating in RC/E but also with forces in RC/S, had been in the Afghan fighting game for some time when General Richards came to Kabul, and their particular approach was embedded in their RC/E PRTs and their OEF chain of command, which operated independently of ISAF. U.S. forces were therefore unlikely to adopt wholesale reform because of a change of pace in ISAF's Kabul headquarters. As for the remainder of the allies, they operated in more tranquil zones—RC/N, RC/W, and the capital of Kabul—and were not poised to grasp the urgency and gravity of the Richards approach. Indeed, one might argue with some justification that General Richards's impact was biggest inside his own national chain of command and therefore inside the British area of responsibility in Helmand.

Still, and this is a critically important point, Afghanistan was a single theater of conflict and in need of an overarching and coherent approach to its problems. Moreover, it follows from the logic of counterinsurgency that the person in charge of the theater campaign must be comprehensive and political. Through 2006 this person was General Richards. He understood the logic, followed it, and ran into political controversy. In researching this book, I had an opportunity to query a NATO ambassador regarding his view of Generals Richards and McNeill, respectively. The latter, General McNeill, was just a soldier, the ambassador replied, but General Richards was very public and active in bringing in the media. It was understood that the North Atlantic Council (NAC) was not always appreciative of this activism.

The NAC had asked for it, though. They had committed forces to a difficult mission and not addressed the fact that the international framework—the Afghan Compact and its JCMB—were irrelevant at best or dysfunctional at worst. NATO had a senior civilian representative in the country—beginning in January 2004 with Turkish Hikmet Çetin, who in 2006 was replaced by Dutch Daan Everts—who was in Kabul to represent the political leadership of the Alliance but who was hamstrung by the leadership vacuum developing in Brussels. General Richards stepped into this vacuum because he wanted to (given his counterinsurgency insights) and because he could (given the leverage coming from his command of forces). By dismissing Richards's framework and bringing in a "regular" soldier, General McNeill, the NAC removed a nuisance but solved little. As General McNeill followed a more classical military approach to the Afghan situation, the political field—the hearts and minds field—opened to the Taliban.

Political Divisions and Counterinsurgency

A phony victory in the Panjwai and the bold leadership of COMISAF General Richards challenged past planning, but unity eluded NATO. NATO did make some progress at the Riga summit of November 2006, though, which took place in the heat of ISAF's southern and eastern expansion. Progress came in the shape of a collective recognition of the type of comprehensive solution that the engagement called out for and that in NATO terms became the Comprehensive Approach. Here we shall first take note of this moderate achievement, then examine the underlying political tensions that bedeviled the Riga summit in a more fundamental way.

Riga was the first occasion on which the allies mentioned the comprehensive approach and thus endorsed it as an important policy area. Looking to NATO's two key operations, ISAF in Afghanistan and KFOR in Kosovo, the allies matter-of-factly concluded that "today's challenges require a comprehensive approach by the international community involving a wide spectrum of civil and military instruments." NATO was at pains to respect the existing mandates of international organizations and thus avoid the kind of debilitating debates on the international architecture that hampered NATO diplomacy in the 1990s when supposedly "interlocking" institutions became "interblocking." NATO's Riga pledge to the comprehensive approach was therefore modest (no change of mandate; NATO is not seeking to imitate the

EU or United Nations) and pragmatic (NATO must seek internal reform and external cooperation).[19]

A centrally placed official from NATO's Political Affairs and Security Policy (PASP) Division explained in a background interview for this book that the comprehensive approach as practice was not new in 2006. It reflected NATO's experience since the early 1990s when it got involved in Bosnian crisis management, and it continued developing through engagements in Kosovo and Macedonia and then outside Europe in Pakistan and the United States in the context of natural disasters (an earthquake and a hurricane, respectively, both in 2005), and in Darfur and Somalia in support of the African Union. The comprehensive approach is a business in growth, he observed, and it has been so for the better part of two decades.[20] This may be so, but it does not explain why it was so difficult to get it on the Riga agenda in 2006 and why the Riga formulation stood until November 2010, NATO being unable in the intervening years to open the formula and render it more precise.[21]

We are thus lead to inquire into the politics of countering insurgencies. NATO was in effect riveted by caveats—meaning allies' reluctance to fully commit to the game plan. The term *caveats* normally refers to the restrictions allies place on their forces as deployed in theater and that limit the forces' ability to operate outside certain areas (for instance, RC/N) or under certain conditions (for instance, at night or far from bases). These caveats have become legend in the history of ISAF because they are concrete expressions of the political ambiguity that is NATO's, and to a large extent they dominated the Riga summit. More than any other ally, Germany came into the line of fire, though France, Spain, and Italy were lined up behind it. These were the big contributors to RC/N, RC/W, and RC/C (the Kabul area), and unsurprisingly they were met with demands from the RC/S countries that they needed to join the fight. This was a serious affair, as we have seen, because the RC/S campaign was intense and bloody. Conscious of the emerging split, Secretary General de Hoop Scheffer took a leading role in the effort to pressure the former group of allies into flexing their caveats.[22] The effort paid off in some respects at the Riga summit because many NATO allies significantly reduced their caveats—among them the Netherlands, Romania, the Czech Republic, Denmark, Greece, Hungary, Slovenia, and Lithuania—but the big ones budged only little, sticking to their guns but agreeing to allow their forces to operate in the south "in extremis."

Caveats inhibited the provision of forces required for the mission. One might think that the resourcing of one's own (NATO's) mission would seem self-evident but not if nations harbor some kind of reservation, seeing the mission as one that the other allies really ought to shoulder disproportionally. In NATO this type of debate takes place in relation to a so-called Combined Joint Statement of Requirements (CJSOR), which is a military assessment of what is needed to fulfill the political ambition as defined by the NAC. The CJSOR by definition defines the minimum requirement of forces: It is not a wish list. Even so, the CJSORs for Afghanistan have been notoriously hard to fill. At the time of the Riga summit, when NATO had just taken over RC/S and was about to take over RC/E, NATO could deliver only around 90 percent of the CJSOR for RC/S and had about 85 percent of the CJSOR ready for RC/E.[23] Again, the Riga summit did help but not much: Five of seven missing battalions were committed, along with a number of critical enablers such as rotary and reconnaissance assets. NATO was now closer to meeting the minimum CJSOR requirements, but it would take some time for the new units and assets to arrive in Afghanistan, and NATO had in the meantime exposed to which extent it would go to frustrate its key unifying actor, the secretary general.

Jaap de Hoop Scheffer had by the time of the Riga summit been NATO's secretary general for the better part of three years and had spent an inordinate amount of time on the Afghanistan dossier. It is only natural that the Alliance's secretary general spend his time and energy defining compromise positions, but through 2005–2006 the office of secretary general was belittled by the allies' reluctance to commit few but critical enablers.[24] The allies were locked in a confrontation over the mission statement and burden sharing and were happy to delay and soft-pedal by having their secretary general spend his own capital beating the drum of force generation where he should have been piecing together an overall strategy for the Alliance. I queried the now former secretary general on this issue, and he noted diplomatically that the early years were "a difficult period because we started from scratch" but also that "the whole issue of force generation has been extremely tedious over the years." NATO has adapted, he noted further, but mostly once the United States was able to free resources from Iraq and enhance its Afghan force generation lead, and this is from 2008 onward. Apart from this, moving NATO "has involved a lot of lobbying and the use of the begging bowl," as de Hoop Scheffer put it.

Force restrictions and burden sharing underpinned a more political and lasting division that pitched the RC/S allies against the rest. This division ran through almost every Afghan issue the Alliance dealt with, but now, in late 2006, it was in some ways formalized and turned into a kind of inner coalition. The RC/S countries—the United States, Britain, Canada, the Netherlands, Denmark, Estonia, Romania, and Australia—began meeting separately in the latter half of 2006. The meetings were informal and held in varying ministerial and ambassadorial formats. One experienced NATO ambassador informed me in 2009 that the group meets every two to three weeks and has open discussions regarding the region.[25] He found that the purpose of the group was primarily linked to "strategic communications," which is to say agenda setting within the Alliance and also the shaping of the public vision of the war. Former Danish Defense Minister Søren Gade (in office from 2004 to 2010) elaborates that RC/S agenda setting could refer to such issues as the comprehensive approach or the use of local militias to encourage reintegration, which was the case during 2007, or to the issue of collateral damage, which brought COMISAF McChrystal to the NAC for discussions in 2009.[26]

Some analysts tend to place more emphasis on the group's impact within the Alliance, though. Daniel Korski, one of the keenest observers of the war, at one point spoke of an "RC/S caucus" given what he perceived as the group's ability to act as a kind of inner NATO directorate. Moreover, the group—or caucus—finds its origins in the Iraq war of 2003 that so divided Europe and that saw a select group of European allies go to war with the United States. This group, at first the Iraq caucus, became the RC/S caucus.[27]

I asked the former secretary general, Jaap de Hoop Scheffer, of his view of this group and whether it gained the kind of political weight that could qualify it for the "caucus" label. "There was an intra-alliance line—not a division but a line—between the allies in the north and west and those in the south. It was a debate and not a division," argues de Hoop Scheffer. And the presence of the group did not preoccupy NATO. "The group made no secret of their meetings. I was invited and attended one of their meetings, and there was always an assistant secretary general present." Still, the formation of such groups was not of the secretary general's preference: "I wasn't that keen on such groupings but in the end also realized that this is important. These allies suffered the casualties. . . . The United States and other allies were unapologetic about it—they were losing soldiers and wanted to have these meetings, and some allies did not like it."[28]

The RC/S group definitely had impact, and it definitely was controversial. Its purpose was to pull other allies into the fight in order to win it, and this purpose, along with the resistance it generated, marked the Riga summit among other NATO events. As the campaign dragged on, though, and as regional concerns became pronounced throughout Afghanistan, the drama became less intense. Germany thus later took the lead in forming a RC/N group. Still, in the course of 2007 the totality of these political issues—from caveats over burden sharing to political fractions—reinforced the lesson from Panjwai and the Richards command experience that NATO was not very capable of "engaging" the Afghan situation—of taking on the adversary, of defining and leading a campaign plan, and of driving local actors to align with NATO/ISAF.

WHOSE ORDER TO UPHOLD?

According to rationalist theory, NATO was for the United States to shape. The United States—a "unipole"—is by virtue of its relatively insular position in North America and level of national power freed of the traditional alliance dilemma. It has the ability to project power into Eurasia at its point of choosing. It does not need to fear "abandonment" by its allies because it can do on its own, and it does not need to fear "entrapment" because it can just say no to beleaguered allies' call for assistance. The allies, on the other hand, are particularly fearful of U.S. abandonment. In short, the United States should be able to shape NATO according to its political whims. This type of dynamic was difficult to observe in 2006–2007, however. NATO's "transformation" U.S.-style ran into trouble. As time went by, beginning in 2001–2002, the United States appeared more and more "entrapped" in Alliance dynamics and less and less willing to simply "abandon" it. All allies thus stuck with the Alliance, but none was able to break the political logjam—and this at a time when the situation in Afghanistan went from bad to worse.

Resisting the U.S. Riga Agenda

The United States came to the Riga summit of November 2006 with an agenda linked to the continuing transformation of NATO. It had been prepared for most of a year and included a broad range of issues, from missile defense, NATO enlargement, and partnership to Iraq and Afghanistan. The key agenda for Afghanistan concerned caveats and force contributions, as we have seen, and modest progress was made at the summit. Perhaps the best way to gauge the ability of the United States to mold NATO for a new global role is the partnership issue because it reveals the way in which Afghanistan connected to world politics.

NATO had built a layered structure of friends and partners in the 1990s: Most were gathered in the Euro-Atlantic Partnership Council, but some were involved by virtue of the Mediterranean Dialogue or the Istanbul Cooperation Initiative that began in 2004. They had geography in common: Combined, they made up the approaches to Europe. NATO's logic was that if NATO can secure a geographic belt of friendly countries around the European core area, then the Alliance's security is more or less guaranteed. It was an impeccable logic from a conventional point of view—a type of Cold War logic according to which threats implied military forces rolling across plains or crossing water to reach the Alliance heartland. To be sure, the allies were aware of the changing security environment, but the European allies in the 1990s wanted to focus on new threats close to Europe and limit NATO to the Euro-Atlantic area. When the Bush administration in 2003–2004 sought to give form to this purpose in the broader Middle East and North Africa, it was met with resistance and a counterproject intended to anchor such missions outside of NATO, in the EU.

Now, in the run-up to Riga, the Bush administration gave the idea of a broader and more political NATO a new go. The theme was once again "NATO transformation," the subheading was the turn from in-place territorial defense to expeditionary and global missions, and the focal point was the partnership policy. Nicholas Burns, who had left the post of NATO ambassador in early 2005 to become under secretary of state for political affairs, outlined U.S. thinking on this issue prior to the summit, identifying a group of "global partners" (Japan, Australia, South Korea, Sweden, and Finland) who had offered NATO significant assistance and now merited closer institutional links with the Alliance. NATO today "is part of a broader and growing web of multinational institutions seeking to address global challenges," Burns explained in early November, and "We need a NATO that works seamlessly with other key actors."[29]

There were two ways to look at this push to accept global partners. One, and the one presented by Nicholas Burns in the run-up to the summit, was that this was merely an additional layer to NATO's existing partnership structure growing out of the Afghan engagement that everyone agreed was NATO's priority number one. It was a functional and pragmatic view. Nicholas Burns—who did not go to the summit in his new capacity but helped define the agenda—later explained that the partnership initiative came out of a long-standing U.S. policy of opening the Alliance to new relationships. It was not particularly related to Afghanistan, though the partnership debate focused on global partners who were active in Afghanistan: It was just one of several items on the Riga agenda, as far as the United States was concerned.[30]

But it was also possible to tie all items together to gain an overarching view of where the United States would like to take NATO—and this was in a global direction. NATO with a new global mission in addition to its remaining regional mission defined the essence of the transformation puzzle that the United States had put together in 2001–2002, which President Bush had reinvigorated with his February 2005 visit to NATO headquarters, and which Secretary of Defense Rumsfeld continued promoting with NATO's Allied Command Transformation (ACT) and the NATO Response Force (NRF), another prominent Riga topic. The new partnership policy was part of this effort: U.S. NATO Ambassador Victoria Nuland opened the partnership issue in early 2006 by suggesting a new global partnership forum for NATO and the folding of the EAPC. Though this fairly radical proposal of closing the old partnership shop and setting up a new global one was toned down subsequently, the continued inclusion of EU members Sweden and Finland in the U.S. proposal gave rise to speculation that the United States was seeking to enhance NATO at the expense of the EU. Moreover, Nicholas Burns's past history as a promoter of a globalized alliance of democracies, along with repeated calls for such an alliance from the hands of prominent Americans, nourished the view that at issue was not just pragmatics but NATO's political destiny.[31]

NATO did not go global at Riga. NATO decided to give its prominent ISAF partners a new status as "contact countries," which was short of real (and global) partnership, and better access to NATO planning, exercises, and operations but on an "ad-hoc" and "case-by-case" basis.[32] A year and a half later, at the Bucharest summit, they would gain "tailored" cooperation packages that slightly improved their status and access but not in a fundamental way. Put differently, while the Alliance struggled in Afghanistan, the allies were not ready to see in this situation a need for new set of principles for international order that NATO could pursue. The United States had proposed one set of principles; the other allies had resisted.

NATO in a Box

NATO's inability to break out of its habitual role as a regional deterrent must also be attributed to the way in which external actors enhanced the status quo inside the Alliance. The first of these was the United Nations, by which we should understand by the Secretariat as well as the General Assembly, albeit with usual reservations for exceptions to the rule, both of which continued to view NATO with suspicion and as a kind of military body that is foreign to the U.N. family. This attitude naturally inhibited NATO's attempt to push the Comprehensive Approach as a general framework for global cooperation.

In Chapter 2 we saw how the catastrophic "dual key" experience in Bosnia, 1992–1995, fed NATO's wish to stand clear of the United Nations during the Kosovo war in 1999. By 2004–2005, things appeared to improve, though, as the difficulty of managing complex crises weighed in on both organizations. David Yost, a prominent NATO analyst, has mapped out a positive movement that began in November 2004 when Jaap de Hoop Scheffer became the first NATO secretary general to formally address the U.N. Security Council. In mid- to late 2005 NATO then proposed both a joint U.N.–NATO declaration and kind of memorandum of understanding defining themes and methods of cooperation. If given a green light, these political agreements would have opened the door to greater NATO–U.N. interaction, improved understanding (clear away stereotypes), enhanced common planning and preparations, and also legitimized innovation in the shape of boundary spanning activities.[33]

The process ran into a red light, however. For almost three years nothing happened. A U.N.–NATO declaration was finally signed in September 2008 but under controversial circumstances. Political backing for the agreement was lacking in the United Nations, which is why U.N. Secretary General Ban Ki-Moon's decision to sign it provoked protest and which explains why the declaration is merely a declaration on "secretariat cooperation." It does not involve the full political weight and purpose of the organizations. Moreover, it was kept secret—though it quickly leaked into the public domain.[34] One NATO spokesperson reflected bitterly on this process, noting that NATO is in Afghanistan under a U.N. mandate and that the United Nations cannot even get around to recognizing that NATO, whose soldiers get killed and maimed, is doing the hard work of the international community.[35]

Many distinct factors are involved in this drama of delay and coyness— from great powers' distrust of one another over organizational stereotypes to real and diverging interests. They all share a theme, however, which relates to NATO's role in the international order that the United Nations is supposed to represent. As we saw in Chapter 2, NATO is committed to the order but not quite to U.N. leadership.

The U.N. ability to put brakes on the Alliance's efforts to pull the Afghan pieces together in an overarching political strategy naturally puts Russia, one of the five permanent members of the U.N. Security Council, at the heart of the matter. In the post–Cold War period, Russia has repeatedly sought to side-track NATO or transform it into something radically different, from a Western alliance into a kind of post–Cold War collective security organization akin to the Organization for Security and Co-operation in Europe (OSCE). Russian leaders from (Soviet leader) Gorbachev to post–Cold War presidents Yeltsin, Putin, Medvedev, and again Putin have sought to deny NATO's its Western character and leadership potential. Russia strongly protested the U.N.–NATO declaration of 2008, labeling it "illegitimate" and "illegal" and denying that such agreements could be confined to cooperation between secretariats and thus could escape the need for political approval.[36] This was in 2008, but in the run-up to the Riga summit in 2006 things were not much different.

The key to understanding this is deeply buried in the Riga summit decla-ration in paragraph 25, which briefly mentions a recently completed missile defense feasibility study and its conclusion that missile defense was techni-cally possible. With this small nod in the direction of missile defense, NATO got further involved in the controversy that involved the U.S. policy of de-fending itself and allies against missile attacks and Russian efforts to obstruct this policy. Russia had reluctantly acquiesced to Washington's desire to let the U.S.–Russian ban on missile defense expire—which became a reality in June 2002, six months subsequent to the Bush administration's announcement that it would not seek to renew the Anti-Ballistic Missile (ABM) treaty—but Russia was in no mood to accept missile defense installations in Europe and certainly not in the new NATO member states close to Russian territory. Poland and the Czech Republic were in 2006 lined up to become hosts to this new defense architecture, and Russia repeatedly warned against it, promising to develop new offensive weapons capable of breaching the shield.[37]

When queried on the Riga summit and the impact that the fighting in southern Afghanistan was having on NATO, former Secretary General Jaap de Hoop Scheffer's first recollection was that "the Riga summit was to some extent dominated by missile defense because of Poland and the Czech Repub-lic and Russian reactions."[38] We have seen how Russia protested the declara-tion when it finally came about, declaring it illegal, and de Hoop Scheffer's recollection is that the process of U.N.–NATO negotiation was "tedious and complex" and that it is "more correct to say that it's an agreement between the secretariats given resistance from some among the P5." Because three of the permanent five (P5) U.N. Security Council members are NATO members (the United States, Britain, and France), and because China did not make much noise, we might surmise that the former secretary general had Russia in mind.

In terms of political strategy, therefore, hostility from the United Nations and Russia combined with allied divisions on partnership and global order to keep NATO in its regional box. The Alliance was busily transforming, but it lacked the capacity to define an agenda for global order and NATO's role within it. For any alliance this is disturbing: The fountain of sound strategy and military planning is political purpose and foresight. NATO might argue that, even if the politics of international order were uncertain, its own course of action in Afghanistan was solidly focused on solving security problems. With grand diplomacy locked down, the "benevolent alliance" was at work on the Afghan ground. But the battle of Panjwai and the growing insurgency belied this line of thinking. NATO was not ready to lead a fight, even if in the name of heralded values. NATO was in double trouble, therefore, lacking in political purpose and military tenacity. The plank that could rescue NATO was the operational dimension of "enabling" the action of others, but this presumed that there was a lead to enable.

THE UNITED STATES IN THE LEAD

By late 2007 and early 2008, and thus in the run-up to the Bucharest summit, there was evidence of hesitant U.S. leadership and Alliance controversy. Appearing next to his boss, Secretary of Defense Robert Gates, before the House of Representative's Armed Service Committee in mid-December 2007, Joint Chief of Staff General Mullen voiced a widely noted view of U.S. priorities: "Our main focus, militarily, in the region and in the world right now is rightly and firmly in Iraq. . . . It is simply a matter of resources, of capacity. In Afghanistan, we do what we can. In Iraq, we do what we must."[39] General Mullen's statement reflected the toll the U.S. "surge" in Iraq was taking in terms of resources and policy attention. The surge was announced by President Bush in January 2007 following an intense debate through 2006, and it involved the deployment of an additional five brigades, or around 20,000 troops, as well as the extension of tours of duty for troops already in Iraq. It was a major effort and a political gamble, and it naturally preoccupied the chain of command.

There was also evidence of Alliance controversy because the United States continued demanding greater efforts of its allies—fewer caveats, more troops, and more critical enablers. It was the same old debate but now given greater urgency by the U.S. decision to bet its money on the Iraq surge. At the December 2007 hearing with General Mullen, Secretary of Defense Gates stated with reference to NATO that "much more can and should be done." The heart of the matter concerned the allies' view of their Alliance, which to Gates was outdated: "NATO must adjust to the challenges associated with conducting operations in distant locations. And NATO needs to ensure that it has the resources and the organizational structure to counter terrorist networks and triumph over insurgencies that threaten to cause instability and failed states." One might think that Gates and the United States could rely on the RC/S group in this respect—the battle-hardened and risk-willing group of countries taking on the Taliban in the movement's heartland—but this group was equally in the line of U.S. fire as Gates criticized not only the resources committed to the fight by NATO allies but also their approach and doctrines. "Most of the European forces, NATO forces, are not trained in counterinsurgency; they were trained for the Fulda Gap [Cold War operations]," and he explicitly compared the troubled experience of RC/S allies to the allegedly more successful efforts of U.S. forces in RC/E. Immediately following the Congressional hearing, on December 12, 2007, Secretary Gates raised this point at an informal RC/S meeting. Unsurprisingly, no allies from this core constituency backed his views. In parallel, the U.S. ISAF commander, General McNeill, let it be known that the United States unofficially had proposed that U.S. forces should take charge of the mission in southern Afghanistan now that the RC/S group and ISAF were incapable of stabilizing the situation.[40] If this was a U.S. lead, it was certainly a curious one involving the privileging of Iraq and the launching of criticism of key allies at all levels, from resources to doctrine.

Yet a lead was coming into being, and the widespread criticism is testimony to it. NATO was in the U.S. line of fire because it was being taken seriously as a lead organization in Afghanistan under ISAF banners. NATO and ISAF had fanned out across that country and by late 2006 established its command: Now the U.S. forces and command needed to adapt their own ways of acting and thinking to this new presence, and with adaptation came expectations that NATO would prove amenable to American ideas and practices. Expectations led to frustrations, but expectations were a priori positive. The United States no longer saw Afghanistan through the primary prism of "coalitions"—OEF—but that of an embedded institution, NATO. Symbolically, NATO's assumption of command over all of Afghanistan's territory—coming with the RC/E command on 5 October 5, 2006—nearly coincided with the (November 8) resignation of Secretary of Defense Rumsfeld, the architect of the coalition-of-the-willing policy that so had stressed the Alliance. This resignation came on the heels of the Republicans' loss in the 2006 midterm elections and represented a culmination of the many controversies that related notably to Iraq, and it was thus not in any particular way motivated by ISAF and Afghanistan. Still, the impact on ISAF business was notable.

The new secretary of defense, Robert Gates, came to office with fresh eyes and a different background. He had no stake in the high-profile transformation agenda of his predecessor and the way in which this connected to and fed civil–military tension within the Pentagon. Gates proved more open to military advice, regular meetings with the military chiefs, and military control of troop movements without his personal review.[41] He also made it his mission to focus on the ongoing wars in Iraq and Afghanistan, which again meant a reduced emphasis on transformation. NATO officials interviewed for this book emphasized how this mission focus challenged NATO but in a different way compared to Rumsfeld: It meant that the Alliance would be judged according to what it delivered here and now and not according to its commitment to future visions—as with missile defense, network-centric warfare, and the like. The onus moved from input (money, plans, policy) to output (troops and effects on the ground) in the shifting balance of NATO diplomacy. Secretary Gates's focus therefore added legitimacy to the complaints voiced by the military ranks of the Pentagon—a "groundswell of complaints" according to one NATO insider—and that targeted European contributions. Secretary Gates's approach to all this was decidedly pragmatic: NATO needs to make decisions, and the United States will work through NATO if it adds value to the mission. The top U.S. general in NATO's organization at this time was General Bantz J. Craddock, supreme allied commander Europe (SACEUR) from December 2006 to June 2009. He recalls that "Gates came to office in 2006 when the United States was focused on Iraq, and in NATO he was trying to keep the focus on a deal—if I do this, you do that." Moreover, "Secretary Gates asked for more informal formats during NATO meetings to get a debate and then a decision. Of course, you'd be uncomfortable with this format if you have nothing to contribute."[42]

The Complexity of a Military Lead

There were really two lines of action along which the United States pushed its allies, with one being military and the other civilian–military or comprehensive.

The military track followed naturally from the expiration of General Richards's command in early 2007 because Richards had brought his own headquarters—the ARRC—and was taking it back with him. This was always the plan, and so NATO prepared through 2006 for a new and more permanent solution to the question of military command and control. The solution became a wholly new headquarters—ISAF HQ—assembled for this specific operation and destined for dissolution once the mission comes to an end. ISAF HQ came neither from the NATO command structure (NCS) nor the force structure (NFS—like the ARRC).

Inventing a new Alliance campaign HQ was largely an exercise in military bureaucracy. The demands of NATO allies for influence and prestige, along with different national cycles of rotation, combined to create a highly complex matrix for staffing the HQ, and this in a theater of ongoing conflict of critical importance to the Alliance. The system, which began operating as the command transferred from General Richards to General McNeill in early February 2007, was almost counterproductive in its complexity. General Craddock, who as SACEUR had to manage the process of setting up the HQ and keeping it in business, recalls, "The ISAF HQ we did get—well, we couldn't have designed it any worse. We had 1,200 people with four different rotational aspects. It was almost unmanageable." And staff numbers grew over the years, reaching the level of around 2,000, which was clearly more than what was needed. A Danish officer speaking on background estimated that the HQ thus grew in size for the simple reason that allies sought prestige, influence, and sometimes a safe Afghan assignment for their troops. In other words, the ISAF HQ was bloated and unwieldy.

There had been other options on NATO's table. If the Alliance felt that NFS headquarters such as the ARRC, though reinforced, were too light and too complex to rotate in and out of the country, it could then fall back on its command structure, the NCS. As we saw earlier, the regional Joint Force Commands (of which there are two) each contain a detachable and deployable command element—the CJTF HQ—that NATO had planned and prepared for expeditionary warfare since the mid-1990s. Such a CJTF HQ, already staffed and trained, could in theory have moved to Kabul to form the nucleus of the new ISAF HQ.

If NATO instead opted for a complex and unwieldy new and temporary structure it was because the United States wanted the military lead but in such a way that the Alliance remained involved. The desire for a U.S. lead precluded the CJTF option because the CJTF would be an extension of and thus be commanded by NATO's Joint Force Command HQ in Brunssum, the Netherlands. Because the Brunssum HQ command rotated between Germany and the Netherlands, one of these countries would be in the operational lead. It would exclude a U.S. command. That option was therefore taken off the table—formally in February 2006. It might have seemed preferable to keep things simple from there on. Simplicity implied drawing on the lessons learned from Bosnia and Kosovo where NATO's theater commander soon communicated directly with SACEUR, at the strategic level, bypassing the operational level of command. Reflecting on this experience and his desire for simplicity, former SACEUR Craddock recalls that "we should have gone directly from COMISAF to SACEUR, but we couldn't: . . . simply connecting the first American COMISAF, General McNeill, to SHAPE, also led by the United States, would have made it look like a U.S. takeover."

The end result was therefore that NATO not only set up a complex and unwieldy Kabul HQ but also inserted the Brunssum CJF HQ into the chain of command, adding even more complexity to the command-and-control organization and stifling SACEUR's ability to operate and respond to the North Atlantic Council agenda. It naturally also eroded the capacity of the local commander—in this case General McNeill—to shape the campaign. General McNeill was commander of ISAF only: He was not involved in the parallel U.S.-led OEF chain of command. We may recall from the previous chapter that NATO's solution to the ISAF–OEF conundrum had been to establish separate commands where an ISAF deputy for security would be responsible for communicating with the OEF chain of command and "deconflicting" missions. From a practical point of view this setup worked well: Missions were indeed deconflicted. But it left COMISAF not only outside the OEF chain of command but now inside a NATO/ISAF chain of command that in complexity resembled that of the reconstruction and PRT effort more generally and that in addition was fraught with command caveats and national force contributions that by virtue of their limited capacities were fixed site forces.

The U.S. desire to take the lead combined with their desire to mobilize NATO behind this lead account for this state of affairs. The key positions were occupied by American officers, but NATO allies could staff various other positions and gain information and presumably also influence. The drivers of this process were not efficiency and simplicity but Alliance diplomacy. The conflicting demands of political coherence and military stringency bring us to the second line of action—the comprehensive integration of civilian and military efforts.

A Comprehensive Lead

The United States took the lead in defining a new comprehensive approach to Afghanistan, though there were several lead actors in this affair, as we shall see. The U.S. lead is important to note, though: It helps us understand the contested nature of the ISAF campaign through 2007; it highlights both the lasting and controversial contribution of General Richards; it opens a new chapter in the ongoing and difficult NATO–U.N. relationship; and it finally and critically illustrates the difficulty of working in perfect tandem with the new Afghan regime headed by President Karzai.

It is appropriate to begin with General Richards and the broad effort he sought to design and implement—the PAG, the ADZ, and military diplomacy. The comprehensiveness of this approach was spot on in terms of counterinsurgency theory, but politics intervened: Neither the NAC nor President Karzai was particularly happy. The NAC felt it was losing control, and Karzai felt little PAG ownership. Moreover, NATO's Secretary General de Hoop Scheffer was hesitant to have NATO organize the "big tent" meetings of the international community because he felt that it would de facto make NATO accountable for efforts and events it did not control. Through 2005–2006 de Hoop Scheffer therefore worked to improve relations to the EU and the United Nations to realize the vision that NATO ended up endorsing at the Riga summit—that the existing mandates of international organizations should be respected but that everyone should work to improve cooperation. It was therefore more or less clear that an ISAF lead was off the table. General Richards's design could have worked had President Karzai and the Afghan government bought into it, but they did not, at least not sufficiently. Something else was needed.

By March 2008 the international community had the answer in the shape of a new U.N. Security Council Resolution that strengthened the U.N. mission in Afghanistan (UNAMA) and expanded its authority to coordinate civilian efforts and interact with ISAF, which remained in charge of security. Security Council Resolution 1806 of March 2008 specifically called on the special representative of the U.N. secretary general—thus the head of UNAMA—to promote "more coherent support" from the international community, "strengthen the cooperation with ISAF at all levels and throughout the country," and expand UNAMA's presence throughout the country and assist Afghan-led reconciliation efforts.[43] Importantly, this enhanced effort was to take place within *existing* mandates. The reigning framework was still the compact dating back to January 2006, and the venue for decision making remained the compact's JCMB board, which Afghanistan and UNAMA co-chaired. The answer therefore amounted to new wine in old bottles: a more concerted effort but through established channels. It was nonetheless a significant step in the direction of recognizing that the "light footprint" of the early years had not worked. The original mandate gave UNAMA authority over "the planning and conduct" of all U.N. operations and urged other actors to consult and coordinate with UNAMA, and this principle had remained in place until now in 2008 when a bigger and more assertive footprint was in demand.[44] Norwegian diplomat Kai Eide was appointed as new UNAMA representative to oversee its creation.

There was therefore a notable shift in the approach to Afghanistan. In the early years, everyone involved in Afghanistan had sought to keep the involvement light—from the United States and OEF over ISAF to UNAMA. Gradually, as the security situation worsened, ISAF and NATO got more involved, culminating in General Richards's ISAF-led effort to bolster the Afghan government. Now, in early 2008, the international community sought to bring UNAMA back to par and shoulder-to-shoulder with ISAF. The new Afghan government remained in charge, of course, but was de facto dependent on outside support, and UNAMA and ISAF/NATO had struck a deal to share more equally in this support. This was new and in some ways encouraging.

In other ways it was not because the deal demonstrated the limits to which even an American lead had to adapt. The drive to bring UNAMA back to par and move from an ISAF–Afghanistan relationship to an ISAF–Afghanistan–UNAMA triangle was U.S.-led, although Britain played an important role as co-lead. This drive had greater ambitions than the "new wine in old bottles" that became the solution: Its original intent had been to revise the mandates to create a significantly stronger U.N. special representative—a kind of international czar of development and governance who would be the trailblazer for the international community and thus also in many ways for ISAF. This drive failed due to Afghan resistance, notably from President Karzai, who rightly perceived that his hands were about to be further tied by assertive international leadership. In the fall of 2007 the United States and Britain put forth British Paddy Ashdown, a former U.N. high representative in Bosnia (2002–2006), where he had become known as the "viceroy" of that country, a label that was not necessarily kindly intended, for the position as new Afghan coordinator. The process got very near to its completion. Paddy Ashdown met with President Karzai early in January during an official visit to Kuwait by Karzai, and they "had apparently got on well," though Ashdown's downbeat view of the campaign's likelihood of success might have been a source of some discord.[45] When U.N. Secretary General Ban-ki Moon asked Paddy Ashdown to accept the job, he did and then started recruiting his staff and organizing his mission.[46]

Later in January Karzai then unexpectedly went into opposition to Ashdown's candidacy—allegedly because an editorial of The Times portrayed him as powerless—as if he suddenly realized the extent to which Ashdown would gain new powers and not simply become another UNAMA head.[47] Paddy Ashdown himself cited Afghan internal politics as the cause of his failed candidacy. It is simply not credible that Karzai or any other at this late point could have been in doubt that the new person would come with significantly enhanced powers. By early December 2007 several things were perfectly clear: The terms of the then current NATO and U.N. representatives (Daan W. Everts and Tom Königs, respectively) were expiring, and neither had, for various reasons, made much of a difference; these two positions would be replaced by the new super envoy who thus would become the single and unifying interlocutor of the Afghan government; this plan was pushed by the actors most likely to make active use of it, meaning the United States in particular but also Britain and NATO more broadly; President Bush had apparently cleared the idea with President Karzai at an early point; and Paddy Ashdown was the favorite candidate.[48] Still, Karzai's blocking move in late January broke the momentum. There would be no "super envoy" to challenge the president, or to work with him, depending on one's point of view, and the international community therefore had to go in search of a new compromise.[49] This compromise became Kai Eide and the deal that he would remain a UNAMA figure but be tasked to provide for greater coordination and unity of effort.

As noted, this was part of the U.S. lead that came about in 2007, and it involved NATO not only in terms of the super envoy diplomacy but also in respect to ISAF's focus and actions. The key issue was to have NATO recognize the comprehensiveness of the campaign and to think in counterinsurgency terms. Counterinsurgency, or COIN, was not part of the NATO vocabulary, but comprehensiveness now was, since Riga, and this became the door through which change could be promoted. Riga took place in November

2006: Six months later, in June 2007, the North Atlantic Council meeting in defense minister format addressed Afghanistan in very comprehensive terms. Their final communiqué enumerated all the ingredients of a COIN campaign: first with reference to the building up of indigenous security forces (ANSF), then to international coordination and unity of effort; the role of neighboring Pakistan; the importance of drugs control; and finally the insurgents' practice of targeting the civilian population.[50] If the Alliance could tie these issues together in an overarching strategy, it would de facto have a COIN strategy: It would become an alliance capable of strategic engagement. But the Alliance was not at this point. It had all the issues but a deficit in strategic capacity. The design to have a U.N. super envoy take the lead was one answer, but it did not answer the question of how NATO was to coalesce behind him or her.

Old Scores

NATO continued through 2007 to be divided on the nature of the mission, which by now is a familiar theme to readers, and it explains why COIN remained an unrecognized term at NATO HQ. Events in 2007 inflamed these divisions, though the comprehensive approach and the super envoy initiative were designed to solve them and advance the campaign. The change of command from General Richards to General McNeill was not so much a change of focus from a comprehensive approach (that of General Richards) to a more traditional military campaign (that of General McNeill) but to another type of comprehensive approach whereby civil–military cooperation was sought anchored in the UNAMA–ISAF–Afghanistan triangle, as we have seen. Still, when viewed from within the ISAF context, it did entail a shift from comprehensiveness to a more military campaign. As the aforementioned NATO ambassador had remarked, General McNeill was "just a soldier" where General Richards had been almost political.

General McNeill was nicknamed "bomber McNeill" because of his supposed inclination to be "kinetic": to rely on the use of firepower. General McNeill had a history with Afghanistan, as we saw in the previous chapter: He headed the OEF coalition at the moment when the regular U.S. army took over from U.S. Special Forces, in 2002, and he was responsible for the strategy of building up PRTs in the army's effort to win hearts and minds. This was an early counterinsurgency effort, and McNeill was leading it. Still, in 2007–2008 some observers found General McNeill's ISAF approach conventional, with large concentrations of forces in "clear-and-sweep" operations and with aggressive entries and quick withdrawals undermining hearts-and-minds tactics (that is, provision of medical services, development aid, or access to government authorities). ISAF's reliance especially on air power and an increasingly visible policy of tracking and killing Taliban leaders by (supposedly) precision strikes had observers worry that "bomber McNeill" was pulling ISAF in an unfortunate direction—away from the stabilization and reconstruction efforts that Afghanistan needed and that European forces arguably favored.[51]

There can be no question that General McNeill did not intend to take over the General Richards dossier: He sought change, in other words, and military diplomacy—the striking of deals as in Musa Qala—was not a priority. This opened the door to critics, but other factors fanned the flames. The U.S. effort to focus comprehensive efforts outside ISAF was one factor because it left ISAF with a reduced and more military task, as mentioned. Another was the skill of the Taliban and the timid commitment of NATO as a whole to the operation. The Taliban had learned from Medusa that they should not challenge ISAF to big fights. But they continued to challenge ISAF by taking territory and holding it, particularly in northern Helmand, just as they continued to develop their skills in asymmetric warfare (blowing up ISAF forces by way of roadside and suicide bombs and terrorizing the civilian population and government officials). NATO committed too few troops to this campaign, and this reflected poorly on all allies. When General McNeill took over as COMISAF in February 2007 there were around 41,000 ISAF troops, of which 15,000 were American and 26,000 from Canada, Europe, and NATO partners. When McNeill terminated his command in June 2008 there were 53,000 in total, with almost 24,000 American and 29,000 soldiers of other nationalities. Though the increase was substantial in relative terms (25 percent compared to the February 2007 level), it was small in relation to what was needed to protect the Afghan population.[52] What struck NATO's supreme commander, SACEUR General Craddock, when asked to reflect on the 2007 campaign was "the volatility of the insurgency" and the fact that "the kinetic side took over." "The Taliban feared the Afghan Development Zones and really fought back," General Craddock recalls, and "they sought to destroy our strategy."[53] Destroying the strategy meant a shift of focus from ADZ to kinetics: This is what the Taliban wanted, and this is pretty much what they achieved.

Adding considerably to the complexity of the Western calculus was the Pakistan issue and the growing realization that Pakistan lacked perhaps both the capacity and interest in going all out in support of ISAF and OEF. COMISAF General Richards had pinpointed the challenge of "infiltration"— in fact, a classical counterinsurgency issue—shortly into his command, and, by January 2008, in the midst of General McNeill's efforts to control a volatile campaign, U.S. Director of National Intelligence, Mike McConnell, informed the White House that "the Pakistani government regularly gives weapons and support to insurgents to go into Afghanistan and attack Afghan and coalition forces."[54] The Haqqani network, one of the groups that supposedly can secure the "strategic depth" to which Pakistan aspires, was behind the assault at the Serena Hotel in Kabul in January and the bombing of the Indian embassy in July 2008, and in both instances there was intercepted evidence of a degree of Pakistani complicity.[55] The Pakistani effort to connect radical groups to foreign policy goals led in November 2008 to the spectacular terrorist attack, this time by the group Lashkar-e-Toiba, in Mumbai, India. A year earlier, in December 2007, radical violence had reached another peak with the murder of Pakistani presidential hopeful, Benazir Bhutto.

The fact of the matter was that the terrain, the population, the skilled opponent, and the radicalization of politics in Pakistan called for a degree of commitment of force and diplomacy that neither the American nor the European part of the Alliance was ready for. General McNeill emphasized this problem and directly countered those who believed it was a question of being "kinetic" or not. At a press briefing in February 2008, General McNeill addressed the coherence of a campaign that had evolved considerably over the years: "It troubled I think a few Europeans when I first came in, and I think a lot of the websites said 'Bomber' McNeill and that kind of jazz. Okay, I got it. But I also knew something about counterinsurgency operations, and I stand by what I've done over the last year." The real problem concerned force levels, he observed. Following the guidelines of U.S. counterinsurgency doctrine, "You'd come to the conclusion you need a huge force, well over 400,000, when you rolled up international force with the indigenous force."[56]

There was enough blame to go around in the Alliance at this point. The United States was betting its money on Iraq, as noted, and the European buildup in Afghanistan was modest, if anything. The non-American contribution had increased by only 3,000 soldiers through the McNeill period, and the ISAF force structure had not become more agile or capable: European allies continued to uphold caveats, and their forces continued to lack the capacity to deploy in theater. David Kilcullen, an Australian expert on modern wars and later a counterinsurgency advisor to General Petraeus, one of the architects of the U.S. surge in Iraq and later COMISAF, stated very early on in General McNeill's tenure as COMISAF that if anyone had a "kinetic" problem in Afghanistan, it was the Europeans. They were naïve about the use of force, placing too much hope on the short-term delivery of development projects, and they committed so few troops that they had no choice but to call in air power when the Taliban turned up the heat.[57]

The European allies had an opportunity to step up to the plate in the civilian domain: The training of Afghan police forces was severely lacking, and such civilian capacity building was part of the EU's profile. Hence, beginning in mid- to late 2006 and as part of the comprehensive approach-diplomacy at this time, NATO began pushing the EU to get involved in the business of training the Afghan police because the lead nation from 2002 up until then, Germany, had bungled the job. In December 2006, in the aftermath of NATO's Riga summit, the EU responded positively, and history's irony had it that it befell to Germany as EU president in the spring of 2007 to manage the process of transferring Afghan police training from itself to the EU. EUPOL was thus created: It was a modestly sized police academy outfit that, if fully staffed, would contain 400 police trainers with a significant number of these operating locally via the PRT structure. But the EUPOL mission was not fully staffed—and it still is not at the time of writing, when around 270 of 400 police trainers are in place; PRT outreach has proven difficult to organize; and EU–NATO cooperation on EUPOL has been hampered by Turkey's ability and notable willingness to arrest this cooperation (especially in terms of intelligence sharing) because of lingering Greek–Turkish disputes over Cyprus. Put differently, EUPOL was no panacea. EUPOL did symbolize the reality of the comprehensive approach agenda, but it did not lift the European contribution to new levels, nor did it solve the problem of how the allies could come together to support a U.S. lead that, considering the history of the campaign and the ability of the Taliban to stress the Alliance, was bound to be contested to some degree.

NATO THE ENABLER

By April 2008 NATO reached consensus on the necessity of it—NATO—stepping in to create strategic coherence. The Afghan track lacked coherence: The Bonn agreement had come and gone, and the Afghan Compact of 2006 was too big and wide to provide it. The international track likewise lacked coherence: Many nations invested in a new Afghanistan but through mainly national channels—though in the spirit of Bonn and the Compact; everyone was talking about a comprehensive approach, but no one was really capable of delivering it, with the United States making an effort but being burdened by the history of its coalition diplomacy and Iraq, with the United Nations hesitating to work closely with NATO, and with Afghan President Karzai refusing to agree to the creation of a "super envoy" who could become the agent of comprehensive thinking and planning. NATO stepped in to redress this situation, which was significant.

What did NATO do? It adopted a plan of action for Afghanistan and embedded it partly in an overarching policy, partly a visible and broad commitment to comprehensive action:

- The plan of action is the (confidential) Comprehensive Strategic Political-Military Plan (CSPMP),[58] which contains four pillars that are defined according to the logic of the campaign and not, say, the institutional competences of any one organization like NATO. The four pillars are ISAF, the Afghan National Security Forces (armed forces and police), civilian authority (disarmament, drugs, justice, and so on), and regional diplomacy (Pakistan and Central Asia). There are sixteen desired strategic outcomes defined in the document and some sixty to seventy particular actions attached to them. An action can involve NATO's lead or NATO's support of another organization's lead. The CSPMP is thus a framework. It needs revision in response to events on the ground, and it has thus been revised several times since April 2008. It is a living document, as any strategy worth its name is.

- This plan of action runs parallel to a general (that is, non-Afghan) "comprehensive approach" policy. This policy, an outcome of the Riga commitment to "do something," comes in the shape of a Comprehensive Approach Action Plan (CAAP). Like the CSPMP, it has four pillars, though they are quite different.[59] The intention behind the CAAP is to bring new people, ideas, and organizations into a hitherto classical civil–military channel of training, exercising, and planning and preparing for operations.[60] Importantly, the intention is also to ensure that other organizations such as the United Nations or the EU open up to NATO and take NATO expertise and viewpoints into account in their own processes of deliberation, training, planning, and so on.

- Finally, the Bucharest summit was a shared NATO–ISAF summit. NATO as ISAF lead organized the summit (and conducted some business of its own) but brought together the major players in and around ISAF: Afghan President Hamid Karzai, U.N. Secretary General Ban Ki-moon, EU Commission President José Barroso and the EU High Representative Javier Solana, and Managing Director of the World Bank Ngozi Okonjo-Iweala, among others (see Chapter 3). It was ISAF that issued the Strategic Vision for Afghanistan at the summit, and all of the participants were there to endow the comprehensive approach—to offer their support for the CAAP but notably also the CSPMP and NATO's lead in Afghanistan.

The CSPMP was in many ways simply another document in the bureaucratic ways of a big organization. One national diplomat who had observed the making of the document from within the headquarters noted that the CSPMP was mostly about public diplomacy and intended to demonstrate mastery of a situation that was spinning out of control. A NATO official who works with the CSPMP and Afghanistan on a daily basis observed that the CSPMP is a kind of "bureaucratic tool"—a consensual document that frames political discussions in Brussels but that no one in Kabul probably has heard of. These experiences doubtlessly reflect the incremental and sometimes painstakingly tedious process of making decisions in Brussels and the fact that the CSPMP was part of it. Nonetheless, the CSPMP signified something quite important: that NATO, with the blessing of the international community gathered in Bucharest, should go from simply organizing forces for ISAF to help bring about the concerted effort that could make ISAF succeed. In other words, NATO had become a designated "enabler."

The Decision: Tasking the CSPMP

So far in this as well as the preceding chapter we have examined the main forces driving NATO toward this enabling position: NATO's loss of a strategic sense of purpose in the War on Terror and its loss of operational coherence in Afghanistan once the fight against the Taliban picked up. If NATO—a benevolent alliance—could not articulate a political vision or fight on behalf of its cherished values, its rescuing plank would have to be its ability to enable strategic action. This was not an easy option. NATO sought to involve the United Nations and the EU but got mired in a network of institutional distrust; COMISAF General Richards laid the groundwork for a comprehensive approach from the bottom up but lacked political backing, even within NATO; and the U.S. effort to move the comprehensive anchor from ISAF to an international super envoy ran into an Afghan veto. In the following pages, we shall trace the process through which NATO, having run out of alternative options, managed to overcome these obstacles and actually become an enabler. Process tracing helps us understand why something happened but also reveals the solidity of political decisions: NATO's new position was very strongly backed but fragile nonetheless.

In some ways the Bucharest decision of April 2008 was portended by the Riga summit of November 2006 and the decision to establish a comprehensive approach (CA) policy track. In the intervening year and a half this CA track got split into two, with one focusing on the general policy (CAAP) and the other on Afghanistan (CSPMP). The interesting question here concerns the making of the second track and the decision that NATO, an ailing alliance, should rescue itself by servicing its leading member in Afghanistan. This second track was formally tasked by NATO defense ministers at an informal meeting in Noordwijk, October 23–24, 2007.

Judging by appearances, the Noordwijk meeting was a conundrum: Informal meetings cannot result in formal tasking. Nonetheless it did. Background discussions with various people at NATO headquarters indicate that the Noordwijk meeting involved controversial debate and that the secretary general resorted to the "silence procedure" to forge a consensus—that he should have tabled a draft decision and challenged reluctant allies by invoking this procedure that will lead to a decision unless one or several allies take it upon themselves to break rank or silence and protest. It would seem to indicate that the CSPMP was the object of dispute and got on track only by a type of institutional coercion. The reality is less dramatic but illuminating still. Secretary General de Hoop Scheffer and Assistant Secretary General (ASG) for Operations Martin Howard have confirmed in independent interviews that the CSPMP was not in dispute but that there were issues of controversy on the agenda.[61] They declined to elaborate on these controversies, but some of the big and difficult issues on NATO's agenda at this time concerned NATO's force in Kosovo (KFOR) and NATO–EU–U.N. relations and thus the overall CA framework—all probable sources of allied disagreement.

The CSPMP figured on a short list—a one-page document with eight to nine issues—that ASG Howard and NATO ambassadors and deputies were working into a decision sheet for the ministers who were meeting separately with the secretary general. When this sheet was passed to the ministers' group, the secretary general suggested that they briefly and exceptionally turn the informal meeting into a formal one to actually get a formal decision on these eight to nine issues, thus including the CSPMP. This was agreed to by the ministers. The formal meeting, the actual decision-making process, lasted less than a minute, as ASG Howard recalls it. Some, and maybe notably the ambassadors, felt that the process had run too quickly and on the issue of the CSPMP that the political framing of it was not yet in place; that the political side of the Alliance needed to discuss further before handing it over to NATO staff. For this reason, to accommodate this viewpoint, the secretary general invoked the silence procedure and thus gave allies an opportunity to reflect and object, if they felt it important. In the end, none did, and the tasking stood.

Looking Upstream: Fountains of the CSPMP
The proposal for the CSPMP came out of a fairly broad process of deliberation within the headquarters where ASG Martin Howard headed the effort to "prepare some ideas," as he put it, for strengthening NATO's political–military action in Afghanistan. This preparation of ideas involved not only ASG Howard's own organization—the Division of Operations and thus that part of NATO's international staff directly in charge of Afghan affairs—but all relevant parts of the international staff as well as allies. It was this set of initial ideas and thoughts that was "summarized" for Noordwijk and became the CSPMP platform. The short story is therefore that NATO headquarters worked: The idea came from the inside and not from some outside expert who happened to gain access to key decision makers—what is known as an "ideational entrepreneur" in the theoretical literature. The institution itself was the entrepreneur. But why did NATO work in this case?

One reason concerns a meeting of British and American minds. There was a tension between the approaches of these two key allies, we might recall. The British approach defined by General Richards was ISAF focused, bottom up, and involved a good measure of local deal making and military diplomacy. The American approach was focused on a new super envoy, was more top down, and was not inclined to support local deals that might give the Taliban breathing space. The two allies sought the same effect—a new Afghanistan capable of securing itself—but by differing means, and ensuing controversies and disputes, often driven by political passion more than facts on the ground, centered on the role of the ISAF Commander General McNeill. This crisis marked the year 2007, but it was overcome because key people crafted the CSPMP as a consensus. The CSPMP represented essentially the philosophy of the battlefield that had been General Richards's, and it offered support to the U.S. lead that had become more and more visible as 2007 progressed. There was more to the CSPMP than this, of course, but this meeting of minds and the momentum it offered should not be underestimated.

One of the NATO officials involved in actually writing the CSPMP told me that, to understand its origins, I would have to look into the effect Martin Howard had on the organization when he became ASG for Operations in August 2007. This is a couple of months prior to Noordwijk, in the midst of the McNeill controversy, and only six months following General Richards's command. Howard had prior to August 2007 been director general of operational policy in the British Ministry of Defence, and he described his new NATO job as quite similar to the old one, namely "to establish the strategic and political context in which we carry out military operations. Here I advise NAC and the Secretary General; then it was ministers. The environment is a bit different of course but in effect it's a very similar job."[62] The British lessons learned from the Afghan experience in 2006–2007 reflected a need to strengthen the political–military planning to obtain comprehensive effects related to governance, development, and also intelligence regarding the opponent, and when moving to NATO Martin Howard found—and this was a widely shared view within the headquarters, he underscored—that there was "no truly political–military plan" at the NAC level.

ASG Howard became NATO's internal entrepreneur, working the CSPMP into being and shape. The recognition that NATO was in need of coherent pol–mil planning may have been widespread, but ASG Howard brought the needed experience to the table. By experience we should understand not only a familiarity with political–military planning and what it can do for an ongoing operation but also a sense for the diplomacy it takes to craft change at the political–military interface. "New ideas need to be socialized," as ASG Howard put it, "and I did spend a bit of time trying to socialize this idea [of a pol–mil plan]. It was done very, very informally. That made it easier for the concept to be agreed." Howard brought along some assets that helped him perform in his new job. His pragmatic approach to Afghanistan contrasted with foreign ministry–led high politics and ran in the vein of defense ministerial and operational thinking that equally characterized the approach of U.S. Secretary of Defense Robert Gates, as we have seen. It was the operational side of the Alliance driving the initiative. Moreover, Howard was British and thus linked to the RC/S group that had formed to give voice to the campaign-intensive experience and to shape NATO's agenda. Howard-the-entrepreneur thus had legitimacy within the key Afghan constituency of the Alliance, but this also raised the question of whether his pragmatic ideas were politically acceptable to all allies.

It brings us to the other key event, the election of a French president, Nicolas Sarkozy, in June 2007. Sarkozy was less intrinsically critical of NATO and more willing to consider new ways of allied cooperation. It soon became clear following Sarkozy's election that he would seek France's military reintegration into NATO—a process that reached its conclusion at the April 2009 Strasbourg-Kehl summit. Organizationally the impact of this move was modest because France already participated extensively in NATO operations and also the NATO Response Force, the showcase of force transformation, but politically and symbolically it mattered enormously. At the Bucharest summit in April 2008, France laid the groundwork for this move by agreeing to deploy an additional 800 troops to Afghanistan and notably commit them to the very difficult RC/E sector, in Khost, under American command. The move was unpopular in France; it brought a vote of no confidence to the floor of the National Assembly, though it failed to pass; and the level of domestic controversy reached unprecedented heights in August 2008 when Taliban forces in the Uzbin Valley ambushed French forces, killing ten of them and wounding another twenty-one. Still, President Sarkozy stayed the course, in effect positioning France as new member of the RC/S club, even though the bulk of the French Afghan contribution remained in and around Kabul.

The new French policy that surfaced at Bucharest had been prepared since late 2007, which helps explain why the CSPMP and NATO's new role did not encounter a French veto or run into opposition that more indirectly drew on long-standing French criticism of the Alliance. According to French press, President Sarkozy had four options on his table ahead of the summit, and all of them were dangerous missions—to deploy more embedded trainers or to deploy a new unit to Kandahar (where the Canadians were threatening to pull out unless reinforced), to Helmand, or to Khost in the East.[63] Naturally, it would have been inconceivable to engage in new and dangerous missions in ISAF while blocking the wider NATO effort to work comprehensively along civil–military lines. France under Sarkozy maintained an overall emphasis on international pluralism or multipolarity, the centrality of the European Union and the Franco–German couple within it, and the need for Europe to stabilize its approaches, notably the Mediterranean area, all of which followed in the traditions of French diplomacy, but the willingness to work through NATO was new. Likewise, France remains wary of NATO's potential incursion into civil affairs, and France never invested in the PRT structure, but the degree of pragmatism on "comprehensive action" issues was new. In Afghanistan, Sarkozy saw, NATO was the only player, and NATO therefore got the task of enabling strategic action.

Looking Downstream: From Tasking to Decision
Following the Noordwijk meeting, the NATO machine kicked into gear and produced the required documents for summit approval. We would expect an international organization to thus respond capably to political tasking but should nonetheless take note of three issues.

First, the process launched NATO into the new business of comprehensive political–military planning. NATO had never before done such planning. The traditional NATO way of preparing operations consisted in essence of military advice, a NAC decision, and then a military plan to achieve political goals.[64] What NATO needed now was a political–military plan to achieve its goals, which required a new and broader planning procedure laying out how civilian and military tools should interact. ASG Martin Howard and the Operations Division led this post-Noordwijk effort to develop and plan in new ways. It involved first a broad process of "middle-management" planning with people from the Operations Division, the military staff, and then the military commands of SHAPE, Brunssum, and ISAF. This process took place under Howard's direction but was organized under a "Tiger Team" headed by Diego Ruiz-Palmer, the freewheeling strategic thinker who then operated in Howard's Operations Division. From here, the process continued with consultations with allies and partners in the Policy Coordination Group—which is NATO's standing committee for overseeing operations.[65] NATO had since Riga in 2006 talked about planning in broader ways, and the development of a general and comprehensive policy (the CAAP) meant that NATO was preparing to do it, but now, with the CSPMP, NATO had to do it, and did. The operational, as opposed to political–diplomatic, part of the Alliance had moved into the driver's seat, and this was due to Afghanistan.

Second, U.S. Secretary of Defense Gates continued to press for a transatlantic deal on Afghanistan and was thus an important external source of support for this internal change of pace. Gates promoted the new policy because it dovetailed with his thinking and cushioned his criticism of the allies as reluctant and not quite up to the task of counterinsurgency—a criticism he and Chief of Staff Mullen launched in late 2007 and early 2008, as we saw. By working within the Alliance to create new unity by way of the CSPMP, Gates was in effect offering the allies a way out. His concrete contributions seem to have been strongest in relation to the Strategic Vision that was made public at Bucharest, with the CSPMP being handled by ASG Howard and the Op Division. The Department of Defense's own press service communicated that Secretary Gates had launched not only the idea of presenting a Strategic Vision to the public but also the idea of generating an underlying comprehensive strategy.[66] ASG Howard maintains that both the Vision and the CSPMP "are truly NATO documents," though. "Secretary Gates was a major player and the United States had major input into the Strategic Vision. Gates was strong part of that. But this wasn't an American draft. Plenty of other people had views and contributed to it. . . . The reigns were held by NATO HQ."[67] What seems certain is that Secretary Gates through this critical period worked the issue of Afghanistan from different angles to mobilize the allies and that this effort coincided with the effort of the headquarters. This tells us that NATO's evolution into an "enabling" Alliance was aided in important ways by continuous U.S. involvement. NATO, to begin its operational transformation and draw back from the brink of failure in Afghanistan, needed a U.S. leadership to enable. Yet it was not easy for the United States to provide this lead at this point in time: It was primarily focused on Iraq, and its history of ignoring NATO in the Afghan context continued to plague its diplomacy. The efforts of Secretary of Defense Gates were therefore quite savvy, combining sticks and carrots to move the Alliance forward—not to have it take the lead (this it had done with ISAF with mixed results) but to have it organize support for, to enable, America's growing lead.

Finally, with the institutional trail and political lead taking shape, it remained for NATO to sort out its broader political cohesion and make sure that all allies agreed on "enabling" as the proper policy. There was a practical dimension to it: NATO could not be seen as an organization that promised support but proved unable to deliver it. It had to make sure that it was able to deliver on its word. Secretary General de Hoop Scheffer got extensively involved in the CSPMP dossier for this reason. According to ASG Howard, the secretary general's involvement following Noordwijk was due to his concern that NATO allies might end up with not one CSPMP but twenty-six different plans—one for each ally. "Once we got to an agreement, he then delegated responsibility to me and the PCG," ASG Howard recalls, but "It took a little while to get to that point, and it involved the Secretary General substantially."[68]

Behind the practicalities of the CSPMP lurked broader questions related to the Alliance's rationale: Was this the right policy for NATO more generally? Should NATO get even more involved in global security affairs and, though on a case-by-case basis and following consultations, "enable" U.S. actions? Afghanistan portended change for the Alliance's basic rationale, in other words. The Bucharest summit of April 2008 was a case in point: It was a grand summit—a big tent meeting—that not only involved NATO in the growing business of complex crisis management but singled NATO out as a lead organizer. We know that Secretary General Jaap de Hoop Scheffer worried about the implications hereof. "The risk of organizing big tent meetings, for instance, is that NATO will be held responsible. But NATO is not a nation builder; it is a political–military alliance that can provide only part of the answer." Therefore, and in the context of intra-Alliance debate, "I have objected to having NATO take responsibility of things it cannot control."[69] It would seem natural to relegate control to the United Nations, the global organization par excellence and the logical counterpart to the "comprehensive approach" idea that in principle is global. This was also de Hoop Scheffer's position: "The problem with the comprehensive approach was and is that NATO cannot steer the process. The leadership should be clearly in the hands of the U.N.: NATO does not have the steering wheel in its hands."

Even if it is accurate that NATO did not have the steering wheels in its hands—and it did not, and certainly not following the eruption of the insurgency in Afghanistan in 2006–2007—it does not follow that the United Nations is capable of grabbing or steering it. The "super envoy" proposal of late 2007 would partly move in this direction, but the idea was denied by Karzai and was in any case dependent on U.S. and British leadership, not U.N. leadership, which was notable by its absence. It became increasingly clear that the lead had to be American, and the United States increasingly drew in NATO as the enabling Alliance. This is one part of the story that will be told in the next chapter. It confirms that NATO, in spite of all its Afghan travails, can operate as an effective alliance. However, NATO is still not ready to digest the consequences of this effectiveness, which is a more robust international role in tandem with the United States and not the United Nations. This is the other part of the story. NATO is working well with the United States in Afghanistan but is driven by its benevolent mission to embrace the United Nations in questions of doctrine. Compared to the 1990s, when NATO set the pace of regional diplomacy irrespective of U.N. willingness to follow suit, NATO has lost in purpose, though it is struggling to recover it.

CONCLUSION

As a benevolent alliance, NATO was challenged in the Afghan context in 2005–2006 because it was not sure which principles it was fighting for. Liberty, democracy, human rights—these were easy rallying points, but they obscured fundamental questions related to the political order: The values are Western in origin but now global in scope; should NATO as a Western Alliance continue to promote them, even if local—Afghan—customs demanded pragmatism? And should it abide by the rules and procedures of the global organization, the United Nations? What happens when the foremost member of the Western Alliance, the United States, gets pitched against much of the international community on this issue? In Afghanistan, where NATO's ISAF lead by 2006 had grown to national (Afghan) proportions, NATO had no good answers to these big questions. Creative ambiguity is perhaps the best way to describe NATO's position in relation to the kind of international order it was fighting to uphold.

Strategic ambiguity did not work in NATO's favor, and the Alliance therefore needed to work its two other dimensions: to prepare or enable a military campaign and actually carry it out and, if needed, engage in combat. Engagement was forced on NATO as it moved south and east in Afghanistan in 2006. NATO was able to fight and hold its ground, especially when the Taliban made the mistake of challenging NATO in classical campaigns, but the Taliban changed their fighting style, and NATO was left to struggle with complex questions of counterinsurgency. NATO's COMISAF through this initial period, General Richards, understood the questions and sought to provide a set of answers—a focused effort in select zones of dense settlements (the ADZs); a strong and coordinated government effort to bring development and governance to these zones (the PAG in Kabul); and the shaping of the campaign environment through the communication and occasional deal making with local tribes and occasional opponents (military diplomacy). It was all controversial, and the war continued.

NATO was divided. Its force contributions and civil–military efforts were Balkanized: Nations preferred to be in control of certain provinces or sectors/regions where they soon became near immune to significant outside policy input and from where they could not move out for reasons of logistics as well as politics. Balkanization continued by virtue of force caveats that tied the hands of NATO force commanders and the piecemeal and reluctant generation of new forces that kept NATO forces slightly short of minimum requirements. The political division of NATO allies into an RC/S group and the rest was significant. It was now visible who wanted to fight and who did not. The force caveats of the non-RC/S allies were a cover for deeper political reservations regarding the mission, but political ambivalence needed to be overcome: If not, the skill of the Taliban, the ineptness of the Karzai regime, and the complexity of Pakistan's involvement would combine to defeat ISAF.

NATO did not have a collective answer to this set of challenges—no design for an order it could uphold—nor a real capacity for engagement. The enabling option was what was left, and NATO succeeded in picking it up. The key was the Bucharest 2008 decision to do comprehensive political–military planning in Afghanistan and have the Alliance do more things, more coordination, rather than just provide more troops. This wider effort would enable those on the ground actually doing the fighting in beleaguered provinces and the talking in Kabul to a government supposed to grow ever more capable. One key element in the design was the U.S.–British effort to generate a coherent and comprehensive engagement in super envoy format but that underestimated the reluctance of the Karzai regime to evolve by the design agreed to in the 2006 Compact. The result was comprehensive action in NATO format. This story involved the downfall of the General Richards design for a comprehensive campaign, a more classical but still controversial ISAF campaign under General McNeill, a new leadership style on the part of U.S. Secretary of Defense Gates, organizational leadership from Secretary General de Hoop Scheffer and ASG Howard, and finally the resurrection of a comprehensive campaign plan in the shape of the CSPMP capped off by a Strategic Vision.

With its Bucharest "big tent" meeting and explicit commitment to a wide and enabling investment in Afghanistan, NATO had opened new fronts in its two wars: It was promising more coherence to Afghans pinning their hope on ISAF, and it had begun the effort to rescue NATO the Western Alliance from irrelevance. It was an important effort, turning around years of diplomatic crisis and responding to the shock of Afghan warfare. If it looked like a comeback, it was only the beginning of one. Much now depended on NATO remaining engaged to sustain the campaign and drawing clear political lessons from it.

6 THE RECKONING

Searching for a Strategic Purpose, 2008–2011

IN THE COURSE OF 2009–2010 it became clear that ISAF's strategy for exiting Afghanistan was to dig in before handing off leadership to the locals. A type of surge akin to the one engineered by the United States in Iraq in 2007 began, with U.S. force numbers reaching the 100,000 mark and the ISAF total that of 140,000. It was done to reverse the momentum of the war, which was not going ISAF's way; to break the Taliban's back; and to incite the type of reintegration of and reconciliation with Taliban forces that would bring about an Afghan political settlement. It would also allow U.S. and allied forces to focus on enemy number one: Al Qaeda and its affiliates, located primarily in the Pakistan border area. This type of "transition COIN" is a balancing act. It demands a lot of resources and quick results, both of which are hard to deliver. It places a premium on good local governance, which takes the steering wheel out of Western hands. COIN classics are not of much help. The French, fighting insurgencies in Indochina and Algeria, never wanted to transition. The British did want to transition from Malaya in the 1950s, and their COIN campaign was successful, but they faced an insulated (Chinese) minority that had no access to outside support in the shape of arms, safe havens, or media coverage. Afghanistan is simply different. As ISAF committed to "transition COIN" in 2009, therefore, they had to invent the strategy and adapt as they went along.

The United States provided the push and the blueprint; the allies and partners supported it. If anything, it exposed the need for strong campaign leadership—the type of leadership that understands regional politics, aligns diverse resources, and puts them to use in an integrated campaign plan. This is strategic leadership, and it was in high demand. In this chapter we shall see the growing but still incomplete U.S. engagement in ISAF through 2008, as well as NATO's decision to enable strategy transformed into a case of campaign leadership by the Obama administration, and how NATO, once again, decided to step in and support it. We shall also see how the resulting strategy, though improved, was imperfect and sows the seeds of political challenges that NATO today must confront. Key among these challenges is the alignment of campaign ambition (COIN as a long-term security engagement) and campaign reality (COIN as a stepping stone to transition), and key for NATO will be its ability to address such gaps and not merely delegate them to lead nations or to a wider and ill-defined international community.

The chapter begins with the section on the leaderless situation in 2008. The ISAF campaign was at this point being rethought in COIN terms under the leadership of COMISAF General McKiernan, with ISAF working along the security line of operation and the United Nations its two lines of operation, governance and development. The challenge of unifying these efforts—of doing so in light of the "transition COIN" logic—was too steep, however, and it ruined both the design put forth by the United Nations and the command of General McKiernan. The fault lay not least with ISAF governments and NATO governments in particular who came up short on two accounts: They failed to provide proper political guidance to COMISAF, and they failed to grasp the futility of doing "transition COIN" in an equal partnership with the United Nations, an organization that is incapable of coercing a corrupt local government within a context of armed struggle.

The realization that "transition COIN" demanded a combined military, civilian, and diplomatic surge, *and* that Western governments needed to provide it, lay behind the Obama Af-Pak strategy of March 2009, which is the subject matter of this chapter's second section. President Obama brought a new strategy to the table and a new military leadership to Kabul, COMISAF General Stanley McChrystal. General McChrystal had a close relationship to the father of the U.S. Army's COIN field manual FM 3-24 of December 2006 and the 2007 surge in Iraq, General Petraeus, who at this point was General McChrystal's immediate boss. It was for General McChrystal and his reinforced command team to work with reinforced civilian agencies and allies to deliver Afghan results. This was clearly a U.S. lead that earlier had been in short supply. NATO, having hesitated through 2008, stepped up to the plate and invested. We trace this movement—how NATO invested but also had

little conceptual input to Obama's strategy and how it resulted in an acknowledgment that the Atlantic Alliance was in need of strategic reinforcement.

The third section of this chapter addresses the parallel efforts through
2010–2011 to reinforce NATO and fight the war in Afghanistan. NATO did
have something going for it—a sense of purpose that had previously been
lacking. President Obama seemed to lose it through the fall of 2009 when he
got caught in a second and considerably prolonged strategic review that the allies excruciatingly watched from the sidelines. NATO endorsed COIN at this
point, which was remarkable when looking back to the early days of ISAF and
OEF infighting. NATO also offered more troops and enhanced its political
presence in Kabul as part of the "transition COIN" campaign, effectively buy-
ing into the transition design laid out by COMISAF, the Karzai government
in Kabul, the United States, and others. Back in Brussels, NATO leaders were
slowly turning the ship around, strengthening the organizational and political instruments the Alliance needed to promote collective strategic thinking.

Yet all was not well. Though investing in "transition COIN" and the mo-
mentary surge, NATO was split. Individual allies caught on to the sense that
the end was near and began preparing to go home, which ran in the vein of
"transition" but not so much "COIN"—and it exposed the frailty of the strategy that Obama had brought to the table and NATO had bought into. The
year 2014 was defined in mid-2010 as the point in time when Afghan security forces would be in the lead in all of the country. It was impossible to tell
whether it could be done, but yet key allies began pulling their combat troops
in 2010. Moreover, and while NATO did step up its effort to shape politics
in Kabul, it remained notably absent from the politics of reconciliation and
thus the process that ultimately must bring the insurgency to a political end,
if such an end is at all possible. This was old NATO, the Alliance that enabled
but did not do strategy. As the concluding section of the chapter outlines, this
raises serious questions regarding NATO's general ability to provide political and strategic leadership. Such leadership is not impossible, but it depends
on informal and extraordinary or heroic leadership efforts. Heroic leadership
may intervene and rescue the Alliance, but heroism is not policy. Moreover,
heroic leadership will be undermined or indeed made impossible to the extent
that the Alliance as a whole nurtures an outlook based on global cooperation
and progress. It is a facile outlook that engenders compromise and broad legitimacy, and it is encapsulated in the "comprehensive approach" that NATO
has turned into its policy. As an outlook it rubs against the dynamism and

engagement that political—heroic—leadership is. Pushed by Afghanistan, NATO is creating a divide between its formal institution and its informal leadership. The chapter ends with this observation and the lesson that NATO needs to build bridges between the two.

A DEFICIT OF LEADERSHIP

General David McKiernan was relieved of his ISAF command on May 11, 2009, less than one year into it, and the orthodox interpretation is that General McKiernan had to go because a new COIN campaign was about to begin and he was not the right man for it. Secretary Gates cited the "new strategy" and "new mission" defined by President Obama as reasons that "I believe that new military leadership also is needed."[1] Others were blunter. General McKiernan brought a "conventional" approach to an unconventional war; he was an "armor officer" who lacked COIN experience; and he had become "deferential" to the complex NATO machine and had begun producing NATO "casserole" instead of real campaign strategies.[2] Retired Army General Keane, who helped General Petraeus develop the successful surge strategy for Iraq, allegedly called Secretary of State Clinton to line her up behind the view that General McKiernan was too conventional.[3] General McKiernan might actually have had the right mind-set, *The Guardian* later affirmed, but he failed on the account of changing the military culture. It was a failure of energy and drive and, as such, a testimony to the kind of political skills that COIN generals need to have and what happens if they do not.[4] What is certain is that the new principals moving in following the election of President Obama—President Obama himself, Vice President Biden, Secretary of State Clinton—came out of the most political of all Washington institutions, Congress, and that their freewheeling and inquiring approach to briefings required considerable political skill of the theater commander. In the spring of 2009, General McKiernan was probably unprepared for this.

The really interesting part of the story is the way in which allied governments, including the U.S. government, responded belatedly or timidly to a number of COIN issues that COMISAF McKiernan was developing. It is fair to criticize General McKiernan on a number of accounts, as we shall see, but the gist of the matter lay in the political realm, where a full COIN campaign was ruled out. The political framework within which General McKiernan was placed was weak, in other words, and it tells us several things: that the United

States sometimes is not able to deliver leadership; that NATO had given up trying; and that the United Nations was no match for the task.

The McKiernan Assessment and COIN Approach

General McKiernan was identified as incoming COMISAF in February 2008, five months prior to his command (and pending Senate confirmation) and seven months subsequent to the U.S. surge in Iraq reaching its peak of 160,000 troops. Afghanistan was not the theater of priority. At this time in Afghanistan COMISAF General McNeill was not able to focus the resources he needed on the Afghan Development Zones that would provide people protection and gain their loyalty in a classical COIN maneuver, and he was instead chasing bandits who were superior in numbers, local knowledge, and agility. NATO was reeling, having managed to confront Taliban strongholds in the south with hard-won success only to find itself hooked on search-and-destroy missions that the new Taliban strategy of pure insurgency fed off. The effort to promote change was for a moment placed in the hands of a new viceroy, Paddy Ashdown, except that Afghan President Karzai vetoed the idea. Where General McNeill was forced to downgrade the ADZs and population-centric COIN, General McKiernan sought to place greater unity of command, enhanced partnering with Afghan forces, regional diplomacy, and a whole-of-government approach at the heart of the ISAF effort.

General McKiernan did not commission an externally resourced commander's initial assessment once he landed in Kabul, which his successor famously did. General McKiernan instead prepared an informal commander's assessment shortly after his arrival in June 2008. It would later inform the Campaign Design and in the end become the operations plan OP TOLO of October, but it was a gradual process of adaptation beginning with the commander's personal assessment. General McChrystal's approach was different. On taking command June 1, 2009, General McChrystal initiated a sixty-day assessment—with key external participants—that was far reaching in its focus and that therefore, when it leaked in August, contributed to the strategic gridlock of the fall.[5] It is certainly possible that General McKiernan should have shaken the tree straight away. However, NATO's secretary general, following Secretary of Defense Gates's suggestion, had in April 2009 mandated the type of far-reaching assessment provided by General McChrystal and thus the making of a fully integrated theater campaign plan.[6] NATO had done no such thing in the spring of 2008. General McKiernan was commander of a force—ISAF—that had a limited mandate with a security focus: He did not have the authority to write an integrated theater campaign plan. His operational plan (OP TOLO) came close to being one, but it was not mandated as such. In short, where General McChrystal could run with change, General McKiernan needed to incite it and then shape it.

General McKiernan's key man in this was the chief of his Strategic Advisory Group (SAG), Brigadier General Gordon B. Davis Jr., who followed McKiernan in his preparations and arrived ahead of schedule in Kabul where he followed the McNeill team and interacted with COMISAF General McNeill to help prepare General McKiernan's startup in Kabul. The assessment divided into four themes, detailing the balance sheet for each one:[7]

- International Political Community. The negatives: The community was fractured and lacked a coordinated plan and overarching strategy. There also was no single voice from the theater but instead a host of commanders talking to their capitals (including several U.S. commanders talking to Washington). The positives: NATO's commitment to comprehensive action (the CSPMP of April 2008) and the U.N. readiness to be involved.
- Security. The negatives: Violence was increasing, ISAF lacked force numbers to hold and build, and Afghan forces were not ready to take over. The insurgents enjoyed significant sanctuaries in Pakistan and were boosted by the narcotics trade. Afghan forces were developing too slowly, and ISAF caveats prevented investments here. The positives: Some additional U.S. forces were coming in (3,500 Marines), and COIN operations in RC/East were having some success.
- Governance. The negatives: Corruption was rampant, there was power brokering as opposed to governance, line ministries were weak, and there was inadequate rule of law and a lack of human capital. The positives: Certain ministries were improving, and the public did not support the Taliban.
- Development. The negatives: There was uneven and slow progress of development as well as a lack of coherence in development assistance. No one was coordinating. The positives: A number of national development programs (notably in education and infrastructure) were going well.

COMISAF's priorities and actions flowed from here. In late June 2008, having run this assessment by some allied ambassadors—but not all and not frequently enough, some would argue—General McKiernan outlined the five things he in particular wanted to expand within the ISAF campaign plan: host nation security force development; counternarcotics support; regional engagement with Pakistan; rule of law and anticorruption efforts; and strategic communications.

This was the agenda in June 2008, and the key question did not concern the management of resources. General McKiernan requested an additional three brigade combat teams along with support (in total 15,000 troops) on top of the reinforcement of one brigade (3,500 troops) announced by President Bush in early September, and this was an issue of sorts, but the real issue concerned General McKiernan's grasp of counterinsurgency. General McKiernan had been ground commander during Operation Iraqi Freedom, thus commanding the armored thrust up the Tigris and the Euphrates. This had made his name, in a way. But it would be wrong to conclude that McKiernan was steeped in armored warfare thinking and unable to grasp a COIN battlefield. In Iraq, General McKiernan was not an advocate of a light footprint, which brought him into confrontation with Secretary of Defense Rumsfeld and CENTCOM commander General Tommy Franks, both of whom saw no need to go ahead with planned reinforcements—the 1st Cavalry Division—in April 2003 when the conventional campaign was over. Likewise, General McKiernan concluded in March 2003, as the armored thrust got under way, that the campaign really had two centers of gravity: the Republication Guard and the insurgent Fedayeen forces that were making their appearance.[8] The history of the Iraq war is about how the entire machinery of the U.S. government made this conceptual shift, but the problem was not the mind-set of the general now in charge of ISAF. Nor was this Iraq history particularly relevant to his ISAF appointment, which seems to have been more influenced by McKiernan's subsequent European command (he was commanding general of U.S. Army, Europe from 2005 to 2008) and the prospect that "his European experience will be a plus in dealing with NATO's disparate forces in Afghanistan."[9]

The key point was the civil–military interface. Brigadier General Davis, General McKiernan's strategic advisor in Kabul, notes that while General McKiernan knew of General Petraeus's work along the civil–military divide and how it enabled the Iraq surge, McKiernan's key strength was his "feel for people and terrain." He "just understood how to put together a very complex plan and execute it," and "he really reordered the battlefield in a very comprehensive way."[10] The civil–military interface was not General McKiernan's key competence, in other words. Background interviews indicate that General McKiernan was slow and timid in his engagement with the diplomatic community in Kabul. This shortcoming in terms of political skill and outreach undid his command. However, it takes two to tango. The civilian side through 2008 was not helpful, which is an often overlooked point, and this hampered the effort in important ways.

Unity of Command: How NATO Helped Undermine COMISAF

The perhaps most clearly defined priority in June 2008 of the new McKiernan team was enhanced unity of command. It implied pulling U.S. commanders under one hat—that of COMISAF—without formally unifying the ISAF and OEF command structures. These structures were politically loaded, and ISAF continued through 2006–2008 with the compromise defined by SACEUR James Jones in late 2005, namely to double-hat the ISAF security deputy (thus, not COMISAF) to deconflict the two chains. General McKiernan wanted greater unity of command, and he saw the main problem as lying on the American side, where a number of commanders, some in ISAF/NATO, others in OEF/ CENTCOM, communicated with Washington. These "tribes" should be pulled together, which in practice meant the double-hatting of General McKiernan as both COMISAF and COMOEF; or, put differently, the single-hatting of U.S. forces in Afghanistan. This would make General McKiernan the supreme voice in Afghanistan and the one talking to both SACEUR/NATO and CENTCOM/ Washington, unifying the message and the effort.

This change happened quite smoothly. NATO raised no challenge to it, partly because General McKiernan had known how to prepare the change through extensive engagements at military and diplomatic levels. Change dovetailed with the NATO wish to unify efforts that informed the CSPMP of April 2008, and the continuing separation of ISAF and OEF meant that all the controversial issues of the past—counterterrorist operations run by Special Forces, ANA training, ministerial development, and detention and interrogation—remained outside NATO's purview. France was briefed on this and made no objections, like the other allies. The U.S. political leadership readily accepted it as well, noted Brigadier General Davis, and the people who needed some convincing were found further down the U.S. OEF chain of command. The Combined Joint Task Force 101 HQ, which commanded OEF operations in Afghanistan's eastern region, initially opposed the idea but eventually was persuaded of both its benefits and inevitability.[11] Acting CENTCOM commander Lieutenant General Martin Dempsey readily accepted the idea, though power now would be concentrated below him, and the OEF training command (CSTC-A) under Major General Cone, which was a major operation, did likewise. General McKiernan could thus add an additional 19,000 U.S. (OEF) troops to his command; he now directed the training of ANSF forces (via CSTC-A); and he had direct access to CENTCOM and the U.S. chain of command in parallel to that of NATO. This new structure was approved in September and declared operational in October. It was certainly an improvement and key to enabling COMISAF to pursue the strategic priorities coming out of his June 2008 assessment.

For all its promise, the command reform had telling weaknesses: The ISAF-OEF distinction lived on, and the ISAF organization—with a very complex multinational corps headquarters in Kabul, a string of complex divisional headquarters in the regions, and then a number of poorly coordinated task forces and PRTs on the ground—was simply cumbersome. It would be fair to argue that General McKiernan should have pushed harder for a real integration of the ISAF and OEF operations, challenging NATO allies to face the reality that the battlefield extended all the way into the Kabul ministries and the training fields for new Afghan recruits. He did not, and one can understand why when looking back at the campaign's history, but the campaign was in no need of continuity. It cried out for major reform. It would only be fair to extend this criticism to NATO governments as well, however, because their timidity structured their commander's thinking. This served to demonstrate the virgin nature of the CSPMP. The allies had talked the talk but now needed to deliver, and they hesitated.

This mutual timidity explains General McKiernan's reluctance to set up a new three-star operational headquarter underneath his own four-star headquarters. In Iraq, during the 2007 surge, this type of four-star versus three-star division of labor had proven immensely fruitful, as the four-star, General Petraeus, worked the theater strategic level, the government scene in Baghdad, while the three-star, General Odierno, ran operations. Many people concluded thereafter that it was essential to free up the top commander for governance issues, and General Petraeus, on becoming CENTCOM commander in October 2008 and thus gaining Afghanistan as part of his area of responsibility, wanted it to happen in Kabul and raised the issue with the local commander,

General McKiernan. The latter resisted, however. He did so because he did not think NATO would give him the strategic tasks that would justify the four-star HQ. Brigadier General Davis explained, "We identified six strategic tasks, and we had one, which was coordination with UNAMA. The rest, which concerned ministerial development, ANSF training, and rule of law support, were not yet NATO-approved ISAF tasks. No one could see SHAPE redo the SHAPE OPLAN to pull these tasks under COMISAF and then submit it to the NAC any time soon, which is why General McKiernan did not want it."[12]

General McKiernan was right—the NAC was not about to move on this issue—but Washington was, and if Washington did, so would the NAC. McKiernan got the Washington politics wrong, in other words. Secretary of Defense Robert Gates and Chief of Staff Admiral Mike Mullen, encouraged by the situation in Iraq and prodded by the newly elected president, Barack Obama, were looking to strengthen precisely the civil–military interface. From their perspective, NATO should be made to move if the campaign demanded it, and it did. The *Washington Post* would later report that they "faulted McKiernan's perceived deference to NATO" because what they wanted in terms of civil–military strategic planning "was sharp thinking from the U.S. military, not a casserole of inputs from a dozen allies."[13] However, background sources indicate that they may have been willing to work with General McKiernan a while longer because they in April 2009—sources indicate—offered for McKiernan to stay on until December 2009. When McKiernan opposed this compromise, they decided—while in Kabul—to replace him by the summer, making the decision official in early May.

General McKiernan misread the Washington situation and paid the price. In the context of this book, though, it is more important to highlight that General McKiernan had been appointed COMISAF by the collective Alliance, including the United States, and that it left its commander in a difficult position. Their reluctance to rethink the campaign through 2008 became part of the command culture. It is possible to argue that the commander alone should have pushed for change, but it amounts to a sad commentary on NATO's ability to provide strategic leadership under dire circumstances.

The Collapse of Alternative Leadership:
The United Nations
NATO's position was all along that NATO did security via ISAF; development and governance were for the United Nations and Afghans to sort out, and it

was really up to them to take the overall campaign lead. The United Nations was a kind of fallback option, therefore. NATO allies knew that things in Afghanistan could not easily be fitted into separate categories (security, development, and governance) and that someone had to look across the board and lead, but they were not willing to establish a NATO lead. They had sought to push the United Nations to the frontline with the viceroy design that had come to naught in early 2008. The U.N. mission (UNAMA) thus remained apart but gained a new head, Kai Eide, who with an expanded mandate for civilian coordination was determined to bring about the UNAMA lead that had been on the table since 2002 but that had never materialized. If Kai Eide and David McKiernan could bring UNAMA and ISAF together in an effective partnership, maybe it would not matter that NATO was strategically inhibited. Maybe the United Nations could provide an alternative.

In theory, it worked. Kai Eide brought with him to Kabul a plan for reinvigorating UNAMA's effort, and this brings us back to General Richards and the Policy Action Group (PAG) he established in 2006. The PAG was intended to bring Karzai and all relevant actors together and garner the civil–military cooperation that the campaign needed, and it did generate a degree of impact. However, the PAG limited its focus to southern Afghanistan, largely RC/S where General Richards' British forces were implanted, and this limited agenda and restrained number of participants may have helped the PAG run along during the difficult year of 2007, but it also meant that there was no real mechanism for handling the national situation. There was of course the Joint Coordination and Monitoring Board (JCMB) that had come out of the Afghan Compact in early 2006, but it was weak and ineffectual, and Kai Eide knew it; by 2008, he later stated, it had become a mere "talking shop."[14] In effect, he wanted therefore to enlarge and nationalize the PAG, still formally underneath the JCMB but now as an effective tool for civil–military coordination across the country. The old PAG had a number of subcommittees, six in all, some of which worked well because participants invested (intelligence fusion and security operations, in particular), some of which did not (including governance, strategic communications, and counternarcotics). Moreover, the PAG itself was supposed to bring the key principals together—from President Karzai to top ministers and COMISAF—but did not. The key principals simply did not invest sufficiently in the PAG: By mid-2008 President Karzai had attended a total of about two PAG meetings.[15]

Kai Eide had UNAMA design a new PAG that was put on the table in July–
August 2008. It had three dimensions:

- The national PAG, formally subject to JCMB lead, should consist of
  three thematic groups: one for security, development, and governance,
  respectively.
- Each group should have a permanent and combined Afghan (GIRoA)
  and U.N. lead.
- Wider participation in each group should be flexible, based on case-
  by-case consideration of who is relevant and important to include.

It would have been natural in the ways of organizational design to depict
this as a three-pillar model, but UNAMA depicted it as three flowers: The
center of each flower contained GIRoA and UNAMA, and the petals around
it contained the flexible names of issues and participants. Thus, UNAMA proposed a "flower" design. Key participants (that is, the Afghan government and
ISAF) endorsed it by October, and by January 2009 it was in operation. To
support it, ISAF not only planned OP TOLO as a campaign to plug ISAF into
wider UNAMA and UNDP efforts—all of which flowed from the three pillars of the Afghan Compact—but also restructured its headquarters. Where
it previously had had a classical military organization along two pillars or
staffs (operations and logistics), it now added a third pillar or staff dedicated to
reconstruction and development. It made for an overarching campaign plan
and wider effort consisting of synchronized and sequential actions directed
toward milestones and end states defined by the Compact.

It did not work, however. UNAMA first of all did not have the resources to
match its intentions, which undermined its credibility with partners who now
had to deliver on UNAMA's behalf. UNAMA's big priority for the "flower" design was to decentralize it and bring "small flowers" into the provinces as part
of a policy of provincial outreach and presence. It made sense, but UNAMA
did not have the personnel. UNAMA could then try to recruit more people,
which it did, but U.N. procedures proved devastatingly slow and unhelpful.
Kai Eide himself repeatedly remarked on this problem, faulting the U.N. headquarters for creating the red tape that inhibited UNAMA on the ground.[16] The
other option was to ask others, and the only real game in town was ISAF. But
ISAF was short on personnel itself, struggling to come to grips with the security situation and increasing casualty figures. "General McKiernan thought he
had too few troops and did not want to provide protection [for UNAMA ac-

tivities] unless really necessary and only once Afghan forces proved unable to do the job," as one ISAF officer remarked on background. McKiernan thus did not want to involve ISAF forces in the business of voter registration in August 2008 in preparation for the presidential elections scheduled for the spring of 2009 (later postponed to August 2009), and "in some ways he was right: ISAF activities were transparent, and UNAMA did make plans for which they had too few resources."[17]

A related problem concerned the way in which the "flower" was intended to work: It clearly would be demanding on the Afghan side in terms of involvement and coordination, while it was not clear how often and to what extent ISAF would get involved. The Afghan side hesitated. Those willing to coordinate already did so in the old PAG subcommittees and were in no need of new mechanisms; those unwilling to coordinate were also unwilling to carry the new mechanism.[18] Getting solid Afghan buy-in was therefore a key problem that bedeviled the UNAMA design from the outset. Faced with both Afghan and ISAF hesitancy, the UNAMA head would have to throw his weight considerably around to move forward. While Kai Eide had extensive diplomatic experience, including a four-year stint as NATO ambassador in the years of international terror (2002–2006), he was also just a career diplomat. Though Eide's opening remark to his UNAMA staff was upbeat—"I may not be Paddy Ashdown, but don't underestimate me"—he did not de facto have political weight.[19] Moreover, he was instinctively critical of ISAF's strategy and in fact applauded the fall of the super envoy design: The United Nations would have become too closely related to NATO and ISAF, he writes in a passage that questions the whole idea of unity of effort.[20] He was no fan of President Bush, going by his memoirs, and he positioned UNAMA in a neutral space that enhanced his local room for maneuver but that as a matter of fact undermined his ability to deliver on the flower model.[21] This ability got undermined at the very outset, in fact, and the occasion was a botched attack on Taliban leader Mullah Siddiq in Azizabad, Herat Province, in late August that killed a large number of civilians. Circumstances were in dispute, but Kai Eide made the choice of not undertaking the joint investigation that COMISAF General McKiernan suggested, instead adopting a high public profile that soothed outraged Afghans, President Karzai among them. UNAMA-ISAF relations plummeted and never really recovered. At a time when UNAMA was rolling out a flower model of cooperation and ISAF was preparing an operational plan premised on unity of effort, it took forty-five days after the incident before

Eide and McKiernan could agree even to meet.[22] UNAMA's staff divided into factions on the issue of whether to work closely with ISAF or to keep ISAF at arm's length to soothe President Karzai, with Eide taking the latter position. UNAMA-ISAF working relations did continue—and they agreed in the fall to have the Afghan ministries of Defense and Interior overlay ISAF's Development Zones and UNAMA's Critical Districts to come up with what became first Action Districts (AD) and then Key Terrain Districts (KTD). At this point they identified about twenty ADs, which became the focal point for the supposedly integrated campaign—but the critical high level of informal relations was broken. Later in 2009, Eide would clash with two American representatives who saw President Karzai as an obstacle to progress and sought to push him: Richard Holbrooke, Obama's special representative for Afghanistan-Pakistan, and Peter Galbraith, UNAMA deputy.[23]

The term *Key Terrain District* was to remain with the campaign from this point on but not UNAMA's level of ambition. The organization never recovered from the 2008 experience, and it got sidetracked further when President Obama as part of the surge decided to place civilian coordination more in the hands of an enlarged U.S. embassy in Kabul. Kai Eide does not deserve all the blame for the misery of the fall 2008, but his August decision to confront ISAF—to align UNAMA closer with Karzai—was fateful: It ran with the flow of Afghan popular sentiment but undermined ISAF and therefore the hope that UNAMA's flower model might get off the ground. However, behind Eide lay a wider deficit in terms of mandate, resources, and leadership capacity at the UN strategic level.

The Campaign Runs along Leaderless

ISAF's security assistance campaign continued, naturally, and as the COIN thinking inherent in General McKiernan's approach made its mark it became readily obvious that the military effort needed to be embedded in a wider civilian effort. There was the UNAMA effort, but it was only unfolding in the fall 2008 and was clearly not going to be an outright success. As testimony to the strategic lethargy of the Alliance, nothing much was done to compensate. We see this in three notable respects.

Training of indigenous forces—the ANSF—was moving up the agenda. Much focus was on the army (ANA), but the police (ANP) was really the end state of the whole affair, as COMISAF's strategic advisor, Brigadier General Davis, remarked.[24] The issue was highlighted in General McKiernan's June

2008 assessment and was one of the five things he wanted improved as a matter of priority. A meeting of minds took place to embed the concept of partnering in the entire organization, which then became a key vehicle for advancing ANSF capacity: It involved General McKiernan on the one hand and General Robert Cone of the training command (CSTC-A) on the other. General McKiernan put the idea into practice with the two-year operational plan that was issued in October and went into effect on November 1. This was OP TOLO, and it was the first operational plan that built on comparatively significant input from senior Afghan military leaders and that was rolled out at a combined ANSF-ISAF commander's conference, which on the Afghan side involved corps commanders and regional police chiefs and which ran in both English and Dari.[25] It was ISAF's first real theater campaign plan, though it came with the label "operational": It defined "focus areas"—later KTD—in terms of clear, hold, and build at the district level, and it made RC/S the center of gravity for the campaign effort.[26] As a collective COIN plan, it was a significant advance for ISAF itself and ISAF–ANA partnering. The ISAF and ANSF chains of command were briefed on the plan, and bases were rebuilt to allow for colocation. All this was challenging because it required money and because ISAF units—depending on national background and regional command standards—differed in their partnering policies that had been allowed to emerge prior to 2008. It was challenging also because the ANSF was not mature. ANSF units lacked training and experience and were generally heavily dependent on ISAF logistics. Partnering was not new, but this was the beginning of a coherently organized approach to partnering and the effort to make ANSF units autonomous.

The push for partnering was generated locally. Brigadier General Davis attributes much of the credit to CSTC-A commander General Cone, who brought the basic idea to the table in the summer of 2008 (he had then led CSTC-A for a year). Another source came from General McKiernan's experience in dealing with senior Afghan leaders during a significant incident in Kandahar, where the Taliban successfully assaulted the city's main prison (Sarposa) and helped at least 1,000 prisoners, many of them Taliban fighters, to escape. It was all the more worrying as the Taliban simultaneously launched an offensive in the Arghandab district north of Kandahar and threatened to move south toward Kandahar city itself. However, the Afghan Defense Ministry managed to take control of the situation, deploying two army battalions and one police battalion in a fairly coherent counteroffensive.[27] "It really boosted the opinion of the senior Afghan leadership in COMISAF's eyes," notes Brigadier General Davis. COMISAF "realized that senior ANSF leaders understood the terrain and the big picture and how to strategize, how to deploy the forces. So he concluded that we've got to stop developing plans on our own; we have to start a big effort to do everything with [the Ministry of] Defense and later with [the Ministry of] Interior."[28]

This brings us back to NATO, the strategic outlook, and the command structure. If partnering was to really get off the ground, then operations and training needed to be tightly integrated. However, operations belonged to the ISAF chain of command, while training (CSTC-A) remained within the OEF chain. NATO was so far happy to maintain the two chains separate and pretend that integration had happened with the double-hatting of General McKiernan. The partnering issue should have been a cause for second thoughts, and in a way it was. The need to move beyond double-hatting and bring training into the ISAF basket was on NATO's agenda in the fall of 2008, a source from NATO's Operations Division explains, but the Alliance failed to move for the reason that a NATO training mission would mean "that success was not only an ISAF matter but also an ANSF matter."[29] The heart of the matter was conceptual: NATO was not ready to define a mission that would place the instruments of success in non-NATO hands. As we shall see, NATO did come around to the idea by the time of the Strasbourg-Kehl summit in April 2009, and the NATO training mission (NTM-A) became operational in the fall of 2009, but the road there had been tortuous.

Training is one window to NATO's hesitancy; counternarcotics is another. NATO allies were divided on the proper course of action against the booming narcotics business that fanned the flames of the insurgency. Through 2007 a type of meltdown threatened. The civilian side of the U.S. team, led by ambassador to Afghanistan, William Wood, made a dedicated push for poppy destruction by aerial spraying. It was a tactic ambassador Wood had implemented earlier in Columbia but "spraying first, reconciling later" was not a military favorite, not among the U.S. military either, because it threatened to destroy local support for the Afghan government and ISAF, especially if the government lacked the capacity to supply governance and development in the wake of the destructive spraying. "Chemical Bill" was the nickname some NATO forces assigned to Ambassador Wood.[30] The allies reached a settlement in October 2008 at a defense ministers' meeting in Budapest, agreeing that ISAF forces could act in concert with Afghan forces against drug dealers and laboratories, though within a stringent set of conditions.[31] This was an improvement of sorts that deflated controversy, but stringent conditions limited the operational impact, and the fact remained that NATO had shied away from reworking its OPLAN, not because it was not needed (it was) but because it was controversial.[32] Secretary of Defense Robert Gates found that the NATO position "was better than nothing," which was hardly a ringing endorsement.[33]

A final window to NATO's hesitancy is Pakistan and the issue of tackling the Pakistani border area to Afghanistan, where key insurgent groups find refuge and support. If the insurgency in Afghanistan was NATO's problem, so were Pakistan's border regions, as we also saw in Chapter 5. To the extent that NATO developed a COIN campaign—and this was OP TOLO of October 2008—NATO needed to address Pakistan to make the Afghan campaign successful. This took time. The Alliance leader, the United States, started shifting its approach to Pakistan in mid-2008, approving Special Forces ground assaults inside the Pakistan border area without advanced approval of the Pakistani government and also beginning the policy of hitting insurgents with drone missile attacks.[34] However, this was done timidly (twenty attacks took place in the latter half of 2008),[35] and it was tactical: It might take out insurgents but not solve the border area problem for the ISAF mission. For this, a strategic policy toward Pakistan was needed, but neither the United States nor NATO as a whole had one in hand. Shortly after President Bush authorized the Special Forces operations in July, NATO's secretary general, Jaap de Hoop Scheffer, publicly ruled out the possibility of any NATO military attack in Pakistan.[36] Of course, that would be stepping outside the ISAF mandate, and NATO's front figure was not likely to define such a hostile policy. But other policy options were possible, notably one of building up Pakistani or joint capacities for intervention in the area. It was critically important because while Pakistan through 2008–2009 had realized the threat that Pakistani Taliban posed to the Pakistani state and society and had launched several large military campaigns to clean up the border regions, Pakistan remained committed to its doctrine of "strategic depth." Never in earnest did its forces enter North Waziristan, a hotbed of the insurgency; in January 2010—by arresting Mullah Omar's deputy, Omar Ghali Baradar—it intervened to shut down or at least gain control of the main current of the Taliban that prepared for peace talks with Karzai and the United States, and questions concerning President Zardari's integrity and skill nourished growing and debilitating civil-military tensions. Instead of developing a regional policy as opposed to an Afghanistan-only policy, NATO relied on the ambiguity of having two chains of command—ISAF and OEF—and having a leading ally taking steps in the latter. Ambiguity was bad policy, however, and proper policy was what NATO needed to bolster the OP TOLO COIN campaign.

Conclusion

NATO's decision to enable leadership in April 2008 was naturally meant to improve the situation on the Afghan ground, but it ended up exposing a deficit of leadership. All allies upheld the idea that ISAF could succeed even if separated from the U.S. effort in OEF and thus from the training of Afghan forces. They were slow to come to terms with a unified counternarcotics policy, and their unified position of October 2008 was riddled with conditions that inevitably would make for varied participation and regional effect. Pakistan was another source of hesitancy. The year 2008 was perhaps the one when Pakistan was really put on the agenda, but NATO—including the United States—struggled to define a policy. The U.N. mission, UNAMA, was no substitute, as we saw. UNAMA's effort to invigorate governance and development at all Afghan levels was overdue but overambitious as well. UNAMA did not match strategy and resources, and it did not manage to define relations to ISAF, the one organization that was indispensable to its flower model.

COMISAF General McKiernan has become a culprit of sorts because he was relieved of command in early 2009. Allegedly, General McKiernan was not insistent enough that the allies must provide the unified organization and command numbers for a COIN campaign; he was too slow in getting OP TOLO defined; he did not manage the civil–military interface; and he focused his ground campaign in the wrong places even if he had the southern emphasis right.[37] It is possible that if begun in June rather than October, OP TOLO could have made a bigger impact or that tactical priority to the Arghandab district north of Kandahar city, as opposed to border interdiction in Spin Boldak and Barham Chah, could have made a difference. However, the bigger point is that by the time General McKiernan took command, the allies had no good answer to the wavering campaign that followed from the flushing out of Taliban strongholds and the subsequent Taliban turn to a strategy of pure insurgency at the turn of 2007–2008 that earned McKiernan's predecessor the nickname "Bomber." Nor had the allies managed to bring development and governance on sustainable tracks, as improbable Kai Eide took over where

Paddy Ashdown was supposed to have forged change. General McKiernan managed to bring COIN to the campaign to a degree that his predecessors had not. Further advance in this direction would depend on a change in the political context.

STRATEGIC LEADERSHIP

The change of political leadership in the United States in January 2009, with President Obama taking over from President Bush, also meant a change of leadership in NATO, or, perhaps more accurately, an infusion of much needed leadership in NATO. President Bush had run his political course and had seen through the successful surge in Iraq but had no energy to begin another surge in Afghanistan. He commissioned a wide-ranging strategic assessment of the Afghan campaign from Lieutenant General Douglas Lute, the NSC deputy for Iraq and Afghanistan. The report was done in late November 2008, but President Bush chose not to make it public, preferring to bypass a potentially critical debate on his own approach to Afghanistan and to leave his successor's hands untied.[38] The new president wasted no time. Two months into his presidency, on March 27, 2009, President Obama announced "a stronger, smarter and comprehensive strategy"—such was the ambition—that placed Pakistan on par with Afghanistan in strategic importance and significantly increased military and civilian efforts.[39] It was ambitious and it needed to be. The insurgency was certainly not growing weaker: In a surprising show of strength, it managed to fight through the winter of 2008–2009. We shall first see how NATO responded positively to the Obama agenda; then we shall interpret what this boost of activism meant for the Atlantic Alliance in a broader perspective.

NATO in Obama's Footsteps

The Obama Af-Pak strategy, as it became known, built on a straightforward "core goal," namely "to disrupt, dismantle, and defeat al Qaeda and its safe havens in Pakistan, and to prevent their return to Pakistan or Afghanistan." The strategy built on three pillars:[40]

- Support the Pakistani civilian government and encourage it to take on Al Qaeda in the western borderlands; in return, offer investments in Pakistan's political and economic development.
- Surge the effort in Afghanistan with an influx of 21,000 troops, including enhanced investments in ANSF training, greater civilian

investments in Afghan development and efforts to root out corruption, and the establishment of a reconciliation process in every province.[41]

- Enhance the diplomatic effort to bring Afghanistan and Pakistan together, including a trilateral dialogue involving also the United States as well as a Contact Group involving all countries with an interest in the region.

This strategy was certainly more comprehensive than that of the president's predecessor. Pakistan figured prominently in it, as did the commitment to a fully resourced COIN campaign. NATO would naturally gravitate toward the latter, given that it was the ISAF lead, but NATO did also address the wider framework.

On Afghanistan, NATO had the CSPMP to match the comprehensive ambition of the Obama administration; what the Alliance added in the spring of 2009 was new substance. The Alliance essentially accepted folding most of OEF into ISAF and widening the portfolio of COMISAF to such an extent that the command organization that COIN enthusiasts had long advocated and General McKiernan had resisted on grounds of political reluctance now became a reality. The first new component was the NATO Training Mission-Afghanistan (NTM-A) that was agreed to at the April 4, 2009, summit, stood up over the summer, and ready for command in mid-November.[42] It was what NATO had done in Iraq as well—with the NTM-I—except that the mission in Afghanistan was an integral part of the security operation (ISAF), whereas in Iraq it had operated in parallel to the international security coalition (Operation Iraqi Freedom, or OIF). NTM-A was a bigger affair and more widely endorsed. France had hesitated in Iraq, limiting NATO's mission and never sending a French trainer to the country. Afghanistan was different. France had from the outset in 2002 provided special trainers for ANA officers' basic training (the United States was responsible for officers' advanced training as well as the training of new recruits, while Britain trained ANA NCOs), and it also supported the operational trainer teams that NATO ran through its operational command—so-called Operational Mentoring Liaison Teams (OMLTs) that were the equivalent of U.S. Embedded Training Teams.[43]

In practice the OEF training mission (CSTC-A) was folded into ISAF. Training was still largely dominated by the United States but now within the Alliance portfolio of responsibilities. This was testimony to more coherent and strategic thinking within the Alliance, though there were limits. CSTC-A had done it all—building up a whole new national defense organization, including the Ministry of Defense—with all its policy, planning, and management facets; recruitment; training of both recruits and officers; and operational and logistical infrastructure. NATO was ready for most of this but not all. It notably did not want to handle the ministerial development tasks, not because they were deemed unimportant but because they overlapped with the kind of civilian development work that NATO allies could not agree to as a matter of principle because some allies, notable among them France and Belgium, wanted this work allocated to the European Union. Paradigmatic comprehensive thinking thus inhibited pragmatic comprehensive action. CSTC-A remained, therefore, as a separate command but now with a much-reduced role defined by the NATO leftovers. To ease matters, NATO agreed to double-hat the new NTM-A commanding general as CSTC-A commander as well. An American—Lieutenant General William Caldwell IV—became commanding general of both commands in November 2009.

NATO's move allowed for a smoother integration of the regular training mission (NTM-A/CSTC-A) on the one hand and operational training (OMLT/ ETT) on the other. Training and operations were run by different commands but now within a more coherent command organization with greater unity of command. Previously, COMISAF had either had no authority over training, which was the case up until 2008, or had held authority by virtue of a double-hat, which is what General McKiernan introduced. Now the organizations fused, which was long overdue, and ambitions therefore increased.

The target figures for ANSF forces (troops and soldiers) were dynamic, as were the current strength figures pulled in opposite directions by aggressive recruitment strategies and high attrition and desertion rates. In April 2009 the ANA stood at around 80,000, and NATO and ISAF succeeding in reaching their target of 134,000 by October 2010. The plan was then to reach 171,600 by October 2011, take stock, and perhaps aim for the target advanced by General McChrystal—240,000—but that President Obama had made subject to annual reviews.[44] Did NATO invest here—matching goals and resources in a true strategic fashion? Not quite, but a movement took place. In April 2009 NATO was at fifty-nine OMLTs, short of the required sixty-eight, but it committed 2,000 new troops to the training effort, bringing the number of OMLTs to seventy. NATO also began a new training initiative, providing paramilitary

police forces for robust Afghan police training, something the European police training effort hitherto had lacked. It also extended its equipment dona-
tion program to the police, the army being included already.[45]

The effort may not have been fully resourced, but it was important and
came in support of a new campaign strategy defined by President Obama and
his administration and adopted by NATO. The logic of enabling the U.S. lead
thus took hold of NATO, which is also clear in relation to the overall command
organization that proved so troublesome to General McKiernan. The aforementioned four-star versus three-star command organization—the Petraeus/
Odierno division of labor in Iraq—now became a reality also in Afghanistan.
COMISAF was four-star General McChrystal, and the commander of ISAF's
new Joint Command (IJC) was three-star and Deputy COMISAF General
Rodriguez, a former OEF (CJTF 76) commander with operational experience
also from Iraq. This team possessed the kind of COIN skills that the U.S. leadership sought, and NATO was ready to approve it—as well as the organization
they needed to carry out their job (Figure 6.1).

NATO gave its approval to NTM-A at the summit in April 2009; the IJC
gained its approval at a defense ministerial meeting in June 2009;[46] and both

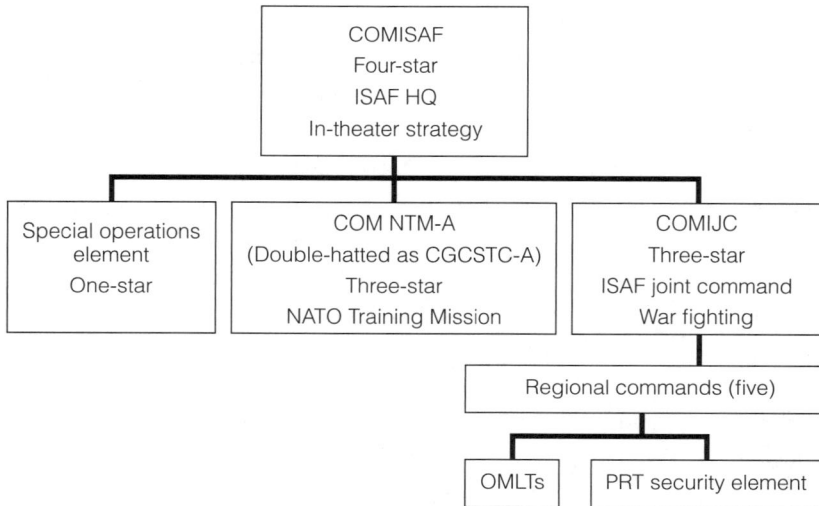

Figure 6.1. New ISAF command, 2009.

SOURCE: Retrieved on January 7, 2011, from the ISAF website (www.isaf.nato.int/en/isaf-command-
structure.html) combined with background interview, ISAF HQ, Kabul, September 29, 2009.

become fully operational on November 12, 2009. The new organization was symbolic of a new political commitment to a unified strategy. Old OEF–ISAF tensions were now (mostly) a thing of the past. There were other spoilers around, though, and Pakistan was one of them. NATO had in the past focused quite strictly on its ISAF mandate, which is to say Afghanistan exclusively, but now the Alliance leader, the United States, wanted to put Pakistan next to Afghanistan in strategic importance. It was a stretch for the Alliance, which had neither the unity to follow up with its proper Pakistan initiative nor the policy instruments. As we saw, NATO Secretary General de Hoop Scheffer had been to Islamabad—twice, in fact, and his deputy to India—and NATO offered a few training courses for Pakistani officers and emergency relief on occasion. It was symbolic and notably lacked in capacity to assist the Pakistani institutions that must be ISAF's strategic partner in the COIN campaign to root out Al Qaeda. What NATO did at the Strasbourg-Kehl summit was therefore to buy time. NATO heads of state and governments declared their desire to "build a broader political and practical relationship between NATO and Pakistan,"[47] kicking this particular can down the road in the hope that strategy would follow.

A Peculiar Community

Few could be in doubt following these decisions that President Obama had infused the Afghan campaign with new political leadership and that NATO had come out in its support. What did this portend for the Atlantic Alliance, though? NATO had zoomed in on enabling leadership as its key competence, as we saw in Chapter 5, and now after stalemate through 2008 the opportunity was there to bring this competence to bear. The spring of 2009 also revealed that the Atlantic community had yet to be renewed. It was on the table as an ambition, but it first had to pass the Afghan test. The Obama administration talked up NATO as a community of values but was inherently pragmatic about it. This led to the realization inside NATO that NATO needed to deliver in new ways in Afghanistan to salvage the Atlantic community.

The atmospherics of the Alliance changed almost from day one of the Obama presidency. The allies knew that an American strategy for Afghanistan was in the making because President Obama had asked Bruce Riedel, a former CIA analyst and Pakistan expert, to chair a strategic review that involved consultations with allies and whose deadline was the April 2009 NATO summit; the United States needed NATO's endorsement to integrate its new strategy with the ISAF mission. Vice President Biden was one of the leading figures in the administration's review effort. He went to Afghanistan and then to NATO headquarters on March 10. As a vice president meeting the group of ambassadors, he was not there to negotiate—which is done among peers—but to boost morale, as one NATO ambassador later remarked.[48] Biden offered the kind of solace—"President Obama and I are deeply committed to NATO"—that Secretary of State Hilary Clinton had offered some days earlier, on March 5—"The United States is firmly committed to NATO, and the Obama Administration will work vigorously to renew a real dialogue within this alliance."[49] Both were followed on March 23 by the new special representative to Afghanistan and Pakistan, Richard Holbrooke, who came to present the findings of the Riedel review. This diplomatic offensive culminated with the president's involvement—first as he presented the new Af-Pak strategy on March 27, invoking NATO as a gathering of "free nations" that provide for a "common purpose today," then as he went to the NATO summit in early April for the collective endorsement of the new strategy.[50]

The pragmatics of the Obama administration ran deep, though. This made for a peculiar community—a type of community of results where outcomes were given as much weight as under the Bush presidency but where institutions and the values they contain trumped the pragmatic toolbox approach. What was left unsaid was the dilemma that would arise if the institution (NATO) could not deliver and the United States had to choose. The approach was instead to assume that the institution would deliver and to put it on alert. Vice President Biden noted on March 10, "I pledged to them [the allies] that we will incorporate their ideas into our strategic review." However, "we, the United States, expect everyone to keep whatever commitments were made in arriving at that joint strategy. It's as simple and as straightforward as that."[51] "The President didn't think Afghanistan should only be an American war," Bob Woodward cites James Jones, Obama's national security advisor, as saying on a trip to Afghanistan later that year, "So what we've tried to do is rebalance the relationships."[52]

This was the pragmatic rationale—to avoid Americanizing the war and to ensure collective buy-in—and it ran through the Riedel strategic review process and the NATO rollout that had already begun in February, shortly after the onset of the review. Bruce Riedel's approach to the review was by necessity pragmatic because he was asked to assess the situation on the ground and devise a strategy for dealing with it. He knew the region and had previously identified Pakistan as the center of gravity for the effort to locate and destroy Al Qaeda.[53] He had traveled with Senator Obama, and both of them saw the war as a necessary war that was under-resourced and poorly conceptualized. The reigning strategy was wrong, in other words. The reviews undertaken in 2008—the Lute review commissioned by the president, another review undertaken by General Petraeus in the Central Command, and finally one in SHAPE by SACEUR General Craddock—were insufficient, Riedel had found. The latter two were focused on the military side of the conflict, with the Petraeus review in addition covering the entire CENTCOM command area that stretches from the Horn of Africa to Central Asia. The Lute review was "the sharpest review, the most self-critical," but it was strategically deficient given its almost exclusive focus on Afghanistan.[54] If Pakistan thus was predestined to figure prominently in the strategy, what about NATO? Did the president bring up this dimension when he commissioned the review, and did he bring it up when briefed on its results?

Bruce Riedel answers in the affirmative. The president brought up the NATO/ISAF dimension in the phone call that he made to ask Riedel to undertake the review, emphasizing the importance of the Strasbourg-Kehl summit for the strategy and making it the deadline for the review process. Moreover, as the review process was in its final stage—March 11–20—and as the interagency process went into high gear, Bruce Riedel gained an opportunity to talk one-on-one with the president onboard Air Force One, as the president flew to California. This was scheduled for March 18, one day following a NSC principals meeting reviewing the strategy and two days prior to a NSC meeting with the president that would settle the review, and it was an occasion engineered by White House Chief of Staff Rahm Emanuel for the president to "get his head into this."[55] I asked Bruce Riedel if the president brought up NATO and ISAF during this exclusive one-on-one and, if so, on what terms. The president did, and he did so because he wanted the strategy not only to be ready for the NATO summit but ready to be ratified and concurred in. It was touch and go, in other words. The key motive, Riedel explains, is that "President Obama does not want Afghanistan to be solely an American problem. Even as we are increasing American troops on the ground, this president and his whole team are determined to keep the mission in NATO."[56]

NATO was not really part of the strategic review process, though. The diplomatic rollout in March looked impressive—with Biden, Clinton, and Holbrooke visiting the NATO headquarters and with Clinton leading the effort to tee off the NATO summit with a large international conference in the Hague on March 31.[57] This changed the atmospherics, as mentioned, but the NATO input into the strategy was negligible. NATO Secretary General Jaap de Hoop Scheffer—whose term ran until August 2009—recalls that "there was not a heavy footprint from NATO. The review process in Washington was extraordinarily complicated, and the big strategic lines were not fully prepared by the time that the Alliance readied itself for the Strasbourg-Kehl summit. The NATO allies and the NAC knew of the process and had insights into it, but they essentially took a wait-and-see approach."[58] Secretary General de Hoop Scheffer went to meet with President Obama in the White House on March 25 in preparation for the NATO summit. At this point the president was two days away from announcing publicly the review results, which had been outlined in the NSC meeting on March 20. Interestingly, "the agenda for this meeting was not dominated by the Afghanistan issue," recalls de Hoop Scheffer:

> NATO knew that something was coming for the summit, and we knew that something had to happen, but, when I visited him, President Obama was very much in the beginning of the debate on his approach to Afghanistan. There was not one line. There was on the issue of training and the NTM-A, which was approved at the summit, but the long-term strategy was not set; it was under development. [We] did discuss Afghanistan, but there was not a form of conclusion presented to me by the president.[59]

The Obama–de Hoop Scheffer meeting was dominated by the issue of "NATO's future," as they stated in the press conference following the meeting.[60] If this future did not so much concern Afghanistan, then what did it concern? De Hoop Scheffer recalls that the matter referred to the Alliance's Strategic Concept—a kind of operational view of the Atlantic Treaty of 1949— that NATO was about to renew. The president "told me that he had a lot of things on his mind and calendar—from the Middle East to China and North Korea—and that he needed a strong NATO and a strong Alliance, and that he hoped for allied support in Afghanistan." It was not an operational meeting, in other words, but one among many that the secretary general had to set up the April summit for success. "I left the Oval Office with the impression that Obama understands NATO perfectly well," de Hoop Scheffer recalls.[61]

The Strasbourg-Kehl summit not only commissioned a new Strategic Concept—this the NAC had done before—but asked the secretary general to provide a draft.[62] Previous Strategic Concepts had been drafted by the International Staff (working for the secretary general) but with significant involvement by the national delegations, which made for complex and drawn-out negotiations. The Strasbourg-Kehl summit was a turn to executive authority, therefore. Moreover, the summit had to pick the successor to Jaap de Hoop Scheffer who would be in charge of drafting the concept, and the choice fell on Danish Prime Minister Anders Fogh Rasmussen. This was another novelty. Never before had the Alliance picked a head of state or government to serve as secretary general: All previous secretaries general had been either foreign or defense ministers. Moreover, Anders Fogh Rasmussen was a sitting prime minister at the time of his appointment. This reinforced the turn to executive authority. President Obama "understood NATO perfectly well," de Hoop Scheffer remarks, and it seems that a significant strengthening of the organization and its executive capacity for strategic planning was part of the president's thinking.

Anders Fogh Rasmussen is certainly not in doubt that this was the case. "This is the first time a secretary general has been picked at a summit of NATO heads of state and government, and they picked one from their own ranks. They told me that I was the chosen candidate because they felt a need to enhance NATO's political-strategic focus." The executive turn was thus the overriding concern. I asked the new secretary general whether in the process of presenting his candidacy—which is done in secrecy, naturally—he had outlined certain issues or priorities as a kind of electoral platform to his colleagues, but this was not the case, Fogh Rasmussen recalls. The fellow heads of state and government knew him, and this was sufficient; he did develop key priorities for his work but in the space of time intervening between the summit and August when he became secretary general.[63] The Fogh Rasmussen candidacy thus distinguished itself not by any issue in particular but rather by its executive character, corroborating the observation that NATO leaders and perhaps President Obama in particular were looking to enhance NATO's capacity at the political-strategic level.[64] This brings us to a final assessment of the Alliance in mid-2009.

NATO was continuously part of the framework within which the Obama team developed a new Afghanistan strategy, and the president explicitly referred to the Alliance's importance. This was the good news for NATO. The bad news was that strategic development was all in U.S. hands, and this during a pro-NATO presidency. The Af-Pak strategy had no NATO footprint because NATO lacked in the capacity to define and carry out strategy. NATO was a strategic enabler in Afghanistan, we know, but this limited role now proved problematic. It threatened the political cohesion that lay at heart of the community—that defined the West, NATO's geopolitical infrastructure. The Obama administration feared for the Americanization of the war and thus needed NATO, but NATO needed to address in greater depth and with greater vision the twin challenge pinpointed by the Riedel review: resourcing and driving a COIN campaign and building up Pakistan's civilian institutions to promote a regional-diplomatic shift and channel resources into combating Al Qaeda in the border area to Afghanistan. To move things forward, the Obama administration first of all offered its own leadership, but it also pushed for an executive tightening of the organization NATO. This resulted in the designation of a sitting prime minister as the new secretary general, and it opened the final stretch of the Afghan campaign that we can engage in this book.

NATO IN SEARCH OF STRATEGIC CAPACITY

Now that the transition train is quite advanced, with half the Afghan population coming under Afghan security leadership, it appears that NATO can emerge from the operation with scars, for sure, but intact. If the allies can agree to prop up the Afghan security forces and engage Pakistan, they will be in a position to sustain transition, turn their backs in earnest on a decade of Afghan combat (though special forces operations might continue), and prepare for a broader diplomatic presence embedded in partnerships. If it turns out this way, the COIN surge of 2009–2012 will have been a major contributing factor to a kind of success. However, the surge is not flawless. COIN specialists will tell you that COIN in Afghanistan is only a couple of years old and that COIN campaigns run in decades. Yet we are seeing surge drawdown and transition, which has to do with Western political calendars—Obama's surge is set to finish a few months ahead of the U.S. presidential elections—as well as exhausted campaign coffers and patience. In consequence, the unfolding of the surge has been marked by a degree of political–military dispute. The political ambition is downgraded, which has to do with the exit strategy, but parts of the campaign are still stuck in Afghan problems that require greater patience and investment. We begin this section with a discussion of the military dimension and the fight on the ground. We shall see that NATO is hanging in there but just barely. NATO got off to a good beginning, but the accelerated tempo of operations, especially the kill-and-capture missions, along with the growing desire to pull out, has made for complexity. It is no longer clear what it means to run a COIN campaign. We then move on to political issues and the question of managing the Kabul scene. NATO's capacity improved at the outset, again, but it has fulfilled its potential and requires renewed investment. This brings us to the third and final subsection on NATO's future capacity in light of the Alliance's new Strategic Concept and the lessons it seems to be drawing from Afghanistan. There are promising signs, but the Alliance needs above all to come to terms with the challenge that benevolent missions, though appealing in moral terms, have no end. To define ends it takes strategic imagination, and NATO should cultivate it.

Fighting for Transition

The U.S. surge in 2009–2012 aside, there is little in NATO's military effort to suggest that the Alliance radically changed its capacity to challenge its enemies to a fight. Proponents of the comprehensive approach might argue that fighting is not the key; governance and development are. Still, NATO sometimes engages in a real fight, such as in Libya in 2011. Moreover, a fully resourced counterinsurgency campaign needs a lot of troops to make for the security that enables governance and development. And unlike the comprehensive approach, COIN builds on a simple proposition that drives the force calculus. The proposition is that you need around one soldier for every fifty people in the population to be at a level where you can prevail. Force planners can then do the math according to the map of the country: To win over the capital of Helmand Province, Lashkar Gah, which transitioned to Afghan leadership in early 2011 and which has a population of approximately 200,000, you need 4,000 troops. For a country the size of Afghanistan with an approximate population of 28,000,000, you need around 560,000 troops. COIN is not rocket science, as an instructor at ISAF's COIN Training Center in Kabul noted, though we should also note that it takes more to design a successful campaign than this.[65] Still, the calculus drove allied planning through 2009–2010: President Obama began his term with an ISAF force contribution of 38,000; he added 21,000 in the spring and another 30,000 in the fall of 2009; counting OEF forces, the U.S. total went up to 100,000; the allies then increased their contributions to the level of 50,000; and the projected force number for Afghan security forces (ANSF) was raised to 400,000. That got the projected collective effort close to the 560,000 mark. In all this, the non-American NATO effort increased only marginally and decreased in relative terms—from 55 percent to 28 percent.[66] COIN math tells us only so much, though. We should instead look at conceptual change, force commitments, and campaign dynamics.

Conceptual change took place in the fall of 2009 when NATO endorsed the COIN campaign of COMISAF General McChrystal. It happened at a defense ministerial meeting in Bratislava, Slovakia, on October 23, and it was akin to a small revolution.[67] This put an end to the political theology of ISAF's purpose, which had fed off the confrontation between stabilization and counterterrorism. ISAF was henceforth—for a little while at least—about COIN. Soon after Bratislava, NATO military authorities were tasked to develop both a COIN doctrine and COIN training requirements for the Afghanistan mission. In December 2009 the military authorities recommended the establishment of a COIN Task Force to drive this process forward; it was set up in January 2010 and has since worked to "ensure that there is focused, rapid and coordinated progress in developing a common approach to COIN doctrine and training, in order to increase Alliance capabilities with a special focus on COIN operations in Afghanistan"—which is its mission statement. NATO's two strategic commands—the operational located in Mons, Belgium, and the transformational located in Norfolk, Virginia, the United States—then issued a set of Joint Operational Guidelines in May 2010, the precursor to a real NATO doctrine (Allied Joint Publication).[68] NATO was filling the gap between ISAF requirements and NATO and national standards, notes General Egon Ramms, commander of joint force command (JFC) overseeing ISAF operations for NATO.[69] To be sure, NATO's COIN doctrine trailed well behind the reality on the Afghan ground, which is almost always the case with allied doctrinal development, but still NATO's overall effort to gear its organization to COIN was an important improvement hidden underneath the public debate on force numbers.

Where controversy used to involve allies, the United States among them, in favor of COIN and those opposed to it, controversy now emerged from below—from the requirements of the campaign as seen through military lenses. More forces and a longer time horizon enhanced the prospects of campaign success, naturally, but troop numbers and time horizons were politically charged. General McChrystal's campaign assessment of August 31, 2009, had leaked into the public domain, and though it flowed from the Obama strategy it also questioned the level of resources committed to the fight. General McChrystal's force request did not leak, but it was widely understood that he put three options on the table—80,000 more troops, 40,000, or 20,000—

and favored the middle option. His forthcoming and frank public remarks were politically sensitive because, inevitably, they weighed in on the strategic decisions that the political leadership had to make.[70] General McChrystal was called to order, and President Obama engaged a prolonged strategy review in the fall. The conclusion of the review was illustrative of civil–military tensions: Obama endorsed a reinforcement of 30,000 troops, thus short of the campaign commander's request; the time line for surge drawdown was accelerated compared to what the Pentagon had wanted; and the deal was written into a highly unusual civil–military business deal.[71]

This tension mostly affected the United States and not so much NATO as such. True, General McChrystal's assessment could have been read as a challenge to ISAF and NATO: "ISAF is not adequately executing the basics of counterinsurgency warfare," General McChrystal wrote, urging ISAF to change its operational culture, become more effective and efficient, invest more resources, and "prioritize responsible and accountable governance"—a euphemism for tackling Afghan government corruption. In short, COMISAF wanted a different ISAF, challenging NATO allies to invest in it.[72] Still, the view from Brussels headquarters was that this was an issue that needed to be sorted out in Washington, though Alliance patience with the Obama strategy review of the fall of 2009 did wear thin. The Bratislava embrace of McChrystal was to an extent a nod in the direction of President Obama. As Obama's review finally reached its conclusions, the buck came back to NATO. Since the president was providing forces 10,000 short of the campaign commander's request, it would be for NATO—the new COIN enthusiast—to fill the gap.[73] The twenty-five NATO/ISAF nations almost managed, offering another 7,000 troops, though almost 2,000 of these were already in Afghanistan but previously scheduled to go back home. COMISAF thus got the approximately 40,000 troops. His entourage—the self-styled Team America—was enthusiastic: "A tremendous amount of things are going to happen," they ventured, "and they are good things."[74]

The new executive turn in NATO following from the selection of Anders Fogh Rasmussen came in handy in this context. A leadership effort was made to minimize the Atlantic divide and drive the Alliance forward as a collective whole. President Obama and his national security team did not wish to Americanize the war, and they, along with NATO's secretary general, Fogh Rasmussen, sought to engage the Alliance. Secretary General Rasmussen had backed COMISAF General McChrystal's COIN strategy early on.[75] Once the Obama team zeroed in on the big strategic issues and identified a gap between additional U.S. forces and COMISAF's force request, NATO's helmsman moved into action. The drive to close this gap resulted in the near 10,000 additional troops announced in December 2009, as we saw. I asked Secretary General Rasmussen whether this decision was marked by a discussion over strategy or priorities, but it was rather, he stated, a case of "close coordination with the White House." In unison, Rasmussen and the Obama team had tasked the strategic command (SHAPE) to provide data on allied contributions and force potentials, and in concert they chose which allies had the greatest potential contributions to make. This led to a coordinated diplomatic offensive through November. In respect to the allies with force potential, "I would present the numbers on behalf of NATO," Rasmussen recalls, and a day or two later "they would be phoned by [President] Obama delivering the same message. I did it in the capacity as NATO's secretary general; he as a prominent ally."[76] This diplomatic offensive did much to unify the Alliance around the new strategy, which was necessary considering the centrifugal pull of eight years of exhausting engagement.

The COIN enthusiasm of these years raised the prospects of a new and prolonged engagement, which is the COIN logic, but the strategy was different. President Obama wanted the surge drawdown to begin in 2011 and the surge to terminate in 2012, and focus inexorably shifted in the course of 2010 to transition.[77] With transition comes impatience, which was visible in the national approaches to the campaign, as we shall see in a moment. However, the quick shift to transition was not the only source of impatience. The accelerated pace of Special Forces operations and so-called kill-and-capture operations had a notable effect as well. Such operations were always part of the campaign, and we saw how the new ISAF command structure gained a SOF component in 2009. However, the lesson that the U.S. military was bringing from Iraq was that a COIN surge worked better if these kill-and-capture missions surged in parallel. Or, in the words of General McChrystal, who ran these shadowy operations in Iraq before becoming overall commander in Afghanistan, "We needed to orchestrate a nuanced, population-centric campaign that comprised the ability to almost instantaneously swing a devastating hammer blow against an infiltrating insurgent force or wield a deft scalpel to capture or kill an enemy leader."[78] The insurgency leadership is an obvious but difficult target given its location inside Pakistan. Al Qaeda leader Osama bin Laden was located and killed in May 2011, but the insurgency continues. The kill-and-capture campaign has therefore notably targeted the middle management level of the insurgency network—the operators moving on the ground in Afghanistan to provide direction and inspiration to the campaign. There are no reliable official data on these missions for obvious reasons, but various background interviews and open sources indicate that an agile command structure (Joint Special Operations Command), top-rate Special Forces, and not least the fusion of multiple intelligence streams—resulting in real-time knowledge of the operative environment but also a reliable target list (Joint Prioritized Effects List)—are the key enablers. It takes a network, as General McChrystal argues, to defeat a network, but it was General Petraeus who became COMISAF in June 2010 and who could explore the kill-and-capture potential to its fullest because U.S. intelligence capacities as part of the surge first had to be transferred from Iraq to Afghanistan and then organized. It has been reported that 12,000 insurgents have been killed as part of this campaign in little over a year, beginning in early 2010, though such data should be treated with care.[79]

The accelerated kill-and-capture campaign—which actually may have slowed somewhat under COMISAF General John Allen, who took command in June 2011—had the side effect of reinforcing the focus on transition. It did so in two ways, though people disagreed on them. One was to decimate the insurgency to such an extent that it lost its capacity to fundamentally challenge the Karzai government and thus the new Afghan regime built on the Bonn process. According to this view, it was impossible to strike a deal with the insurgents, and so the campaign had to kill off their radical potential. The view was prevalent under General Petraeus's command and perhaps within the wider military chain of command, which, as we saw, foresaw the need for an extended surge, up until 2016, and which therefore were inherently critical toward a transition plan that did not follow—in their view—conditions on the ground. Another was to incite the insurgents to negotiate. The surge, including the kill-and-capture operations, was a means to negotiate from strength and with the aim of bringing the Taliban into the constitutional regime and thus bringing an end to the war. It remains the stated option of Western diplomacy, though it has proven virtually impossible to get off the ground. The December 2011 Bonn conference, as we saw in Chapter 3, has shifted emphasis from reconciliation to continued international engagement for this very reason, and whatever advance that had been made in regards to Qatar-based talks between the United States and the Taliban on confidence-building measures—the talk before negotiations—ground to a halt. They could start anew, but the strategy of transition has encountered a fundamental obstacle—the fairly compressed transition plan incites the insurgents to tough it out, and the kill-and-capture campaign has not been a game changer. It enhances the need for robust and long-term strategic partnerships and regional diplomacy, which are on the international agenda, just as it enhances the sense that there is not much more that combat operations can achieve.

The Netherlands became the first ally to pull its force contingent (approximately 1,700 troops) out of Afghanistan, which it did in August 2010. It left the province of Uruzgan north of Kandahar as well as the Australian forces who had hitherto operated there along with the Dutch, exposed. Afghanistan had become too much to handle for the Dutch government, which fell apart on the issue in late February 2010, failing to undo a parliamentary decision (from October 2009) to pull out by the end of 2010. The Christian Democrats had hoped to placate its governing partner, the Labor party, with this parliamentary decision but then regretted it. NATO weighed in, requesting in early February 2010 a Dutch decision to prolong its stay in Uruzgan, only now with a lesser force of 900 troops, mostly focused on training. It came to naught as Labor defected and the government fell.[80] The Americans moved into Uruzgan beginning in August 2010 (with a force of 900); the Dutch left some helicopters behind for a while to support the Australians; and the new Dutch government ended up committing new forces to police training. Compensatory gestures mattered, and the Netherlands remained within ISAF, but still ISAF's first combat withdrawal was a matter of fact. It had come from within the RC/S core that once drove the NATO campaign.

Another RC/S ally, Canada, officially terminated its combat mission in mid-2011 and brought out its near 3,000 troops by the end of the year. The withdrawal deadline is of old vintage, having been established in March 2008 as part of the parliamentary elections that caused Canada to make demands on NATO—to which NATO responded by reinforcing the Canadian presence with American troops made available by a French decision to deploy a battalion to the Kapisa province in RC/E. A fragile conservative–liberal governing coalition, combined with a public opinion turned decidedly against the war, has made the government reluctant to engage the Afghan issue at all. It refused a NATO request for more troops to monitor the presidential elections of August 2009 and then refused to discuss the issue in any depth.[81] At the Lisbon summit of November 2010, Canada agreed to deploy 950 trainers but in a Kabul-centric mission (anything but Kandahar!) that is "behind the wire" and with zero offensive combat action.[82]

The U.S. surge brought 20,000 troops to Helmand and Kandahar in an effort to break the Taliban in their heartland. Britain—the dominant RC/S ally—thus got moved into the hot spot. With Kandahar set to lose its Canadian forces, the U.S. command team favored pulling the British forces from Helmand to Kandahar, making the city the focus for a renewed British campaign and leaving Helmand and other neighboring provinces to surging U.S. forces. British voices differed on what to do. Lieutenant General and Deputy COMISAF Sir Nick Parker as well as RC/S commander Major General Nick Carter both favored the change with reference to "the coherence of command" and "the interests of maintaining relations with the [U.S.] Marine Expeditionary Force" operating in Helmand. However, in London, the Ministry of Finance opposed on the grounds of costs; the Ministry of Foreign Affairs on the grounds of facilitating an exit strategy; and some in the armed forces on the grounds of continuing investments in an area the British forces knew well.[83] By May 2010 the latter position prevailed: The British forces would remain in Helmand inside the new ISAF regional command (RC/SW). In late 2010 the ISAF offensive to regain the momentum, which had moved from a minor but strategically important settlement in Helmand, Marja (Operation Moshtarak), to Kandahar city (Operation Omid), was squarely in American hands: All the three hot regional commands (RC/E, RC/S, and RC/SW) were American led, as were the operational and the strategic commands. It was a testing time for the U.S.–British relationship, at least in an operational sense. Questions related to the nature of COIN abounded: Had the British footprint been too light? And what had really happened in Iraq in 2007 when the British pulled out of the city of Basra just as the United States was surging? Was the American COIN approach too heavyhanded in general? And were the U.S. Marines, which surged in the south, in particular incapable of the patience and restraint that COIN demands?[84]

The good news for NATO and ISAF was that the earlier bêtes noires of the campaign, France and Germany, sustained it. France was never central to the effort on the ground, though it played a strong role in securing Kabul and, since 2008, prodded by President Sarkozy's desire to break the French–NATO stalemate and Canada's clamoring for Afghan reinforcements, maintained a battalion in U.S.-dominated RC/E—in the district of Surobi and neighboring province of Kapisa. This area—an approach to Kabul—thus became the focal point of the total French force of 4,000, the La Fayette brigade, and France fully aligned with the COIN campaign. It also fully aligned with the transition plan, though, and even accelerated it. President Sarkozy announced in January 2012—shortly before Secretary of Defense Panetta's wish to mark the transition to Afghan national lead in mid-2013 was misunderstood as an accelerated U.S. transition schedule—that France would accelerate the handover to Afghan leadership.[85] Sarkozy's deadline of late 2013 was manageable within the framework of Alliance solidarity; however, the December 2012 deadline of his successor, François Hollande, broke it. Germany has been less quick to head for the exit. It extended the mandate of its troops and augmented them through 2010 to the level of almost 5,000 to sustain the training and thus transition strategy. Moreover, its political leaders, Chancellor Merkel and Defense Minister Guttenberg (who resigned in April 2011) labeled the mission one of resolving an "internal armed conflict," as opposed to stabilizing the country, which added to the realism of the policy and notably relaxed the legal constraints operating on German soldiers.[86] The government's February 2010 Afghan strategy—labeled Responsible Transition—foresees the beginning of a drawdown in mid-2011, which was confirmed by the political leadership on several subsequent occasions in shows of support for the official NATO strategy.[87]

In sum, the fight for transition has brought a mixed balance sheet. NATO as a collective whole has stepped up to the plate by way of its conceptual turn to COIN and by gearing its military organization to it. The turn to executive authority in the organization helped realize the force commitment that followed from Obama's strategy review in late 2009. However, the COIN campaign has morphed into a transition strategy. Transition is now happening at such a pace that it is at least partially incompatible with COIN. Also, the accelerated kill-and-capture campaign has to an extent become *the* critical military mission because it promises relief in the urgent effort to stabilize Kabul and degrade the insurgents. Allies have been quick to adopt the U.S. transition plan, which means that military withdrawals will pick up pace in 2012. It is therefore appropriate to define 2011 as the last big campaign season of the COIN effort. It is thus all the more critical that NATO enhances its ability to structure the political playing field, to which we now turn.

Breaking Bad Political Habits

Investments in Kabul politics were what NATO needed. It could of course eschew responsibility by referring to the ISAF "assistance" mandate or the role of the United Nations or others, and it had repeatedly done so in the past.

This approach was legally sound but a political calamity. NATO would have to shape the political conditions on the ground if it were to shape the conditions under which it could exit the country. Beginning in late 2009, NATO actually made headway in this respect. It stepped up its presence in Kabul; it devised ways and means of enticing other organizations, such as the United Nations, to support NATO; and it embedded this approach in its new Strategic Concept. It did not amount to a revolution but the beginning of a necessary political transformation.

The key lever for NATO was its Senior Civilian Representative (SCR) in Kabul. It was NATO's political voice in Kabul, where the ISAF command structure was military and where other political voices tended to be either national (that is, the embassies) or non-NATO (the United Nations and other IOs). Once merely a personal representative of the secretary general, the SCR had been upgraded in 2008 to become the civilian representative in Kabul of the entire Alliance and with a greater say in PRT affairs, and Italian Fernando Gentilini was the first such NATO SCR, appointed in mid-2008 (see Chapter 5 for more on the SCR position). In January 2010, at a London Afghanistan conference, NATO announced the replacement of Gentilini with British ambassador to Afghanistan, Mark Sedwill, and a reinforcement of the SCR office: Its core staff of civilian advisers was upgraded from six to twenty-four, and the SCR himself was placed at the four-star level, on par with COMISAF. These were minor changes in the big Afghan picture, perhaps, but significant changes nonetheless. These meant that NATO finally had decided to change the situation whereby allies pretended to coordinate their PRT teams and the Alliance as a whole pretended to have the mechanism for coordination.[88] This past leadership by committee produced a stalemate and neither mandated or encouraged the SCR to drive the process forward. NATO's civilian lead, the SCR, had been a mere reporting and advisory agent. The reinforced SCR was notably to take charge of the PRT element and design a plan for transitioning the PRTs into a new model of Afghan governance in line with the logic of transition.

The "new" SCR, in the person of Mark Sedwill, was notably instrumental in helping devise the Afghan "leadership and ownership" that was the guiding theme of the Kabul conference of July 2010. It was at this conference that President Karzai pledged that Afghanistan would be in the security lead by 2014, which was a hugely important goalpost for the allies. The conference communiqué makes no mention of the PRTs because they are yesterday's tool;

instead, it sets new goalposts, namely the channeling of more international aid through Afghan government budgets and greater alignment of international and Afghan priorities.[89] Mark Sedwill also contributed to the security transition paper known as *Inteqal*, though this paper, as with most papers, was formally Afghan led. The *Inteqal* paper foresees security transition province by province according to a broad assessment of the full set of factors affecting security, governance, and development. If conditions for security transition are ripe—and a Joint Afghan–NATO *Inteqal* Board (JANIB) will prepare recommendations for the Afghan government formally in charge—then a four-stage process of transition will begin. It begins modestly with civilian leadership of the PRT in question but ends with complete Afghan ownership of security, governance, and development.[90]

In this we detect NATO's realization that it needed to enhance its civil–military effort—which was not new—and embody the effort in capable actors on the ground. This was new, though the reinforced SCR was only a beginning and a modest one compared to the parallel efforts taking place. These parallel efforts ran at all levels—the national level where individual allies sought to integrate their national toolbox of defense and other ministries and agencies, the international level where the allies met and coordinated among themselves and with the United Nations and others, and the Afghan level where this comprehensive approach was supposed to engender effects. The United States, like other allies, had been swept up in this process, and it framed the making of the Af-Pak strategy. The Obama administration could build on the whole-of-government approach that had been developed through 2008 by a nonpartisan and independent organization prodded into action by President Bush, who saw the misery of uncoordinated action.[91] Standing on this whole-of-government platform, U.S. Ambassador to Afghanistan Karl Eikenberry and COMISAF General McChrystal developed the "integrated civil–military campaign plan" that embedded the military surge in a civilian surge.[92] Two things are noteworthy here, though. One is that whole-of-government thinking, which ran through all Western capitals, as noted, is about policy coordination as part of a strategy: It is not strategy. A comprehensive approach does not tell you what to achieve but how to achieve it, and there is a world of difference between the two. Bruce Riedel, who drafted the Af-Pak strategy, saw that the United States had no shortage of toolbox assessments but was short on real strategy, meaning the goal setting that aligns resources and drives the campaign. In respect to the comprehensive approach, Riedel noted, "It is obvious that everyone would want it," but "it was not a major part of what I did at all."[93] Second, strategy in action demands agile actors on the ground. Complex civil–military campaigns cannot be run by organizational fiat and standard operating procedures; they must be run by leadership capable of adapting means and ends in respect to an evolving operational reality. This is why the joint Afghan–international community board supposed to run things (the JCMB) is irrelevant to the campaign. The international Kabul scene is dominated by the U.S. ambassador and COMISAF, and the U.S. ambassador meets regularly with other leading ambassadors—not just ISAF ambassadors but typically the ambassadors of China, India, Pakistan, Russia, and Japan as well. The U.N. representative (SG SR)—Stefan di Mistura succeeded Eide in March 2010 and was in January 2012 succeeded by Jan Kubis—joins them, though the clout of this office has been in decline since 2008.[94]

It is in this context that the SCR reinforcement gains its particular significance. It is essentially NATO's entry into the scene of civilian strategy making in Kabul (COMISAF was always there to handle military strategy making)—and a sign that toolbox tinkering, which is the comprehensive approach, requires leadership to succeed. Reinforcing the SCR creates a direct link from Kabul politics to the North Atlantic Council for whom the SCR labors. The choice of Mark Sedwill was significant because he served in Kabul and was from the group of willing and able allies. He was also not American, which served NATO now that the American footprint had grown large. Sedwill and COMISAF McChrystal quickly established a tight working relationship that placed the two on par. When COMISAF was out of town and could not run briefings, SCR Sedwill and not Deputy COMISAF would take over meetings—an unprecedented situation in a military headquarters such as ISAF.[95] The change resulted not only from good personal relations in Kabul: It was NATO's express intention to put the SCR on the four-star level next to COMISAF.

NATO could have done more to reinforce the SCR, and the fact that it did not is part of the explanation as to why the SCR lost momentum in late 2010 and into 2011. NATO could have revised the SCR terms of references and thus formally empowered him to become a leading Kabul actor. It did not but instead opted for his informal reinforcement (more staff; political gestures). Background interviews indicate a mixed set of reasons for this.[96] Some allies did not see a role for a reinforced SCR and therefore hesitated to invest resources in the office; others (such as Italy) felt that Fernando Gentilini had been dealt poor cards and now unfairly was asked to step down to make way for improvement; yet other allies enthusiastically sought a strengthened NATO civil–military actor in Kabul and assigned their best and brightest to the reinforced SCR staff. These enthusiasts sought to strengthen the terms of references; the others resisted. In the end, the enthusiasts dropped the issue, seeking out a new representative who by way of personality and modus operandi could generate change on the ground. Here was an opportunity to pull in a new Paddy Ashdown—a heavy political mover and shaker—and word has it that NATO Secretary General Fogh Rasmussen, who appoints the SCR, was scanning the European diplomatic scene for such an experienced political figure. The SCR posting lacked in weight, though, and the new SCR instead became a serving ambassador. Mark Sedwill's successor, British Simon Gass, who took over in April 2011, was likewise a serving ambassador prior to his appointment. Interestingly, Gass came from a two-year posting to Iran—one of the countries whose importance in the regional diplomacy is increasing.

The lack of formal reinforcement became a handicap in the wheeling and dealing of Kabul politics, though it should be noted that Sedwill's tenure as SCR has been regarded in consistently positive terms. Kabul is just a tough and complex environment, and political backing is therefore critical. The operating environment degraded beginning with the fraudulent presidential elections of August 2009. President Karzai found his mandate renewed but international standing undermined, and he has reacted by asserting his independence from the international community. Among other things, Karzai refused to fundamentally engage the January 2010 London conference on the grounds that important matters could be handled in Kabul in the summer, a challenge Sedwill, appointed at London, picked up. The Kabul summit was widely perceived as being successful because it established both *Inteqal* and the 2014 deadline, and it has come to represent the height of comprehensive cooperation.

Deteriorating relations fed off suspicion that Karzai's regime was not only weak but fundamentally corrupt and inept. Ambassador Eikenberry voiced this concern in 2009 in a confidential assessment of President Karzai, whom he saw as "an inadequate strategic partner"; the assessment was leaked and became common knowledge, yet Eikenberry remained in place until July 2011.[97] Ambassador Richard Holbrooke—the U.S. point man on Af-Pak issues in 2009–2010—had such a falling out with President Karzai over the elections that he failed to recover his ground in Kabul and had to hand more initiative to the local ambassador—who was Eikenberry. The U.N. mission (UNAMA) broke in two over the electoral fraud, with SG SR Kai Eide bending backward to stress positive issues while his deputy Peter Galbraith vetted his criticism in public and got fired as a result. Part of the UNAMA staff simply left with him, and the appointment of Stefan di Mistura in early 2010 failed to redress the UNAMA situation, though his contribution to Kabul diplomacy is noted positively.[98] When General McChrystal again aroused political controversy in the context of a *Rolling Stone Magazine* portrait and subsequently got fired, this did not simplify matters.[99] The new COMISAF, General Petraeus, had a reputation and a degree of political immunity—could President Obama politically afford to fire a third commander, having fired Generals McKiernan and McChrystal?—that reset relations in Kabul. Petraeus and Eikenberry were in the front seat and SCR Sedwill in the backseat. Ambassador Crocker, who succeeded Eikenberry, was Petraeus's partner from the Iraq surge, but Crocker came to Kabul just as Petraeus left (to take up the CIA directorship), and General Allen of the U.S. Marines moved in.

It is remarkable how little coverage COMISAF General Allen has received compared to Generals McChrystal and Petraeus. This serves to underscore the hope and ambition that went into the COIN surge and that inflated the public relations role of COMISAF—though General Petraeus was sure to draw cover given his role in Iraq—and also how COIN has now given way to transition, which has put diplomacy and diplomats in the driver's seat. This turn of events highlights the limits of the SCR because Simon Gass has become invisible in the public domain, like COMISAF General Allen. Both are solid players on the ground, but they are not shaping the public domain and the campaign strategy. The relative decline of the SCR began with General McChrystal's firing and General Petraeus's entry into Kabul, notes one national official who has been in a position to observe these events, because General Petraeus came in with so much weight. To Sedwill's credit, the official continued, he was skillful in designing the type of transition process with which Petraeus could be comfortable—Petraeus being an ardent critic of the accelerated transition plan for the surge. Sedwill thus became a team builder and a source of campaign coherence, which was critically important, but the leadership was Petraeus's. With Petraeus off the stage in mid-2011, a new phase has opened where execution rather than design marks the work of both COMISAF and SCR.[100]

The incomplete political engagement reverberates through the effort to promote reconciliation between the Kabul regime and Taliban leadership. The process is difficult to gauge from the outside, but it picked up pace in 2010, with the Consultative Peace *Jirga* of June 2–4, 2010, formally kicking off a structured attempt by President Karzai to dialogue with supposedly moderate Taliban (see overview in Chapter 3). The big ISAF nations, the United States and Britain in particular, along with Saudi Arabia and Turkey and others, have been reported to work in favor of dialogue but under cover, of course. It has thus become common to talk of a "Kabul process" that is the Afghan equivalent to NATO's transition strategy.[101] The Istanbul conference of November 2011 deepened a regional diplomacy track in this regard, but much work needs to be done. The NATO Lisbon summit of November 2010, along with the Bonn December 2011 conference, pointed in the direction of more partnership, and NATO duly decided at the Alliance's May 2012 summit in Chicago to upgrade these efforts.

The allies have been slow to agree on a course of action in regards to reconciliation. It was not until the unfolding of the surge in 2010 that the United States formally moved on the issue, a commitment long urged by allies such as Britain and Germany.[102] It is inconceivable that NATO as a whole could become engaged in reconciliation: The North Atlantic Council is simply not adapted to secret peace negotiations. However, it is not unreasonable to expect an allied position that explains how such negotiations run by individual nations tie in with NATO/ISAF efforts. The official NATO position—which is to encourage an Afghan-led process that meets three conditions (the government must be in the lead, reconciliation must build on the constitution, and the government must be in a position of strength)—tells us very little. This is old NATO, mainly camped on formality. New NATO should be more forward leaning on the issue of the Bonn process—which produced the regime that cemented the Northern Alliance's leadership in Kabul and became the framework into which disgruntled Pashtuns had to step if they wanted a stake in the new Afghanistan. NATO should have addressed this issue much earlier, perhaps as early as 2005, and certainly in the intervening years as it became clear that President Karzai was not up to the task of transforming his country's political landscape.[103] His unpopularity is now a Taliban asset: A Western diplomat speaking on background noted that the Taliban could kill Karzai but would be foolish to do so. NATO should have been and should be more actively engaged in defining the heart of the matter—the underlying political bargain in Afghanistan. Instead we observe a campaign-reconciliation detachment, which reflects poorly on NATO's political-strategic ability. There have been improvements, as we saw with the reinforced SCR, and this underscores NATO's enhanced ability to enable operational adaptation. However, the SCR is a mostly a window to the kind of alliance that NATO could be if its members came to realize the full implication of Sun Tzu's admonition that failure in every battle will follow from the insufficient knowledge of the enemy and oneself.[104]

Breaking Out Is Hard to Do

NATO is not only ready for change but has changed already, and in fundamental ways: Current NATO is in fact "NATO 3.0"—a new version compared to Cold War NATO (NATO 1.0, 1949–1991) and post–Cold War NATO (NATO 2.0, 1991–2011)—and it began at the Lisbon summit, November 19–20, 2010. This is NATO's own line, promoted in the run-up to the summit, notably by NATO Secretary General Rasmussen and U.S. NATO Ambassador Ivo Daalder.[105] The summit produced a range of decisions to support this claim.[106] One was the decision to balance the commitment to nuclear deterrence with a vision, first laid out by President Obama in the spring of 2009, of a nuclear-free world. Another was the decision to build a collective missile defense (MD) shield that one day could bolster the move to nuclear zero, though this progression remained controversial. A third was to link missile defense and partnership to Russia, offering Russia a concrete MD partnership as a symbol of "reset" relations. A fourth was to enhance the use of political partnerships across the globe (with both countries and organizations) in flexible formats. A fifth was to direct NATO to become better at building up local security forces in zones of conflict and states threatened by failure, which amounted to a first real advance into the politics of comprehensive planning since Riga in 2006. In sum, NATO turned its back on old issues (nuclear deterrence and Russia as a problem) and engaged new tasks (missile defense, a large network of partners, and security building) that unmistakably associated NATO with the "emerging security challenges" it highlighted and that it has made the focus of a new part of its HQ in Brussels.[107] NATO clearly sought renewal, and it sought to convey the impression that it was ready for a global role more focused than in the past on strategic dialogue with great powers and interventions in deteriorating regions from where threats to NATO members are likely to emerge.

This was an agenda that also applied to Afghanistan, although it was stated only implicitly. The summit produced two documents on Afghanistan: one on partnership and one on transition.[108] The latter was adopted in ISAF format and confirmed the *Inteqal* approach, and it set the stage for the handover of Afghan areas—from provinces down to districts—to Afghan leadership: President Karzai announced the first tranche in March 2011, the second in November. The former document on partnership was a NATO–Afghanistan Enduring Partnership Declaration focusing on the potential for dialogue, training, and capacity building post-2014. It was confirmed in an Enduring Partnership declaration issued by NATO and Afghanistan at the May 2012 summit in Chicago, which confirmed NATO's noncombat, security capacity building role post-2014. NATO's partnership was important partly because it gave new impetus to bilateral partnership negotiations between Afghanistan and the United States, which advanced at a tortuous pace, partly because it was one step in keeping NATO engaged in a conflict that is sure to last beyond the transition end point in 2014 and whose regional impact is of direct concern to the allies.

Still, something was missing. NATO 3.0 was a public relations gimmick that reflected an ambition but not really the historical record. NATO had been there before, in Prague in 2002 when it wedded itself to the great transformation agenda in response to international terrorism. Back in those days, this was NATO 3.0, supposedly radically different from the crisis manager of the Balkans that NATO had become during the 1990s. Now, in 2010, NATO 3.0 reemerged because the Prague summit and lessons were inconvenient. The 2010 ambition was honorable and reflected Afghan lessons: We see it in respect to all three dimensions of the new Strategic Concept—a mutual defense clause omitting references to territorial limits, a crisis management ambition with a beefed up civil-military interface, and a partnership agenda that is if not global, then more flexible.[109] Still, what was missing was the answer to the lingering question of why we should trust NATO this time, if NATO had not delivered after Prague 2002 in spite of its promises. The answer related partly to the dynamic between political leadership and institutional adaptation, to which we are about to turn, but also more fundamentally to the collective mindset because NATO, by seeking refuge in the optimism of global governance, was in risk of giving up on the business of war.

With regards to institutional adaptation NATO's Secretary General Rasmussen feels confident that NATO can improve its strategic capacity within the current institutional framework, which is to say with the existing North Atlantic Council (NAC). In his view, if the North Atlantic Council is approached in the right way, it can be a vehicle of renewal and strategic deliberation and action.[110] Critical in NAC adaptation is an emphasis on political discussions as opposed to operational briefings, the enumeration of national positions (of which there are twenty-eight), and issues of minor concern. To make the NAC work in strategic ways, a wider reform of headquarter affairs has been necessary, and we see it in the actions and approach of Secretary General Rasmussen. He has subordinated the permanent representatives or ambassadors to enhance executive leadership.[111] He operates visibly at the level of heads of state and government.[112] And he has sought to remove routine matters from the NAC agenda to focus discussions.[113]

Yet reform in the headquarters is not the end of the story of Alliance leadership. When queried on the kind of leadership it takes to promote change in NATO, apart from these refinements of the Council workings, Anders Fogh Rasmussen invokes two processes. One is a process of raising awareness and generating the kind of attention and support that allows for goal setting, and then the development of strategy and tactics. The "burning platform" is critically important, he noted, because the problem must be apparent to everyone, and the way to create this platform, he continued, is notably with "keynote speeches."[114] In addition, one might add, and as observers of NATO cannot have failed to notice, Anders Fogh Rasmussen has stepped up the use of media communication, using a variety of electronic and print platforms to communicate NATO's agenda.[115] The creation of burning platforms—of agenda setting—is an inherently political process. It is a tool of political leaders, and with the appointment of a prime minister as secretary general, NATO has gained a more prominent use of it in house. The other process invoked by the secretary general is hardly surprising and consists of working with the allied governments to generate the consensus necessary for collective decision making. In contrast to his predecessors, Anders Fogh Rasmussen seeks to generate consensus by engaging the capitals more directly, as we saw, but the task of mobilizing unity is the same.

The gist of this approach to leadership is informal and political, and it offers the clue to NATO's future. It is the center of transatlantic gravity, this informal and political process, and in a way it always was: Heads of state and government and other high officials always worked in a type of community that was formed by way of a whole range of meetings and gatherings, and NATO was the formal and structured face of this interaction. Afghanistan— and the other wars and conflicts of the new decade—has reinforced the importance of this informal community, however. The NATO heads of state and government are unlikely to meet in NAC format more than once a year—the approximate pace of summitry for the past decade—but they meet often in other formats, and they—the Blackberry generation of leaders—have all the means to stay in running touch on the big issues. Together they must create the "burning platform" that Anders Fogh Rasmussen emphasizes and that enables NAC decision making, which on a routine basis will meet in the format of foreign and defense ministers or permanent representatives.

In NATO we thus see a broader trend in international affairs that has to do with globalization and the changing meaning of state sovereignty and cooperation. There is first of all a tendency for heads of state and government to become very visibly involved in the day-to-day affairs of high diplomacy (they were always involved in summitry) because of the need to carry the public and mobilize support for complex solutions. There is then also the tendency to search for new and flexible patterns of cooperation that suit the issue at hand. The mission must determine the coalition, as Rumsfeld once argued. This remains a valid point. Informal groups thus run high diplomacy: The informal formats of G8 and G20 have grown in importance in the regulation of international finance and trade; the Contact Group/Friends of Libya shaped the high politics of the 2011 Libya campaign; and the Friends of Democratic Pakistan have become the mobilizing mechanism for policy coordination in relation to Pakistan. They connect back to institutions—be it the International Monetary Fund, the United Nations, or NATO—but they cross fertilize and provide the leadership and direction that guide the operational work of these institutions.

The question is whether NATO can avoid becoming the mere tool of such shifting coalitions. If that happened, it would rob NATO of political meaning, causing it to wither. Afghanistan tells us that not all is lost for the Alliance. The ISAF format is a considerable success for the Alliance in the sense that it has succeeded in bringing ISAF partners almost fully into the NAC. Prompted by ISAF partner frustrations with the old model of decision making, decisions have for several years been made in ISAF format only. There are no NAC deliberations followed by ISAF deliberations, therefore, but only ISAF deliberations and then decisions. Naturally, the NAC reserves for itself the right to act on behalf of the Alliance, but the operational partnership format is extensive and was turned into a NATO model for future operations with the revised partnership policy of early 2011. Yet we also know that NATO's key challenge does not concern the NATO–ISAF relationship but the relationship between the

United States and its most committed allies on the one hand and the remaining allies on the other—between the core coalition and the Alliance.

The great danger is that NATO allies will come to believe that globalization and the prevailing idea of global and complex or multilevel governance is the answer to this challenge. Such thinking pretends there are no fundamental problems in world politics because everyone—the coalition and the alliance, the nations and the international organizations—supposedly can be made to work for the same purpose, which is to advance liberal goals of democracy, transparency, and human rights. It is vision of "globality" or "global functionality" according to which it would make no difference whether NATO, the African Union, or China solves a given problem. However, functionality as a vision is inadequate and in the end dangerous because it builds on the illusion that political differences are ephemeral and not central. It leads us to focus our efforts on means—the heralded comprehensive approach that allegedly enables concerted action anywhere in respect to every kind of problem. It has become an important idea inside NATO because it is comforting: Cooperation and unity are both the ends and means of global functionality. NATO is therefore setting up its organization up for comprehensiveness, opening up channels of communication and coordination and allowing for "plug-and-play" among headquarters and other actors in the field. However comforting the thought, global functionality and comprehensive action are disconnected from the core reality of the Afghan campaign, as this book has made clear, which is the deficit in political goal setting and strategic approach. It is one thing to admonish what needs to be done in Afghanistan; it is quite another to define why you are there.

This is the stuff of the conclusion, but it connects to the debate on informal and political leadership and how NATO can mend its ways. If NATO is to continue as an able Alliance with purpose, it must draw a distinction between NATO the Alliance and NATO the organization—a favorite theme in French thinking, where Gaullists wanted to belong to the former but not the latter. In the present-day era, the distinction lives on but to remind us that the allies' investments in the latter hide a deficit of investment in the former. They should take comfort in the fact that a prime ministerial secretary general has wrought considerable change to the organization, updating it to connect it to the nations' concerns and rationalizing this change in the Strategic Concept. They should worry that they are losing the Alliance.

President Obama is an appropriate end point to this discussion. His political leadership has on the one hand set the course for where the Alliance must go. "We must begin by acknowledging the hard truth," President Obama observed in his Nobel Peace Prize acceptance speech in December 2009, "We will not eradicate violent conflict in our lifetimes. There will be times when nations—acting individually or in concert—will find the use of force not only necessary but morally justified." There are indeed great visionaries of peace and reconciliation, the president continued, "But as a head of state sworn to protect and defend my nation, I cannot be guided by their examples alone. I face the world as it is, and cannot stand idle in the face of threats to the American people. For make no mistake: Evil does exist in the world."[116]

The realism of this speech struck observers at the time because it was given at a peace prize institute, but the matter of fact is that it would create ripples in NATO had it been given there. NATO does not deal in evil; it deals in cooperation and progress. Such realism as that can help NATO the Alliance resurrect itself, nonetheless, because it is the antidote to facile ideas of global functionality. Yet, and on the other hand, President Obama has had his own particular toolbox approach to NATO, devising strategy in Washington and asking NATO to pitch in. His conception of security policy is contractual: Just as he made a business contract with his own military leadership in the context of the surge, so he has reminded allies that they get the kind of Alliance they pay for. When Robert Gates stepped down as secretary of defense, it was widely noted that he put the point in blunter terms than the president could permit himself to do.[117] There can be no doubt that European allies are not doing enough to build an Atlantic bridge in terms of defense capabilities, but it is worth underscoring that NATO's sense of realism in this and other domains would be heightened if the Alliance leader took NATO seriously not only as an organized conglomerate of nations but as an alliance with a distinct Atlantic or Western character.

CONCLUSION

COIN became a household term in the course of 2008–2010 and not only because of the Afghan campaign. The surge in Iraq through 2007–2008 was the catalyst of popularity and offered hope that the Afghan campaign might experience a similar turn to the better. The math of COIN is simple—one soldier for every fifty people—but the practice is breathtakingly hard. Through 2008 NATO eschewed the challenge in Afghanistan. No one in the North Atlantic

Council, including the United States, had the will or resources to roll out a full COIN campaign in Afghanistan. President Bush initiated a strategy review that pointed in this direction but so late in his presidency that it made no difference. Some months earlier, he had given greater attention to the transnational nature of the insurgency, stepping up the covert campaign in Pakistan's border territories, but the overall strategic framework vacillated. NATO allies, having decided that they excelled in enabling leadership, found it hard to make a difference.

Efforts on the Afghan ground naturally stalled. COMISAF General McKiernan brought to the ISAF table the most comprehensive design for a COIN campaign hitherto seen. Some of its key pillars continue to the day; notably the population-centric approach and the concept of widespread partnering with Afghan forces. In the U.N. track, Special Representative Kai Eide sought to revive the UNAMA mission after President Karzai had denied ISAF and UNAMA unified efforts—with his veto of Paddy Ashdown's candidacy for robust international leadership in Kabul. Kai Eide put on the table a new design—the flower organization analyzed in this chapter—that would build on General Richard's PAG and enlarge it to a national model for development and governance. Both efforts failed. The UNAMA effort failed because it was beyond U.N. capacity and because Eide never managed to eradicate the sense that he or his UNAMA mission worked in a type of rivalry with ISAF. The campaign desperately needed a burst of ISAF efforts, but this was politically denied at home, where NATO allies hesitated to invest in COIN. General McKiernan saw this and refused to set up his organization for full COIN. As the United States changed its political mind, it dismissed General McKiernan and asked General McChrystal to do it in his stead. NATO at this point agreed and got caught up in a type of COIN enthusiasm.

COIN has many faces, though, and one of them is transition and the ability of forces to prepare a handover of security responsibilities to the local government. This facet of COIN soon came to dominate allied thinking. They set up a transition track internationally, running through a string of summits, which was supposed to work broadly along all three lines of security, development, and governance. As the allies looked to draw down the engagement and terminate the combat missions, the security track came to dominate, though. The *Inteqal* framework remains broad, but the political focus has narrowed: Security is the name of the game. NATO has promised to do better. It is now NATO 3.0, it claims. NATO had not conceived of its campaign in broad political–military terms, but now it will, and it will bring the tools to the table to get other missions right from the beginning. Secretary General Rasmussen has with success reformed the workings of the North Atlantic Council and contributes to the extraordinary leadership that it takes to move a large political–military organization into gear.

The challenge is thus cut out for the underlying Atlantic community. This community is built around progressive principles, and it has come to make the comprehensive approach both its tool and outlook. The community works better if there is a peace to enforce or a local government to assist. Going one-on-one in a classical strategic encounter is not NATO's core competence, and this is not merely because alliances are fraught with collective action problems; it is because it has begun growing into a liberal and non-strategic community. Inevitably, if NATO is to act strategically, it will be due to a strong dose of ad hoc political leadership. President Obama provided such leadership through 2009, and the result is now being played out. Working with key allies, Secretary General Rasmussen has done his bit, perhaps notably in engineering the reinforced SCR that signals NATO's entry into the politicking of the Kabul scene. This clash between leadership and community is eased by the fact that NATO is on its way out of Afghanistan: The community can bend to the leadership because the community at the end of the day will rediscover its liberal peace. Such is the promise, and it is needed in the Afghan context. One can only wonder what will happen to NATO, though, if determined leadership seeks to engage the Alliance in another troublesome conflict. The Arab Spring is hopeful, and NATO's Libyan intervention turned out well, but something could still blow up, and NATO will have to reconcile its leadership and community before the next conflict tears at its seams and perhaps fatally so.

CONCLUSION

IN WAR, IDEAS ARE PARAMOUNT. They inform the political goals for which forces fight, and they shape the strategy that will lead to victory. Capabilities such as logistics, resources, and organization matter, naturally, but they matter in relation to a purpose, the foundation for strategy. Not coincidentally, knowledge and understanding are the first two qualities emphasized by Chinese strategist Sun Tzu in his "Five Essentials for Victory," and Hans Morgenthau, a power analyst par excellence, defined political power as a "psychological relation" between those who exercise it and those over whom it is exercised.[1] To grasp NATO in Afghanistan, we must therefore grasp ideas and then relate them to power. In Afghanistan, NATO has been more than an alliance: It has been an alliance with purpose, a "benevolent Alliance," and it has struggled because Afghanistan has not been receptive to it.

Much of the literature on NATO and Afghanistan dwells on NATO's shortcomings in terms of capability. It fields too few troops, who are poorly trained and equipped for counterinsurgency warfare in Southwest Asia; it lacks the combat support teams and logistics to sustain large operations; and it lacks the political and financial commitment to move troops in theater in response to the evolving campaign. Moreover, it lacks the capacity to coordinate civil–military relations and synchronize efforts across the three lines of operation—security, development, and governance. The criticism is to the point, and NATO is acutely aware of it. NATO summits prescribe greater investments in the right kind of military gear, and NATO's command structure is reformed to plug-and-play with civilian organizations. If successful, these efforts will improve NATO's capabilities and go some way to address the criticism. Yet we should be aware that NATO's key deficit concerns its purpose.

When going to Afghanistan in 2002–2003, NATO had purpose. It was not perfectly coherent because alliances never are. However, NATO had overcome the challenge posed by the end of the Cold War and the new world of the 1990s. NATO's response was contested, at times inadequate and contradictory, but in time it gained coherence. NATO activated its means for liberal ends and became a "benevolent alliance." This purposive alliance faced challenges, notably because NATO in effect had become a kind of collective security gendarme in the Euro-Atlantic region and needed to integrate its own sense of mission with the concerns of outsiders—the other big powers in the Security Council, the United Nations as an organization, and many others. Afghanistan therefore provided relief early on. It lifted NATO's gaze from the Balkans, though NATO is still there, and it eased tense relations to Russia. Fighting for a new Afghanistan was a noble and just cause following the September 2001 attacks, and it became all the more noble as the controversial War on Terror moved to Iraq. NATO gained a role in 2003 when taking over the ISAF mission that it felt it had initially been denied by the Bush administration, and it was an inherently benevolent mission of providing security assistance to an emerging democracy.

NATO emerges from an Afghan war that went awry with a reinforced sense of benevolence and a diminished sense of alliance. We see this in the temptation to question the current mission and not the purpose from which it springs. If NATO is downgrading ambitions on behalf of Afghan governance and development, it is not because the underlying values are not noble; it is because the conditions are too tough. The Afghan government, once destined to be a partner in reconstruction, has proven inadequate; the Taliban is too strong and too deeply embedded to defeat; Pakistan is a conundrum; and NATO resources and patience are wearing thin. There is a debate on early mistakes of the campaign, but it tends to provide comfort: The purpose was right, but the organization and effort were inadequate. More resources should have been poured in at an early stage; more should have been done to wrestle control of the new political institutions from the old guard; and more should have been done to bridge traditional and modern conceptions of justice. Adherents of the NATO-is-dying school believe this is all pie in the sky: NATO is finished and could not have done right even if someone at the outset had provided the Alliance with a different strategic blueprint. It is this die-hard criticism that feeds the NATO-must-globalize school's conclusion that NATO must learn how to cooperate more broadly with other institutions, from the EU and the United Nations over the Asian Investment Bank to new national partners across the globe. In this lens, NATO has a vibrant future, and it is called the comprehensive approach. This embeds NATO in a wider liberal community, adding to NATO's comfort and legitimacy. It has become a mind-set estranged from the idea that politics may have its own logic but war its own grammar and thus from the necessity of defining political concepts of order within the realm of the war in which one is engaged. Politics is part of the war, in other words. It is thus poor strategy to erect a Bonn/Karzai regime, consecrate it with a national development strategy, and then pretend that a dogged war can be made to fit into this ambition. Where the allies should have devoted attention to the political basics of the war, they preferred to search for greater resources for its development strategy, which became the comprehensive approach. This approach holds great operational value but it is not strategy.

This drift toward liberal ease is confirmed by the tendency in NATO to depict the Alliance not as an alliance but as a security institution. NATO integrates with global partners and institutions to manage the global commons. This is not NATO trying to learn and to become able to handle a strategic challenge akin to Afghan war; it is NATO looking for something else to do. It brings us to the classical view of NATO and its prescriptions for Alliance renewal.

AFGHANISTAN REDUX

The important success story of this book is NATO's ability to improve on the brink of defeat. NATO allies collectively came to recognize in 2007–2008 that their mission in Afghanistan could neither run on separate tracks from the main U.S. effort (OEF) nor cope with the insurgency. It led to the April 2008 adoption of a strategic pol-mil plan (CSPMP), which was embedded in a more general action plan to realize the comprehensive approach as an all-around tool. NATO—now including the United States—began pulling in one military direction, and it sought to bring in a wide and predominantly civilian toolbox in its support. It was a qualified success, as we saw. The CSPMP emerged into a vacuum of leadership in 2008. The ISAF commander on the ground pushed for an embrace of a fully resourced COIN campaign and laid out ISAF's first de facto theater campaign (OP TOLO). However, European allies hesitated,

UNAMA faltered, and the Bush administration, having gone through a tough Iraq surge, had neither the time nor the appetite for an Afghan surge. Still, there was improvement, and the effects gradually became apparent. NATO allies became COIN enthusiasts in the course of 2009, supporting President Obama's decision to surge in Afghanistan. They agreed to a new command structure, a new training mission, and an enhanced effort led by the senior civilian representative to tie together the PRTs and prepare for stage 4 transition to Afghan leadership, and they have managed to engage the first tranches of transition without falling out over their spoils, which is to say that they have shared the diminishing burdens fairly equitably.

Missing from this adaptive success is the decision to place the CSPMP within a context of political reconciliation in Afghanistan, which would have amounted to a desire to get the Pashtuns included in a real peace deal, a willingness to question the extent to which Western policy merely supported power brokers—including Karzai—whose reigns fanned the flames of discontent and therefore the insurgency, a sense that Pakistan and India needed to be brought into a regional deal, and then an ability to shape the CSPMP to these ends. It became harder over time because players got entrenched. The effort should have begun in 2002 "because sooner or later these people [the Taliban] would come back," as an insightful UNAMA staffer concluded at the time.[2] In late 2009 Britain advocated reopening Afghanistan's constitutional bargain as a complement to the Obama surge, but by this point in time it was hard to get agreement.[3] President Karzai sought actively to take charge of reconciliation, as did Pakistan; Britain promoted it but the U.S. military wanted to degrade first, then negotiate; and President Obama sought compromise. In short, NATO adaptation happened within a static approach to the most critical question of the campaign, the adequacy of the Bonn institutions that ISAF labored to defend.

What will happen next in Afghanistan? We know the plan for 2011–2014, which is the *Inteqal* plan. If it works out, Afghanistan will have gained so much by way of security, governance, and development by 2014 that it can stand on its own feet as an independent and moderate state. This will not happen. To compensate, the December 2011 Bonn conference, along with NATO's May 2012 Chicago summit, therefore acted as stepping stones toward the definition of the "enduring partnership" that NATO and Afghanistan sketched in November 2010 and also toward a comprehensive regional engagement. Western allies will primarily seek to have the Afghan government stand on its own security feet, and the ambition to ensure proper governance and development has been downgraded and pushed beyond 2014. The COIN effort remains but is therefore transforming into one of training Afghan security forces to maintain a type of political order in urban areas and along vital arteries of communication and trade. Rural communities will have an opportunity to make peace with the help of village stabilization programs, but the effect will be varied, especially now that the surge drawdown begins in the Taliban stronghold of southern Afghanistan. The accelerated SOF campaign designed to eliminate or at least seriously hurt the insurgent middle management operatives will continue, notably in eastern Afghanistan, where the Haqqani network and Al Qaeda operate out of Pakistan's northern Waziristan province. It will happen to eliminate insurgents and terrorists but as part of an evolving policy on reconciliation and stabilization. It all amounts to a distinctively narrower campaign that the one designed during the heydays of COIN enthusiasm—in 2009—and one whose ultimate rationale resides in the political bargaining that the main protagonists and stakeholders engage.

This leads to the question of whether we are facing a Najibullah rerun. Afghan President Najibullah defied expectations and survived four years past the Soviet withdrawal in 1988 but then fell from power in 1992 as the collapse of the Soviet Union led to the collapse of external support for his regime. He was killed by the Taliban in 1996. A rerun is unlikely, though. The NATO allies are not about to disintegrate as did the Soviet Union, and they benefit from the lessons of history. Moreover, the United States in particular is now so committed to the security situation in Southwest Asia that a withdrawal in any short- to medium-term perspective is inconceivable, and, if the United States remains engaged, so will key allies. The question is therefore not whether the allies will engage but whether they will be able to engage in such a way that their interests are secured. To do so, they must not believe that peace will grow out of the Afghan security forces.[4] They must instead promote a new political deal inside Afghanistan and then help tailor and sustain the kind of Afghan security force that this deal requires (the current COIN-sized force will be much too big and expensive). They must also notably engage Pakistan and address its security concerns, including India's role in the Southwest Asian security structure.

NATO and Afghanistan's "enduring partnership" as of 2012 tells us only a small part of the story. It is focused on aspects of Afghan security sector reform, notably the continuation of training, further capacity building in relation to threats of terrorism and narcotics, and improved access to NATO partnership tools, including political dialogue and access to NATO schools. This focus is by now fairly traditional, and the real novelty would be if NATO agreed to go further in the rule-of-law missions that are also part of security sector reform but that NATO hitherto has eschewed on the grounds that these are civilian missions, or if NATO engaged in regional diplomacy to secure a stable Afghan environment. Given the general downgrading of Western ambitions in Afghanistan, we should expect no NATO rule-of-law mission. It is rather the missing diplomatic effort that should be noted. Because diplomacy is ongoing but taking place outside NATO—variously in bilateral relations, multilateral formats such as the Istanbul process, or the Friends of a Democratic Pakistan—we can predict a continuation of this division of labor: Multilateral and institutionalized NATO will run security sector reform policy while informal coalitions will shape the high politics of regional reconciliation. Critically, the two efforts must be closely coordinated. Just as security institutions will wither in the absence of political settlement, so reconciliation will be shallow in the absence of functioning security institutions to sustain a political deal. The challenge for Western allies is not to continue on parallel tracks, therefore, but to coordinate them. The worst-case scenario is a repeat of the theological debate on stabilization versus counterterrorism that undercut NATO in the early phase of the campaign. This is a scenario to which the allies must pay close attention. The accelerated engagement of politically active allies in volatile regional affairs in parallel to NATO's slower-moving Afghan partnership policy has all the ingredients for burden-sharing recriminations and political misunderstandings. Political negotiations by a political coalition and institution building by NATO make for a difficult balancing act but nonetheless the act that NATO now must engage.

NATO's future in Afghanistan has the complexity of classical theory and none of the straightforwardness that NATO-is-dying or NATO-must-globalize proponents thrive on. The case for complex engagement divided between coalition and collective institution follows from the political ethics inherent in classical theory. The alternatives—a withdrawal (following from the NATO-is-dying school) or the abdication of leadership in favor of network governance (following from the NATO-must-globalize school)—would have severe consequences in terms of Southwest Asian instability, political radicalization, the loss of Western cohesion, and an accelerated global power shift that could well prove unmanageable. The prudent option is therefore to support security sector reform by NATO and political coercion and persuasion by coalitions. It is a difficult balancing act, as mentioned, and it brings us to some general conclusions regarding NATO's future as a Western alliance.

STATESMANSHIP AND NATO'S FUTURE

This book tells us that a reversal of fortunes is not impossible. NATO is adaptable. It can come to recognize the nature of a campaign, its limits, and the need to compromise behind a U.S. lead; it might also prove capable of proactive diplomatic change now that the combat phase is coming to an end. In addition to being adaptable, NATO is resilient. A decade of war in Afghanistan suffices to wear down most alliances, but NATO is still there. These are important qualities that should not be overlooked.

Critics tend to take aim at NATO burden sharing, the preponderance of U.S. power, and the limited force contributions provided by European allies. The Alliance is unbalanced, goes the argument, and the ills can be traced back to power—and to power disparity. This was an argument made by departing Secretary of Defense Gates, as we saw in Chapter 6. Yet the gap has marked the Alliance from the very outset—from the reaction to the Korean War in 1950 and the making of a Medium Term Defense Plan that soon proved impossible to realize to the present. Power distributions change from bipolarity to unipolarity and soon to be multipolarity, and yet the Alliance and its burden-sharing debate continue. The debate is an important facet of the Alliance, and only the foolhardy would deny it, especially when major operations raise the stakes of solidarity, but admonitions to do more are simply integral to the dynamics of the Alliance, and they go both ways. The United States wants Europe to put more tools in the toolbox; the Europeans want the United States to stop treating the Alliance as a mere toolbox for U.S. policy. The really critical question for the Alliance is rather whether it can get its campaigns right in terms of strategic focus and whether it can adapt sufficiently to adverse campaign conditions. If it cannot, it is strategic inability that will undo the Alliance, not burden sharing. If it can, burden sharing will simply be part of the background noise.

We know from this analysis and some of the literature reviewed in Chapter 1 that NATO has not been apt at strategic thinking and action in Afghanistan. It failed to question the appropriateness of the end state of the ISAF campaign, which was the state-building agenda of the 2001 Bonn conference; and, when the Afghan state needed a nation, NATO and ISAF turned to counterinsurgency to win hearts and minds, and so the mission expanded. In the end NATO lost its balance, being roundly benevolent and hardly strategic at all. The conclusion is not that NATO should become a unitary and strategic actor, however. NATO is, as we also noted in Chapter 1, an amalgamation of nations and geopolitical experiences. The conclusion is rather that NATO must seek unity in diversity, which brings us back to the relationship between coalitions and institutions and the role of political leadership in connecting them. There are three general lessons. The first relates to the task of leadership, the second to organizational modernization, and the third to the geopolitical character of NATO's future missions.

Political leadership depends above all on charisma, though legality and custom matter as well. It is to say that leadership cannot be disconnected from the individuals who lead, and that leadership depends on people and not institutions. We cannot gauge NATO leadership by way of NATO documents or procedure but by way of observing NATO heads of state and government and their capacity for responding to events. Leadership is a question of vision and ability to connect to the "human apparatus" in Max Weber's words—the people and popular support—that enables leadership.[5] It is complicated by the existence of two distinct ethical imperatives, one of responsibility and another of conviction. The former demands a cool head and focus on consequences of action; the latter demands a pounding heart and focus on visions and dreams.

NATO lost its balance in Afghanistan, as we know. NATO's leadership was too focused on liberal convictions in the abstract and too unaware of campaign consequences. The implication is not that they should give up on liberal convictions, in what would amount to an embrace of stark realism. Instead they should turn these broad convictions into Alliance convictions as a type of fusion between value and consequence, striking a balance between the responsibility to follow liberalism's impulse and the responsibility to act in the national interest. The Alliance could be the lieu of this balancing act. This requires that Alliance leaders imagine the Atlantic community and speak of it. They must recognize that the allies are different but yet belong to a Western community. There can be no denying that transatlantic differences—summed up in the image of Mars and Venus—are real. However, the Western community gains its potential from the liberal undercurrent that is inherent to both European and North American political traditions and from the fact that they are both in their separate ways incomplete road maps for foreign policy. Political traditions distort reality to make sense of it. What the Alliance needs, therefore, is not a transatlantic divorce but a balance of Atlantic political pathologies.[6] It is by sticking together that Western allies can make real and solid contributions to international order. In short, the leaders of NATO nations must make a capable NATO part of their vision to gain it.

Imagining the Atlantic community in terms of its internal balance and external actions is the overriding task of Atlantic political leadership. It may sound abstract to observers of military hardware and organization, but without this investment by the leaders of NATO nations in the political capital of the Alliance, its organization and capabilities will mean less and perhaps nothing at all. This brings us to the second lesson regarding organizational modernization. NATO did well to appoint a prime minister as secretary general in April 2009. This move has reinvigorated the effort to reform or modernize the headquarters and the wider organization beyond what a former defense or foreign minister could hope to achieve. Anders Fogh Rasmussen may be a secretary general, but he remains a politician—one who lives for politics as opposed to administering political decisions.[7] As a result, the North Atlantic Council is today less cushioned by protocol and more directly challenged by the political needs of the Alliance as a whole. The permanent representatives or ambassadors, in particular, have been made more aware of their status as political servants, with the secretary general placing himself among not the servants but the chiefs. Headquarter reform has likewise followed for the purpose of gearing NATO to focus on "emerging security threats" and to better serve national interests. There is an argument to be made that the pace of organizational reform in NATO has been rapid, following Anders Fogh Rasmussen's blitz campaign of reform in 2010–2011, and that it is now time to implement reforms and bring substance to "new" NATO. The capacity promises inherent in the Strategic Concept and other guiding documents must be realized, and this requires a change of pace from the organizational leadership. Two demands on NATO heads of state and government follow.

They must first of all continue the practice of appointing one from their own ranks to lead the organization, and not only because it enables modernization. It is a mechanism to ensure that the secretary general is a distinctively political "agent" of the "principals." The latter will regularly channel some of their diplomatic efforts through informal coalitions to gain speed and flexibility, but they will need connections back to NATO as an institution and collective alliance. A political "agent" at NATO's helm eases this task because he or she will be (almost) on par with the chiefs and thus better positioned to shape some of the decisions that will have to be made to bridge coalition initiative and Alliance policy.

Second, the NATO chiefs must enhance their investment in the strategic capacities of the office of the secretary general. At present, the secretary general has a small private office as well as a deputy secretary general to support him. The secretary general is also head of the International staff, but this is the background organization. What matters is that the private office is a small outfit greatly dominated by national appointments and that governments are happy to keep the secretary general institutionally weak. It protects their political turf, especially on issues they would rather not confront. But governments in the North Atlantic Council should be made to confront the realities of campaigns—how they require coherent resourcing and above all agile diplomacy to connect the grammar of war to the logic of politics. They should therefore invest in an enhanced private office—a kind of secretary general's cabinet—where the secretary general gains a greater control of appointments and ultimately a greater capacity to push the North Atlantic Council in the direction of strategic coherence by way of analysis and agenda setting. An enhanced office of the secretary general will at times be politically inconvenient, but it will be the right thing for the Alliance, and it will become reality if the Alliance's leaders show political courage.

We come to the final lesson, which concerns the geopolitical nature of NATO's future missions. NATO missions should reflect a combination of liberal purpose and geopolitical interest, where interest is defined in terms of the ability of the allies to manage political relations in the regions that are essential to their own security and stability. NATO must balance values and interests; otherwise, it will lose its balance and sow the seeds of political failure. This ought to put an end to debates on NATO's global reach because NATO is not global. Its geopolitics is regional: NATO is about Atlantic relations and Europe's security order. Sometimes the Alliance will be drawn into the wider world, as in Afghanistan, because an enemy challenges it to a fight. However, Germany and Russia remain key focal points of the Alliance, even if they are not always explicit: Germany because German restraint underpins Europe's institutionalized order, notably in relation to the EU, and Russia because its estrangement from Western policy will radicalize Europe's security. These are common concerns to all allies, and operations in Afghanistan or other theaters of conflict do not remove their urgency. To the contrary, expeditionary warfare, which requires a dedicated focus on the fight itself, also requires the political mastery of underlying and geopolitically diverse concepts of order.

NATO's future missions and activities should follow from here. NATO is in Afghanistan, and Afghanistan should be an enduring NATO concern. Reconciliation in Afghanistan, disruption of Al Qaeda, and Pakistani moderation—these are the goals, and NATO should stay engaged behind them though with a greater emphasis on political reconciliation and regional diplomacy, as described in this conclusion. Looking to the broader Middle East that is experiencing promising but uncertain political transitions, NATO should carve out a role in security sector reform: It should not only bomb to win, as in Unified Protector in Libya, but become an advisor and partner in the building of democratic security institutions. Enhanced training and institution building could revive the NATO-EU dispute along the fraught civil-military boundary, but it should manageable. Both organizations are essential to Europe's security order, especially in regards to Germany's position, and both can contribute to geopolitical stability outside Europe. Moreover, the high politics of Iran's nuclear program, missile defense, and the future of political alignments in the region will provide for a continuing NATO-EU division of labor. Finally, now that the global commons are becoming a buzzword in the Alliance's planning scenarios, it would do the Alliance well to cut through the global governance thicket and shape a geopolitical policy that connects the growing interest of the United States in Asia to Europe's security order. NATO should undertake a permanent naval mission in the Indian Ocean to shape its thinking on these issues. The mission would target piracy and thus build on NATO's current mission, but the key would be to broaden the mission to involve a dialogue with the growing Asian powers, notably India and China, on trade and communication among Europe, Africa, the Middle East, and Asia.

These missions, from Afghanistan over the Middle East to the Indian Ocean, are virtuous insofar as they embody both liberal values and Western interests. They are balanced missions. They connect political conviction and responsibility, and they could help NATO overcome the liberal disconnect it has experienced in Afghanistan. The Western alliance will remain diverse and beset by burden-sharing debates, and allies will sometimes divide their energies between coalition diplomacy and NATO engagement. This is not necessarily bad news. What matters is the willingness and ability of NATO leaders to speak of the Atlantic community and engage it, as this book has shown. It is one thing to be in control; it is something quite different to actually take control. If NATO leaders engage the Alliance in earnest, they commit to an Atlantic project that may irk observers who believe NATO is either dead or just a cogwheel in a global network but that is inscribed in the Atlantic Treaty's wedding of liberal values and political geography. With Atlantic commitment, they can undertake the ultimate task of statesmanship: to shape the future.[8]

REFERENCE MATTER

NOTES

Introduction

1. ISAF Facts and Figures as of October 18, 2011; available at www.isaf.nato.int/images/media/PDFs/18%20october%202011%20isaf%20placemat.pdf.

2. Rasmussen, Interview with author, October 29, 2010.

3. Edward H. Carr, *The Twenty Years' Crisis, 1919–1939* (London: Macmillan, 1991), 88–89.

4. James Sperling and Mark Webber, "NATO: From Kosovo to Kabul," *International Affairs* 85/3 (2009), 491–511.

Chapter 1

1. Adda B. Bozeman, *Politics and Culture in International History: From the Ancient Near East to the Opening of the Modern Age* (New Brunswick, NJ: Transaction, 1994), 113–114.

2. Dan Moran, "The Great Game and the Quagmire: The Anglo-Soviet Wars in Afghanistan, 1838–1989," in Theo Farrell, Frans Osinga, and James Russell, eds., *Fighting the Afghanistan War: States, Organizations, and Military Adaptation* (Stanford, CA: Stanford University Press, forthcoming).

3. See David Yost, *NATO Transformed: The Alliance's New Roles in International Security* (Washington, DC: U.S. Institute of Peace Press, 2001); and James Gow, *Defending the West* (Cambridge, UK: Polity Press, 2005).

4. Ahmed Rashid, *Descent into Chaos: The World's Most Unstable Region and the Threat to Global Security* (London: Penguin, 2008).

5. This would include, according to Ahmed Rashid, building up President Karzai as a force for good rather than vilifying him, though it may be too late for that. "NATO's Dangerous Wager with Karzai," *New York Review of Books Blog*, November

22, 2010; available at www.nybooks.com/blogs/nyrblog/2010/nov/22/nato-karzai-afghanistan/.

6. Seth G. Jones, *In the Graveyard of Empires: America's War in Afghanistan* (New York: Norton, 2009); also *Counterinsurgency in Afghanistan* (Santa Monica, CA: RAND, 2008).

7. Jason Burke, *The 9/11 Wars* (London: Allen Lane, 2011); and Peter Tomsen, *The Wars of Afghanistan* (New York: Public Affairs, 2011).

8. Stephen Tanner, *Afghanistan: A Military History from Alexander the Great to the War against the Taliban* (Philadelphia: Da Capo Press, 2009), is a more regular military history of Afghanistan than Tomsen's work that has been updated to provide current perspectives, like Tomsen.

9. Sherard Cowper-Coles, *Cables from Kabul: The Inside Story of the West's Afghanistan Campaign* (London: Harper Press, 2011).

10. Tim Bird and Alex Marshall, *Afghanistan: How the West Lost Its Way* (New Haven, CT: Yale University Press, 2011).

11. Ahmed Rashid, "NATO's Failure Portends Wider War," *New York Times*, October 30, 2006; *Economist*, "The Future of NATO," November 25, 2006, 381/8505, 12.

12. *Wall Street Journal*, "NATO's Afghan Failure," February 1, 2008, A14,; also Robert D. Kaplan, "Equal Alliance, Unequal Roles," *New York Times*, March 27, 2008.

13. John Feffer, "Afghanistan: NATO's Graveyard?" *Foreign Policy in Focus*, September 29, 2009; available at www.fpif.org/fpiftxt/6465.

14. Julianne Smith and Michael Williams, "Threats from Within: Four Challenges inside NATO," *International Spectator* 43/3 (September 2008), 21–26; and David E. Johnson, "What Are You Prepared to Do? NATO and the Strategic Mismatch between Ends, Ways, and Means in Afghanistan—and in the Future," *Studies in Conflict and Terrorism* 34/5 (May 2011), 383–401.

15. Alexandra Gheicu, "Divided Partners: The Challenges of NATO–NGO Cooperation in Peacebuilding Operations," *Global Governance* 17 (2011), 95–113; and Luis Peral, "Transforming an Unrealistic War," *Georgetown Journal of International Affairs* 11/1 (2010), 65–72.

16. Richard Rupp, *NATO after 9/11: An Alliance in Continuing Decline* (New York: Palgrave, 2006), 3; also Sean Kay, "What Went Wrong with NATO?" *Columbia Review of International Affairs* 18/1 (April 2005), 69–83. Anand Menon and Jennifer Welsh add that adaptability is not sustainability: Institutional change may enhance distributional conflict among the allies; "Understanding NATO's Sustainability: The Limits of Institutionalist Theory," *Global Governance* 17/1 (January 2011), 81–94.

17. Azeem Ibrahim, "Testing the NATO Alliance: Afghanistan and the Future of Cooperation," *Harvard International Review*, Summer 2009, 80.

18. James M. Goldgeier, *The Future of NATO*, Council on Foreign Relations, Special Report No. 51, February 2010, 3. See also Goldgeier's "Commentary: Afghani-

stan Seen as Crucial Test," *Washington Times*, March 22, 2009; and "NATO's Future: Facing Old Divisions and New Threats," *Harvard International Review* (Spring 2009), 48–51.

19. "RUSI interview with General David Richards," *The RUSI Journal* 152/2 (April 2007), 24–33, at 27.

20. Rick Hillier, *A Soldier First: Bullets, Bureaucrats and the Politics of War* (Toronto: Harper Collins, 2009), 288, 477. The observed lack of strategy is echoed in Bird and Marshall, *Afghanistan*, as well as in Johnson, "What Are You Prepared to Do?" 383–401.

21. Andrew J. Bacevich, "NATO at Twilight," *Los Angeles Times*, February 11, 2008.

22. Andrew J. Bacevich, "Let Europe Be Europe," *Foreign Policy* March/April 2010.

23. Michael Cox, "Beyond the West: Terrors in Transatlantia," *European Journal of International Relations* 11/2 (2005), 203–233.

24. Donald J. Puchala, "The Atlantic Community in the Age of Terrorism," *Journal of Transatlantic Studies* 3/1 (Spring 2005), 89–104.

25. Robert Kagan, *Of Paradise and Power: America and Europe in the New World Order* (New York: Vintage, 2004).

26. T. V. Paul, "Soft Balancing in the Age of U.S. Primacy," *International Security* 30/1 (Summer 2005), 46–71; Barry Posen, "ESDP and the Structure of World Power," *The International Spectator* 39, no. 1 (2004): 5–17; Barry Posen, "European Union Security and Defense Policy: Response to Unipolarity?" *Security Studies* 15, no. 2 (April–June 2006), 149–186; and David C. Ellis, "U.S. Grand Strategy Following the G. W. Bush Presidency," *International Studies Perspectives* 10/4 (November 2009), 361–377. For the view that EU soft balancing is real and will succeed, see Andrew Moravcsik, "Europe: The Quiet Superpower," *French Politics* 7 (2009), 403–422.

27. Ellis, "U.S. Grand Strategy," 374.

28. For a geopolitical version of this argument, see John J. Mearsheimer, *The Tragedy of Great Power Politics* (New York: Norton, 2001). For a realist argument inspired by social criticism of ruling elites see Christopher Layne, *The Peace of Illusions: American Grand Strategy from 1940 to the Present* (Ithaca, NY: Cornell University Press, 2006); and "Who Lost Iraq and Why It Matters: The Case for Offshore Balancing," *World Policy Journal* 24/3 (Fall 2007), 38–52.

29. Sarah Chayes, "NATO Didn't Lose Afghanistan," *New York Times* July 10, 2007. See also her book, *The Punishment of Virtue: Inside Afghanistan after the Taliban* (New York: Penguin Press, 2006).

30. Stephen Walt, "Alliances in a Unipolar World," *World Politics* 61/1 (January 2009), 86–120; and Galia Press-Barnathan, "Managing the Hegemon: NATO under Unipolarity," *Security Studies* 15/2 (July 2006), 271–309.

31. For a similar criticism of the unipolar perspective, see Martha Finnemore, "Legitimacy, Hypocrisy, and the Social Structure of Unipolarity," *World Politics* 61/1 (2009), 58–85. For a favorable evaluation of alliance strength versus coalitions, see Sarah Kreps, "Elite Consensus as a Determinant of Alliance Cohesion: Why Public Opinion Hardly Matters for NATO-Led Operations in Afghanistan," *Foreign Policy Analysis* 6/3 (2010), 191–215.

32. See notably Peter Viggo Jakobsen, *A Work in Slow Progress: NATO's Comprehensive Approach to Crisis Response Operations*, DIIS Report 2008:15; "Right Strategy, Wrong Place: Why NATO's Comprehensive Approach Will Fail in Afghanistan," *UNISCI Journal* no. 1 (January 2010); Martin Smith, "Afghanistan in Context: NATO Out-of-Area Debates in the 1990s," *UNISCI Journal* no. 1 (January 2010); and Peter Dahl Thruelsen, *NATO in Afghanistan: What Lessons Are We Learning and Are We Willing to Adjust?* DIIS Report 2007:14; available at www.diis.dk/graphics/Publications/Reports%202007/DIIS_2007-14_UK_F_WEB.pdf.

33. See Michael J. Williams, *NATO, Security and Risk Management: From Kosovo to Kandahar* (London: Routledge, 2009). Williams's point is that NATO has failed to adapt and is in risk of dying.

34. Celeste A. Wallander and Robert O. Keohane, "Risk, Threat, and Security Institutions," in Helga Haftendorn, ed., *Imperfect Unions: Security Institutions over Time and Space* (Oxford, UK: Oxford University Press, 1999), 21–47; and Celeste A. Wallander, "Institutional Assets and Adaptability: NATO after the Cold War," *International Organization* 54/4 (Autumn 2000), 705–735.

35. Andrew R. Hoehn and Sarah Harting, *Risking NATO: Testing the Limits of the Alliance in Afghanistan* (Santa Monica, CA: RAND, 2010).

36. Joshua Walker, "NATO's Litmus Test: Prioritizing Afghanistan," *Journal of Transatlantic Studies* 5/2 (Autumn 2007), 169–178 at 170; also Andrew T. Wolff, "The Structural and Political Crisis of NATO Transformation," *Journal of Transatlantic Studies* 7/4 (December 2009), 476–492.

37. Ellen Hallams, "The Transatlantic Alliance Renewed: The United States and NATO since 9/11," *Journal of Transatlantic Studies* 7/1 (March 2009), 38–60.

38. The citation is from Sean Kay and Sahar Khan, "NATO and Counter-Insurgency: Strategic Liability or Tactical Asset?" *Contemporary Security Policy* 28/1 (April 2007), 163–181 at 177. The NATO–EU problem—and solution—is dealt with by James Goldgeier, *The Future of NATO*, 16–18; see also Franklin D. Kramer and Simon Serfaty, "Recasting the Euro-Atlantic Partnership," Initiative for a Renewed Transatlantic Partnership, CSIS, February 1, 2007.

39. At this point liberal analysis slips into constructivist garbs. A "teacher" (NATO) can help "students" (prospective NATO members) learn new norms of conduct and in time alter their identities; Alexandra Gheciu, "Security Institutions as

Agents of Socialization? NATO and the 'New Europe,'" *International Organization* 59 (Fall 2005), 973–1012.

40. Mark Webber, "NATO: The United States, Transformation and the War in Afghanistan," *British Journal of Politics and International Relations* 11/1 (January 2009), 46–63. New thinking may not possible, of course; see Michael J. Williams, "Empire Lite Revisited: NATO, the Comprehensive Approach and State-building in Afghanistan," *International Peacekeeping* 18/1 (2011), 64–78; and "(Un)Sustainable Peacebuilding: NATO's Sustainability for Postconflict Reconstruction in Multiactor Environments," *Global Governance* 17/1 (2011), 115–134.

41. David Brown makes a compelling and similar case in relation to counterterrorism: "'The War on Terrorism Would Not Be Possible without NATO': A Critique," in Martin A. Smith, ed., *Where Is NATO Going?* (London: Routledge, 2006), 23–43.

42. The allies are managing a capability gap created by expeditionary warfare but not one created by the Afghan war and its strategic requirements; Theo Farrell and Sten Rynning, "NATO's Transformation Gaps: Transatlantic Differences and the War in Afghanistan," *Journal of Strategic Studies* 33/5 (2010), 673–699.

43. Zbigniew Brzezinski, *The Grand Chessboard: American Primacy and Its Geostrategic Imperatives* (New York: Basic Books, 1998); also "A Geostrategy for Eurasia," *Foreign Affairs* 76/5 (September/October 1997), 50–64. For the roots of this thinking, see his *Game Plan: A Geostrategic Framework for the Conduct of US–Soviet Relations* (New York: Atlantic Monthly Press, 1988).

44. Zbigniew Brzezinski, "An Agenda for NATO," *Foreign Affairs* 88/5 (September–October 2009), 2–20; "Balancing the East, Upgrading the West," *Foreign Affairs* 91/1 (January–February 2012), 97–104.

45. Two notable reports argue that NATO can renew itself only by renewing its sense of Western purpose: Klaus Naumann et al., *Towards a Grand Strategy for an Uncertain World: Renewing Transatlantic Partnership* (Lunteren, NL: Noaber Foundation, 2007); and Rafael L. Bardají and Manuel Coma, *NATO 3.0: Ready for a New World* (Madrid: Strategic Studies Group/GEES, 2009). For the circumscribed view of the West, see particularly Charles Kupchan, *The End of the American Era: US Foreign Policy and the Geopolitics of the Twenty-First Century* (New York: Vintage, 2003); and "The Atlantic Order in Transition: The Nature of Change in U.S.–European Relations," in Jeffrey Anderson, G. John Ikenberry, and Thomas Risse, eds., *The End of the West? Crisis and Change in the Atlantic Order,* 111–126 (Ithaca, NY: Cornell University Press, 2008).

46. Henry A. Kissinger and Lawrence H. Summers, chairs, *Renewing the Atlantic Partnership: Report of an Independent Task Force Sponsored by the Council of Foreign Relations* (New York: Council on Foreign Relations, 2004), 4. See also Henry Kissinger, *Does America Need a Foreign Policy? Toward a Diplomacy for the 21st Century* (New York: Simon and Schuster, 2001).

47. Karl-Heinz Kamp, "NATO after Afghanistan," *US Naval Institute Proceedings* 136/6 (June 2010), 54–59.

48. David P. Calleo, "The Broken West," *Survival* 46, no. 3 (Autumn 2004), 29–38; "Transatlantic Folly: NATO vs. the EU," *World Policy Journal* 20/3 (Fall 2003), 17–24. These articles are included in Calleo's book, which expands on the theme of trans-atlantic partnership in the face of divergent worldviews, *Follies of Power: America's Unipolar Fantasy* (Cambridge, UK: Cambridge University Press, 2009). See also Sten Rynning, "Realism and the Common Security and Defence Policy," *Journal of Common Market Studies* 49/1 (January 2011), 23–42; "Strategic Culture and the Common Security and Defense Policy? A Classical Realist Assessment and Critique," *Contemporary Security Studies* 32/3 (December 2011), 536–551.

49. Henry Kissinger, *A World Restored: Metternich, Castlereagh and the Problems of Peace, 1812–1822* (London: Phoenix Press, 2000); Stanley Hoffmann, "Obstinate or Obsolete? The Fate of the Nation-State and the Case of Western Europe," *Daedalus* 95/3 (1966), 862–915.

50. Hans Morgenthau, *Scientific Man vs. Power Politics* (Chicago: University of Chicago Press, 1965), 203.

51. The argument is that social and historical reality is evolving to such an extent that it cannot be meaningfully generalized. "There are sciences to which eternal youth is granted, and the historical disciplines are among them . . . ," is the way Max Weber phrased it. Weber also wrote that "there comes a moment when the atmosphere changes. . . . The light of the great cultural problems moves on. Then science too prepares to change its standpoint and its analytical apparatus and to view the streams of events from the heights of thought"; Weber, "The Methodology of the Social Sciences," in E. A. Shils and H. A. Finch, eds., *The Methodology of the Social Sciences* (New York: Free Press, 1949), 104 and 112.

52. To conceive of alliances in terms of power and purpose is in fact Weberian and a hallmark of traditional alliance analysis. George Liska, whose treatise on alliances remain a cornerstone in the literature, wrote that "if allies are to stay together despite setbacks, the grounds for alliance must be rationalized. To do so is the function of ideology, which more than anything else makes alliances into social institutions"; Liska, *Nations In Alliance: The Limits of Independence* (Baltimore: Johns Hopkins University Press, 1968), 61. See also Morgenthau, *Politics among Nations: The Struggle for Power and Peace* (Boston: McGraw-Hill, 1993), 200.

53. Weber, "The Methodology of the Social Sciences," emphasis added.

54. Weber, "The Methodology of the Social Sciences," emphasis in original. The ideal-type thus reflects reality: It is not simply the invention of the analyst. This marked off Weber's approach from the tradition of pragmatism, which, as the name indicates, was pragmatic about the origins of tools as long as they generate insight.

However, the use of the ideal-type can be pragmatic in the sense that one may use it to generate not general knowledge but insight into particular events or issues.

55. The citation is from George Liska's depiction of a typical mutual-assistance alliance; *Nations In Alliance*, 33.

56. Weber, "The Methodology of the Social Sciences," 90. In Weber's slightly tortured language: "An ideal type is formed by the one-sided *accentuation* of one or more points of view and by the synthesis of a great many diffuse, discrete, more or less present and occasionally absent *concrete individual* phenomena, which are arranged according to those one-sidedly emphasized viewpoints into a unified *analytical* construct" (Emphasis in original).

57. Lawrence Freedman, *A Choice of Enemies: America Confronts the Middle East* (London: Phoenix, 2009), xxvi. Amassing the available evidence and considering it was also what classical scholars did. They did so within the tradition of ideal-typical analysis. In fact, Hans Morgenthau, generally considered the founder of the modern discipline of realism, was a Weberian who constructed an ideal-typical model of the rational and responsible statesman. Realism was not a depiction of reality: it was an analytical construct to help us grasp the essence of reality. See Stephen Turner and George Mazur, "Morgenthau as Weberian Methodologist," *European Journal of International Relations* 15/3 (September 2009), 477–504. See also Ido Oren, "The Unrealism of Contemporary Realism: The Tension between Realist Theory and Realists' Practice," *Perspectives on Politics* 7/2 (June 2009), 283–301; and Casper Sylvest, "John H. Herz and the Resurrection of Classical Realism," *International Relations* 22/4 (December 2008), 441–455.

58. Classical scholarship was always in the business of speaking truth to power but never in the business of prediction. Ideal types are not accurate depictions of reality: They are tools of interpretation, and good interpretations of security affairs can identify problems and opportunities and thus help statesmen make politically wise and morally courageous choices.

Chapter 2

1. Retold in Ryan C. Hendrickson, *Diplomacy and War at NATO: The Secretary General and Military Action after the Cold War* (Columbia: University of Missouri Press, 2006), 58–60.

2. This was one of four "fundamental security tasks" outlined in the Alliance's Strategic Concept of April 1999. To enhance security and stability in the Euro-Atlantic region, the Alliance affirmed, it must be ready to engage in crisis management operations and develop its network of partnerships. This was the key novelty in the enumeration of fundamental security tasks; the other three tasks, which preceded this fourth one, were security, consultation, and deterrence and defense. See *The Alliance's*

Strategic Concept, April 24, 1999; available at www.nato.int/cps/en/natolive/official_texts_27433.htm, paragraph 10.

3. See NATO's *London Declaration* of June 1990 and its proposals for a strengthened CSCE; available at www.nato.int/cps/en/natolive/official_texts_23693.htm, paragraphs 21–22.

4. *Charter of Paris for a New Europe*, Paris, November 19–21 1990; available at www.osce.org/documents/mcs/1990/11/4045_en.pdf, 4.

5. France and Britain led the peace talks to demonstrate greater European skill following the U.S. lead in negotiating an end to the Bosnian war. France and Britain were the initiators of the EU's defense dimension (the ESDP), which they had put on the agenda in November 1998 at a St. Malo meeting.

6. Slovenia, Croatia, and Bosnia-Herzegovina sovereignty were considered not cases of *succession* but of state (Yugoslav) *dissolution*. They had no choice but to go for independence, in other words. In addition, the option of claiming statehood was part of given Yugoslav constitutional practice; Marc Weller, "The Rambouillet Conference on Kosovo," *International Affairs* 75/2 (1999), 211–251 at 214. Kosovo was never a Yugoslav republic, and Serbia was not in a process of dissolution in 1998–1999. In February 2008 Kosovo's parliament declared Kosovo's independence from Serbia, and this revisionist policy seems to have borne fruit, undermining what was once Western policy. More than sixty countries have recognized Kosovo's independence, though some European allies such as Spain hesitate for domestic reasons, and Russia and China have declared the declaration unlawful. Following a Serbian appeal, the International Court of Justice ruled in July 2010 that Kosovo's declaration of independence did not violate international law but also that the question of recognition remained inherently political.

7. NATO claimed the attack was a mistake resulting from planning based on an outdated map. However, reports subsequently indicated that China's embassy during the conflict rebroadcast Serb army signals that the Serb forces no longer could transmit themselves. The missile strike could have occurred in retaliation of this covert assistance; *Observer*, "NATO Bombed Chinese Deliberately," October 17, 1999.

8. Kofi Annan, "UN Peacekeeping Operations and Cooperation with NATO," *NATO Review* 47/5 (October 1993), 3–7.

9. *Statement by Kofi Annan, Secretary General of the United Nations*, NATO HQ, Brussels, January 28, 1999; available at www.nato.int/docu/speech/1999/s990128a.htm. Emphasis added.

10. *UN Security Council resolution 1244*, June 10, 1999; available at http://daccess-dds-ny.un.org/doc/UNDOC/GEN/N99/172/89/PDF/N9917289.pdf?OpenElement; see paragraphs 6 and 10.

11. Lawrence S. Kaplan, *NATO and the UN: A Peculiar Relationship* (Columbia: University of Missouri Press, 2010), 181–185.

12. Anthony F. Lang Jr., "A Realist in the Utopian City," in Kent. J. Kille, ed., *The UN Secretary-General and Moral Authority: Ethics and Religion in International Leadership* (Washington, DC: Georgetown University Press, 2007), 265–286 at 270–272.

13. This subcontracting would happen in accordance with Article 43 of the U.N. Charter, whereby member states are encouraged to assign forces to the United Nations via "special agreements"; *An Agenda for Peace: Preventive Diplomacy, Peacemaking and Peace-Keeping*, A/47/277 - S/24111, June 17, 1992; available at www.un.org/docs/SG/agpeace.html, especially paragraphs 42–46.

14. Had NATO been a U.N. "regional security arrangement," it would have been subjected to oversight by the U.N. Security Council, where the Soviet Union was a permanent member, and its decisions could have been vetoed by the Soviet Union. See Kaplan, *NATO and the UN*, chapter 1.

15. NATO's Article 3 is perfectly compatible with the U.N. Charter's Article 51, which recognizes the inherent right to individual and collective self-defense. However, in preparing for it, in setting up a durable alliance (NATO's treaty is unlimited in duration but does foresee a review of the treaty after ten years [Article 12] and allows for individual withdrawal from it after a twenty-year period [Article 13]), the NATO allies were in effect saying that the United Nations did not suffice.

16. Oscar Schacter, "United Nations Law in the Gulf Conflict," *The American Journal of International Law* 85/3 (July 1991), 452–473 at 469. The U.N. Charter's principle of sovereign equality was engraved in the Gulf War's peace settlement, which preserved the right to Iraqi self-government and made no demands for constitutional change.

17. Anthony F. Lang Jr., "A Realist in the Utopian City," 280–281. Boutros-Ghali's memoirs are phrased diplomatically, but he makes repeated references to "opposing positions in the Security Council" and "diametrically opposed pressures," which refer predominantly to French-British disputes with the United States but also to Russia's opposition to air strikes and Islamic governments' support for them; Boutros Boutros-Ghali, *Unvanquished: A US–UN Saga* (London: I. B. Tauris, 1999), 145–148.

18. Kaplan, *NATO and the UN*, 150.

19. Boutros-Ghali notes that Woerner "had always been constructive and optimistic when working with me" and had "come to believe in a strong NATO partnership with the United Nations"—an appreciation of the deceased NATO secretary general that comes on the heels of the observation that Claes had taken the reins; Boutros-Ghali, *Unvanquished*, 237.

20. The dual-key remained but was delegated to military commanders (UNPROFOR's military commander [at first French General Janvier, then British Lieutenant-General Rupert Smith] and NATO's commander of southern forces Europe, Admiral Leighton Smith); Ryan Hendrickson, "History: Crossing the Rubicon," *NATO Review* 3

(Autumn 2005); available at www.nato.int/docu/review/2005/issue3/english/history .html. On Boutros-Ghali's condition, see Boutros-Ghali, *Unvanquished*, 240.

21. John Woodliffe, "The Evolution of a New NATO for a New Europe," *The International and Comparative Law Quarterly* 47/1 (January 1998), 174–192 at 185.

22. Resolution 1031; available at http://daccess-dds-ny.un.org/doc/UNDOC/ GEN/N95/405/26/PDF/N9540526.pdf?OpenElement.

23. Mary Ellen O'Connell, "The UN, NATO, and International Law after Kosovo," *Human Rights Quarterly* 22/1 (February 2000), 57–89 at 69; also Mats Berdal, "Whither UN Peacekeeping," *Adelphi Paper* 281 (London: International Institute for Strategic Studies, 1993).

24. Jarat Chopra and Thomas G. Weiss, "Sovereignty Is No Longer Sacrosanct: Codifying Humanitarian Intervention," *Ethics and International Affairs* 6 (1992), 95–117; Thomas G. Weiss, "Triage: Humanitarian Interventions in a New Era," *World Policy Journal* 11/1 (Spring 1994), 59–68; Richard K. Betts, "The Delusion of Impartial Intervention," Foreign Affairs 73/6 (November–December 1994), 20–33; Stephen D. Krasner, "Compromising Westphalia," *International Security* 20 (1995–1996), 115–151; and Samuel J. Barkin, "The Evolution of the Constitution of Sovereignty and the Emergence of Human Rights Norms," *Millennium* 27 (1998), 229–252.

25. See Martin A. Smith, "Afghanistan in Context: NATO Out-of-Area Debates in the 1990s," *UNISCI Journal* 22 (January), 16–32; also Mats Berdal and David Ucko, "NATO at 60," *Survival* 51/2 (2009), 55–76.

26. Adam Roberts, "Humanitarian War: Military Intervention and Human Rights," *International Affairs* 69/3 (July 1993), 429–449 at 429.

27. See Ronald Tiersky, "France in the New Europe," *Foreign Affairs* 71/2 (Spring 1992), 131–146; Owen Harris, "The Collapse of 'the West,'" *Foreign Affairs* 72/4 (September–October 1993), 41–53; Jonathan Clarke, "Replacing NATO," *Foreign Policy* 93 (Winter 1993–1994), 22–40; Frank Costigliola, "An 'Arm Around the Shoulder': The United States, NATO, and German Reunification 1989–1990," *Contemporary European History* 3/1 (1994), 87–110; and Kees van der Pijl, "From Gorbachev to Kosovo: Atlantic Rivalries and the Re-incorporation of Eastern Europe," *Review of International Political Economy* 8/2 (Summer 2001), 275–310.

28. See Charles L. Glaser, "Why NATO Is Still Best: Future Security Arrangements for Europe," *International Security* 18/1 (Summer 1993), 5–50; Ronald D. Asmus, Richard L. Kugler, and F. Stephen Larrabee, "Building a New NATO," *Foreign Affairs* 72/4 (September–October 1993), 28–40; Ivo Daalder, "Are the United States and Europe Heading for a Divorce?" *International Affairs* 77/3 (2001), 553–567; and Alexander Moens, "European Defence and NATO: The Case for New Governance," *International Journal* 56/2 (Spring 2001), 261–278.

29. Kori Schake, "NATO after the Cold War, 1991–1995: Institutional Competition and the Collapse of the French Alternative," *Contemporary European History* 7/3 (November 1998), 379–407.

30. The CSDP option began in 1998–1999, as we shall see, and it was then called the European Security and Defense Policy (ESDP). The change from European to Common took place with the Lisbon Treaty of 2009.

31. Franco–British Summit, *Joint Declaration on European Defense*, St. Malo, December 4, 1998, paragraph 1. For an upbeat assessment of the potential of the ESDP, see Charles Cogan, *The Third Option: The Emancipation of European Defense, 1989–2000* (New York: Praeger, 2001). For a prudent evaluation of the compatibility of underlying French and British motives, see Jolyon Howorth, "Britain, France, and the European Defence Initiative," *Survival* 42/2 (2000), 33–55.

32. NATO upgraded its 1996 Berlin agreement to a "Berlin Plus" agreement that gave the EU assured access to NATO planning but only presumed (case-by-case) access to collective NATO assets.

33. France has generally longed for the influence granted by the Standing Group of early NATO. The Standing Group was composed of the United States, Britain, and France (Germany was not yet an ally). It called most military shots, though it formally reported to a collective Defense Committee and relied on a collective Military Committee composed of allied chiefs of staff. The Standing Group was marginalized by the integrated command structure set up from 1951 and the Supreme Allied Commander Europe (SACEUR). It lived on, though, and formally closed only in 1966 when France left the integrated command. The Military Committee then changed in nature to become the leading interlocutor of the military commands it is to this day.

34. In 1995–1996 French President Chirac lost his bid to arrest NATO enlargement in favor of improved NATO–Russia relations (NATO ended up seeking both). Instead, at the July 1997 Madrid summit Chirac sought to rebalance a northern enlargement (Poland, Hungary, and the Czech Republic) with a southern enlargement (Romania and Slovenia). Germany's Chancellor Kohl, who held the key to tipping the scales within the Alliance, sided with the United States, however. See Ronald D. Asmus, *Opening NATO's Door: How the Alliance Remade Itself for a New Era* (New York: Columbia University Press, 2002), 238–250. On the Contact Group and Kosovo, see Kaplan, *NATO and the UN*, 178.

35. Boutros-Ghali, *Unvanquished*, 328; Albright, *Madam Secretary*, 223; William Shawcross, "France Ambushes America in UN Leadership Battle," *Sunday Times*, December 1, 1996; and "French Diplomatic Intransigence Makes Waves across the Atlantic," *Guardian*, December 13, 1996.

36. France gained a promise that a number of posts in the U.N. system would be offered to francophone candidates—in the name of strengthening the U.N. bilingual

policy; "UN Picks Annan from Ghana as Leader; France Drops Opposition to Consummate Insider," *Globe and Mail*, December 14, 1996.

37. President Chirac did not single-handedly engineer the turnaround in Bosnia, but he certainly contributed decisively to it. See Dominique Moïsi, "Chirac of France: A New Leader of the West," 74 *Foreign Affairs* (November–December 1995), 8–13; and Charles Grant, "France's New Relationship with NATO," *Survival* 38/1 (1996), 58–80. The contribution of allied efforts is conspicuously missing from Madeleine Albright's *Madam Secretary* (New York: Miramax Books, 2003), 204.

38. The agreement of June 1996 was reached in Berlin and became the "Berlin agreement," according to which NATO would create an option for all-European action within its organization.

39. Ronald Tiersky, "French Gamesmanship and NATO's Future: The Context of 'AFSOUTH,'" *French Politics and Society* 15/2 (1997), 49–56. Chirac lost control of the government because the socialist opposition won the parliamentary elections in 1997. Socialist Prime Minister Lionel Jospin and President Jacques Chirac "cohabited" for the next five years, therefore. It may be noted that another historically reluctant ally, Spain, completed its integration into NATO's military command at this time, in 1997.

40. *Conférence de presse de M. Hubert Védrine, ministre des affaires étrangère, Bruxelles le 8 décembre 1998*; available at http://lesdiscours.vie-publique.fr/pdf/993000016.pdf.

41. *Conférence de presse de M. Jacques Chirac, Président de la République, Moscou le 13 mai 1999*; available at http://discours.vie-publique.fr/notices/997000096.html.

42. British Prime Minister Blair famously enunciated a doctrine of "international community" in Chicago in April 1999 that saw the Kosovo war as a just war and that notably did not link certain political conditions for armed intervention (of which Blair mentioned five) to UNSC authorization. See the PBS site on "The Blair Doctrine"; available at www.pbs.org/newshour/bb/international/jan-june99/blair_doctrine4-23.html.

43. Hubert Védrine, *History Strikes Back: How States, Nations, and Conflicts Are Shaping the Twenty-First Century*, foreword by Madeleine Albright (Washington, DC: Brookings, 2008), vii–viii.

44. Védrine, ibid., 9–10.

45. See, for instance, James Gow, *Triumph of the Lack of Will: International Diplomacy and the Yugoslav War* (London: Hurst and Company, 1997).

Chapter 3

1. John le Carré, *A Small Town in Germany* (London: William Heinemann, 1968).

2. *Agreement on Provisional Arrangements in Afghanistan Pending the Reestablishment of Permanent Government Institutions*, December 5, 2001; available at www.un.org/News/dh/latest/afghan/afghan-agree.htm.

3. One delegation represented the Northern Alliance that always fought the Taliban and that was now in control of Kabul; another "Rome" delegation represented the former Pashtun king Zahir Shah who was exiled to Rome in 1973; a third "Cyprus" delegation represented exiled Afghans mainly related to Western Afghanistan and with ties to Iran; and a fourth "Peshawar" delegation, as the name indicates, represented Pashtun forces closely aligned with Pakistan.

4. The constitution's Chapter 8, Paragraph 2, states that the government "must delegate certain authorities to local administration units" while "preserving the principle of centralism"; *The Constitution of Afghanistan*, available at www.supremecourt .gov.af/PDFiles/constitution2004_english.pdf.

5. U.N. Security Council, *Resolution 1386 (2001)*, December 20, 2001; available at http://daccess-dds-ny.un.org/doc/UNDOC/GEN/N01/708/55/PDF/N0170855.pdf? OpenElement.

6. *The Afghanistan Compact*, London, January 31–February 1, 2006; available at http://unama.unmissions.org/Portals/UNAMA/Documents/AfghanistanCompact-English.pdf.

7. *Afghanistan National Development Strategy, 2008–2013*; available at www .embassyofafghanistan.org/documents/Afghanistan_National_Development_Strategy_ eng.pdf.

8. Alessandro Minutto Rizzo, *Speech*, Kabul, August 11, 2003, available at www .nato.int/docu/speech/2003/s030811a.htm.

9. ISAF I was led by Britain, from December 20, 2001, through June 19, 2002; ISAF II by Turkey, from June 20, 2002, through January 31, 2003; ISAF III by Germany and the Netherlands, from February 1, 2003, through August 10, 2003.

10. NATO, *Statement by the North Atlantic Council*, NATO Press Release (2001) 124, September 12, 2001; available at www.nato.int/docu/pr/2001/p01-124e.htm.

11. George Robertson, *Statement*, October 2, 2001; available at www.nato.int/cps/ en/natolive/opinions_19011.htm.

12. George Robertson, *Statement to the Press*, October 4, 2001; available at www .nato.int/docu/speech/2001/s011004b.htm.

13. Operation Eagle Assist lasted for a little more than half a year, from October 9, 2001, through May 16, 2002.

14. NAC Statement, *NATO's Response to Terrorism*, December 6, 2001; available at www.nato.int/cps/en/natolive/official_texts_18848.htm.

15. Yves Brodeur (NATO Spokesman), *Press Briefing*, April 16, 2003; available at www.nato.int/docu/speech/2003/s030416a.htm.

16. Diego A. Ruiz Palmer, "The Road to Kabul," *NATO Review* (summer 2003); available at www.nato.int/docu/review/2003/issue2/english/art3.html.

17. NATO, *Prague Summit Declaration*, Press Release (2002) 127, November 21, 2002; available at www.nato.int/docu/pr/2002/p02-127e.htm.

18. Lieutenant Colonel Steve Beckman, *From Assumption to Expansion: Planning and Executing NATO's First Year in Afghanistan at the Strategic Level*, U.S. Army War College Strategy Research Project, March 18, 2005; available at www.dtic.mil/cgi-bin/GetTRDoc?Location=U2&doc=GetTRDoc.pdf&AD=ADA431768, 6.

19. This is the wording of Resolution 1510. *United Nations Security Council Resolution 1510 (2003)*, October 13, 2003, available at www.nato.int/ISAF/topics/mandate/unscr/resolution_1510.pdf. For the dual-track NATO planning (Kunduz and CONOPS), see Beckman, *From Assumption to Expansion*, 9–12.

20. NATO North Atlantic Council, *Final Communiqué*, December 4, 2003, paragraph 4; available at www.nato.int/cps/en/natolive/official_texts_20271.htm.

21. The task forces were brigades that broke into a number of battle groups or battalions, and the nationality of the brigades varied while the task force command remained with one nation.

22. NATO North Atlantic Council, *Final Communiqué*, December 8, 2005, paragraph 3; available at www.nato.int/cps/en/natolive/official_texts_21715.htm.

23. NATO, *Riga Summit Declaration*, Press Release (2006)150, November 29, 2006, paragraph 5; available at www.nato.int/docu/pr/2006/p06-150e.htm.

24. Ibid., paragraph 6.

25. Ahmed Rashid, *Descent into Chaos*, p. 355.

26. James Jones cochaired with Kristin Krohn Devold the Strategic Advisory Group of the U.S. Atlantic Council that in January 2008 published *Saving Afghanistan: An Appeal and Plan for Urgent Action*; available at www.acus.org/files/publication_pdfs/1/012808-AfghanistanbriefwoSAG.pdf. Jones also cochaired with Thomas Pickering the Afghan Study Group at the Center for the Study of the Presidency whose report, *The Afghan Study Group Report: Revitalizing Our Efforts, Rethinking Our Strategies*, was published just two days subsequent to the Saving Afghanistan report; available at www.thepresidency.org/pubs/Afghan_Study_Group_final.pdf.

27. NATO, *Bucharest Summit Declaration*, Press Release (2008)049, April 3, 2008, paragraph 6; available at www.nato.int/cps/en/natolive/official_texts_8443.htm?mode=pressrelease.

28. NATO, *ISAF's Strategic Vision*, Press Release (2008)052, April 3, 2008, available at www.nato.int/cps/en/natolive/official_texts_8444.htm?mode=pressrelease.

29. *New York Times*, "2008 Becomes Deadliest Year for the United States in Afghanistan," September 11, 2008.

30. *Observer*, "NATO Pact to Send 5,000 Troops for Afghan Polls," April 5, 2009; *New York Times*, "Europe Offers Few New Troops for Afghanistan," April 4, 2009.

31. NATO, *Summit Declaration on Afghanistan*, April 4, 2009; available at www.nato.int/cps/en/SID-49089266-5BE88E36/natolive/news_52836.htm.

32. Barak Obama, *Remarks by the President in Address to the Nation on the Way Forward in Afghanistan and Pakistan*, December 1, 2009; available at www

.whitehouse.gov/the-press-office/remarks-president-address-nation-way-forward-afghanistan-and-pakistan; and NATO, *Statement on Afghanistan by Ministers of Foreign Affairs of Nations Participating in the International Security Assistance Force (ISAF)*, December 4, 2009; available at www.nato.int/cps/en/natolive/news_59701 .htm.

33. *New York Times*, "NATO Pledges 7,000 Troops, but Avoids Details," December 4, 2009.

34. General Stanley A. McChrystal, *Commander's Initial Assessment*, August 30, 2009, pages 2–5; available at media.washingtonpost.com/wp-srv/politics/documents/ Assessment_Redacted_092109.pdf?hpid=topnews.

35. *New York Times*, "NATO Ministers Endorse Wider Afghan Effort," October 23, 2009.

36. Afghanistan: The London Conference, *Communiqué: Afghan Leadership, Regional Cooperation, International Partnership*, January 28, 2010; available at http:// afghanistan.hmg.gov.uk/resources/en/pdf/Communique-final.

37. NATO does not issue communiqués following informal meetings, but the secretary general outlined the transition plan in his *Closing Press Conference*, April 23, 2010; available at www.nato.int/cps/en/natolive/opinions_62896.htm.

38. White House, *Overview of the Afghanistan and Pakistan Review*, December 16, 2010; available at www.whitehouse.gov/the-press-office/2010/12/16/overview-afghanistan-and-pakistan-annual-review; also *New York Times*, "Obama Cites Afghan Gains as Report Says Exit Is on Track," December 16, 2010; and White House, *Remarks by the President on the Way Forward in Afghanistan*, June 22, 2011; available at www.whitehouse.gov/the-press-office/2011/06/22/remarks-president-way-forward-afghanistan.

39. *New York Times*, "Karzai Calls on U.S. to Pull Back as Taliban Cancels Talks," March 15, 2012.

40. NATO reached agreement on this policy at a meeting in December 2009. See *Backgrounder: ISAF support to reintegration and reconciliation* (no date is given, but the document is from December 2009); available at www.isaf.nato.int/images/stories/ File/Dec%202009-Backgrounder%20Support%20to%20reintegration.pdf. In concrete terms, ISAF Headquarters in Kabul has organized a Reintegration Cell to support the Afghan reintegration effort. At the July 2010 Kabul conference the internationally funded "peace and reintegration trust fund" created at the London conference in January was transferred to an Afghan High Peace Council in charge of reintegration, and the ISAF Cell is working with this Council.

41. Rabbani was notably a bridge between that part of the Northern Alliance that is most hostile to reconciliation, which was his background, and the Taliban. His death will no doubt harden Northern Alliance hostility. Moreover, and following Taliban electoral intimidation in their own strongholds, Afghanistan's parliament elected

in September 2010 is strongly dominated by non-Pashtuns and thus people affiliated with the Northern Alliance. To gain reconciliation, President Karzai must thus invent new bridges between these hostile camps.

42. Ahmed Rashid, "How Obama Lost Karzai," *Foreign Policy*, March/April 2011; available at www.foreignpolicy.com/articles/2011/02/22/how_obama_lost_karzai.

Chapter 4

1. On structural change, see Robert Kagan, *Paradise and Power: America and Europe in the New World Order* (London: Atlantic Books, 2003); on the poorly managed process, see Philip H. Gordon and Jeremy Shapiro, *Allies at War: America, Europe, and the Crisis over Iraq* (New York: McGraw-Hill, 2004), 92.

2. William Drozdiak, "Attack on U.S. Is Attack on All, NATO Agrees," *Washington Post*, September 13, 2001. James Mann sees this as the origins of the Article V declaration in his book *Rise of the Vulcans: The History of Bush's War Cabinet* (New York: Viking, 2004), 303.

3. Lord Robertson's recollection of that dramatic day does not address the source of the idea. Robertson refers to the ambassadors' emergency meeting and then also work undertaken by Assistant Secretary General Edgar Buckley and Private Office Director Jon Day, noting somewhat obliquely that "one of the most momentous options considered was whether this assault on the US meant invoking Article 5 of the North Atlantic Treaty—the self-defence clause"; Robertson, "Being NATO's Secretary General on 9/11," *NATO Review*, September 8, 2011; available at www.nato.int/docu/review/2011/11-september/Lord_Robertson/EN/index.htm. However, U.S. Ambassador Burns recalls that "the Canadian Ambassador, David Wright, called me late in the afternoon of September 11, 2001, to suggest that we consider invoking Article V of the NATO Treaty in response to the attacks on the U.S.," and that he thereafter conferred with Lord Robertson, among others; Interview with author, August 25, 2010. See also *Washington Times*, "Diplomacy Adapts to New Threats," March 15, 2004; and Ryan Hendrickson, who cites Ambassador Burns to the same effect that Wright was the source of the idea, in *Diplomacy and War at NATO: The Secretary General and Military Action after the Cold War* (Columbia: University of Missouri Press, 2006), 120. Edgar Buckley, assistant secretary general for defence planning and operations (1999–2003), reports that the first reference he heard to Article V came from Ambassador Wright but at the emergency meeting in the secretary general's office; "Invoking Article 5," *NATO Review* (Summer 2006); available at www.nato.int/docu/review/2006/issue2/english/art2.html. The next couple of phrases in this paragraph draw on Buckley.

4. Ambassador Burns explains that he called both the NSC and State and gained support (interview with author, August 25, 2010); the "welcome" is from Condoleezza Rice, *No Higher Honor: A Memoir of My Years in Washington* (London: Simon &

Schuster, 2011), 78. On learning of the Article V initiative, "I choked back tears and told him [Ambassador Burns] that we would welcome the action."

5. Buckley, *Invoking Article 5.*

6. *Independent*, "Terror in America: NATO—Robertson Calls for New Ideas in War on Terrorism," September 14, 2001.

7. Robertson, "Being NATO Secretary General on 9/11."

8. Author's interview with Ambassador Burns, April 12, 2010.

9. *New York Times*, "For First Time, NATO Invokes Joint Defense Pact with U.S.," September 13, 2001.

10. *New York Times*, "For First Time . . ."; *Independent*, "NATO Clears Way for Joint Response to Attack on US," September 13, 2001.

11. *Daily Telegraph*, "US Asks Nato for Help in 'Draining the Swamp' of Global Terrorism," September 27, 2001.

12. Dick Cheney, *In My Time: A Personal and Political Memoir* (New York: Threshold Editions, 2011), 331; Donald Rumsfeld, *Known and Unknown: A Memoir* (New York: Sentinel, 2011), 354. Rumsfeld later published a much-noted article on military transformation in which he failed to refer to NATO at any point: "Transforming the Military," *Foreign Affairs* 81/3 (May–June 2002), 20–33.

13. Buckley, Invoking Article 5.

14. Rice, *No Higher Honor*, 79.

15. George W. Bush, *Decision Points* (London: Virgin Books, 2010), 191.

16. Bob Woodward, *Bush at War* (London: Pocket Books, 2004), 136 and 154. The Shelton plan for Afghanistan is outlined in Woodward, 79–80, but see also *The 9/11 Commission Report*, July 2004, 333; available at http://govinfo.library.unt.edu/911/report/911Report.pdf.

17. Rumsfeld, *Known and Unknown*, 358–359.

18. On ground forces, see Woodward, *At War*, 314. On other force numbers, see Anthony H. Cordesman, *The Lessons of Afghanistan: War Fighting, Intelligence, and Force Transformation* (Washington: CSIS Press, 2002), 11.

19. For this note of caution see Cordesman, *The Lessons of Afghanistan*, and Stephen Biddle, "Afghanistan and the Future of Warfare," *Foreign Affairs* (March–April 2003).

20. Bush, *Decision Points*, 197; Woodward, *At War*, 195. Rice's memoirs contain no reference to this event.

21. James Dobbins, *After the Taliban: Nation-Building in Afghanistan* (Washington, DC: Potomac, 2008), 11.

22. See Steve Coll, *Ghost Wars: The Secret History of the CIA, Afghanistan, and Bin Laden, from the Soviet Invasion to September 10, 2001* (London: Penguin, 2004).

23. Author's interview, April 12, 2010.

24. Rumsfeld presented his approach in the following terms in February 2003:

From the outset of the war our guiding principle has been that Afghanistan belongs to the Afghans. [. . .] The objective is not to engage in what some call nationbuilding. Rather it's to try to help the Afghans so that they can build their own nation. This is an important distinction. In some nationbuilding exercises well-intentioned foreigners arrive on the scene, look at the problems and say let's fix it. This is well motivated to be sure, but it can really be a disservice in some instances because when foreigners come in with international solutions to local problems, if not very careful they can create a dependency (*Beyond Nation Building*, Remarks as Delivered by Secretary of Defense Donald H. Rumsfeld, February 14, 2003; available at www.defense.gov/speeches/speech.aspx?speechid=337)

See also Rumsfeld, *Known and Unknown*, 483 and 682–683.

25. The CIA's field commander, Gary Berntsen, claims to have filed the request for more U.S. troops for the Tora Bora assault, only to find it ignored in the chain of command. *Jawbreaker: The Attack on Al Qaeda and Bin Laden* (New York: Crown, 2005). See also *Tora Bora Revisited: How We Failed to Get Bin Laden and Why It Matters Today*, A Report to Members of the Committee on Foreign Relations, U.S. Senate, November 30, 2009; available at http://foreign.senate.gov/imo/media/doc/Tora_Bora_Report.pdf, and Ahmed Rashid, *Descent into Chaos* (London: Penguin, 2008), 91. In his memoirs President Bush writes that "Years later, critics charged that we allowed bin Laden to slip the noose at Tora Bora. I sure didn't see it that way." U.S. commanders "assured me they had the troop levels and resources they needed," and "we would have moved heaven and earth to bring him to justice" had they known for sure where he was; *Decision Points*, 202. Rumsfeld aligns, arguing that General Franks could have had more troops if requested; Rumsfeld, *Known and Unknown*, 402.

26. Kathy Gannon, "Afghanistan Unbound," *Foreign Affairs* 83/3 (May/June 2004), 35–46; Antonio Giustozzi, *"Good State" vs. "Bad Warlords"? A Critique of State Building Strategies in Afghanistan*, LSE Crisis State Research Centre, Working Paper no. 51, October 2004; M. L. Roi and G. Smolynec, "End States, Resource Allocation, and NATO Strategy in Afghanistan," *Diplomacy and Statecraft* 19/2 (2008), 289–320; and Seth G. Jones, *Counterinsurgency in Afghanistan* (RAND counterinsurgency study, vol. 4, 2008).

27. Bush, *Decision Points*, 205–207.

28. Author's interview with Dobbins, January 15, 2010.

29. In a meeting among National Security Council principals called to discuss a U.N.-led debate on the issue of ISAF expansion, Rumsfeld "simply steamrolled the decision through" that no more international troops or peacekeepers would be called on; Deputy Secretary of State Richard Armitage, quoted by Seth G. Jones, *In the Graveyard of Empires: America's War in Afghanistan* (New York: Norton, 2009), 115. James Dob-

bins, at this point overseeing U.S. Afghan reconstruction policy, recalls: "The issue was not raised again through 2002"; Author's interview, January 15, 2010.

30. Three ambassadors (Finn, Khalilzad, and Neumann) have gone on record on this; see *New York Times*, "How the 'Good War' in Afghanistan Went Bad," August 12, 2007. See also Rashid, *Descent into Chaos*, 135; and Woodward, *At War*, 225.

31. Ahmed Rashid, *Taliban: Militant Islam, Oil and Fundamentalism in Central Asia* (London: I. B. Tauris, 2009), 207.

32. See especially James Dobbins, *After the Taliban*, 35, 39–40, and 70.

33. *New York Times*, "U.N. Insisting Afghans Get a Government They Want," October 24, 2001.

34. Lakhdar Brahimi, *Briefing to the Security Council*, Tuesday, November 13, 2001; available at www.un.org/News/dh/latest/afghan/brahimi-sc-briefing.htm.

35. Lakhdar Brahimi, Speech at the Opening of the 55th Annual DPI/NGO Conference: Rebuilding Societies Emerging from Conflict, A Shared Responsibility, New York, September 9, 2002.

36. See *The Atlantic Monthly*, "The Pragmatist," July–August 2004, 44–46; and Richard J. Ponzio, "Transforming Political Authority: U.N. Democratic Peacebuilding in Afghanistan," *Global Governance* 13 (2007), 255–275 at 261–262. Brahimi was notably working in tandem with U.S. ambassador Zalmay Khalizad, a skilful diplomat close to the principals of the Bush administration and a later ambassador to Iraq.

37. Britain provided around 1,500 soldiers of the 5,000 soldiers that ISAF I comprised, in addition to the theater's strategic (divisional) headquarters and operational (brigade) headquarters. The British deployment became Operation Fingal.

38. *Times*, "SBS Risked Attack from the Alliance," January 23, 2002; also Sean M. Maloney, "International Security Assistance Force: The Origins of a Stabilization Force," *Canadian Military Journal* (Summer 2003), 4.

39. See, for instance, *Washington Post*, "Turkey, Britain, France to Head Peacekeeping Forces," November 16, 2001.

40. *Independent*, "Campaign against Terrorism: Blair Will Send Troops for Three Months," December 15, 2001.

41. *Guardian*, "British Forces' Role Remains in Doubt: Hoon Warns of Dangers Facing Security Mission," December 20, 2001.

42. "More Turmoil for Turkey? The Military Keeps Watch," *Strategic Comments* 8/5 (2002), 1–2.

43. Author's interview, January 15, 2010.

44. The JDP had been created only nineteen months prior to the general elections that enabled it to form a single-party government. Erdogan, banned from taking office in 2002, became prime minister in March 2003, replacing his confidant Abdullah Gül.

45. Elizabeth Pond, *Friendly Fire: The Near-Death of the Transatlantic Alliance* (Pittsburgh: EUSA, 2004), 89–96.

46. I interviewed both ambassadors and officials who had been present in the NAC. See also *International Herald Tribune*, "3 Block NATO Aid for Turks on Iraq: France, Germany and Belgium Trigger One of the Biggest Crises in Alliance's History," February 11, 2003; *Independent*, "Iraq Crisis: Robertson's Gamble Misfires and the Alliance Ruptures," February 11, 2003; and *New York Times*, "Threats and Responses: 3 Members of NATO and Russia Resist U.S. on Iraq Plans," February 11, 2003.

47. Lord Robertson, the architect of NATO's decision-making process through these events, was at the White House three days later for a meeting with President Bush, who led his team in a standing ovation in Robertson's honor. See Michael Gordon and Bernard Trainor, *Cobra II: The Inside Story of the Invasion and Occupation of Iraq* (London: Atlantic Books, 2007), 130.

48. Interview with author, April 12, 2010.

49. *Press Briefing*, April 16, 2003; available at www.nato.int/docu/speech/2003/s030416a.htm.

50. Woodward, *At War*, 310.

51. Quoted in U.S. Army, *A Different Kind of War*, U.S. Army Combined Arms Center, Fort Leavenworth, Kansas, June 2009, 240.

52. The DDR lead was not the U.N. assistance mission to Afghanistan, UNAMA, but the U.N. Development Program, UNDP.

53. The DDR program and its successor program (DIAG) ultimately allowed the international community and in particular the U.N. organizations "to avoid admitting failure by dragging on despite ever decreasing returns"; Antonio Giustozzi, "Shadow Ownership and SSR in Afghanistan," in Timothy Donais, ed., *Local Ownership and Security Sector Reform* (Zurich/Berlin: LIT Verlag for the Geneva Centre for Democratic Control of Armed Forces (DCAF), 2008), 219.

54. Obaid Younossi et al., *The Long March: Building an Afghan National Army* (Santa Monica, CA: RAND, 2009), 13.

55. Fahim had to concede defeat on this issue by December 2002, and from this point on international donors led by the United States could plan for substantial change. See Antonio Giustozzi, "Military Reform in Afghanistan," in Mark Sedra, ed., *Confronting Afghanistan's Security Dilemma: Reforming the Security Sector*, BICC Brief 28, September 2003, 26–27.

56. This point is made by Antonio Giustozzi in "Auxiliary Force or National Army? Afghanistan's 'ANA' and the Counter-Insurgency Effort, 2002–2006," *Small Wars and Insurgencies* 18/1 (March 2007), 45–67.

57. The agencies in question were typically, and from a U.S. perspective, USAID, the Department of Defense, the Department of State, the Department of Agriculture, the Afghan Interior Ministry, UNAMA, and various NGOs (nongovernmental organizations). The "galvanizing" perspective is from Barbara J. Stapleton, *A Brit-*

ish Agencies Afghanistan Group Briefing Paper on the Development of Joint Regional Teams in Afghanistan, London, January 2003; available at www.reliefweb.int/library/ documents/2003/baag-afg-08jan.pdf.

58. This point and the next paragraph draw on U.S. Army, *A Different Kind of War*, chapter 7. See also *New York Times*, "US Sees Hunts for Al Qaeda In Pakistan Lasting Into Fall," May 6, 2002.

59. This task force was the Coalition Joint Civil–Military Operations Task Force (CJCMOTF).

60. U.S. Army, *A Different Kind of War*, 234.

61. Olga Oliker et al., *Aid During Conflict: Interaction Between Military and Civilian Assistance Providers in Afghanistan, September 2001–June 2002* (Santa Monica, CA: RAND, 2004), 68–70.

62. Ibid., 234. James Dobbins writes that he already in January 2002 sought to insert a greater civilian component into the CHLC structure but that the idea came to nothing on the grounds of Pentagon opposition; *After the Taliban*, 133.

63. Robert Kaplan, *Imperial Grunts: On the Ground with the American Military, from Mongolia to the Philippines to Iraq and Beyond* (New York: Vintage, 2006), 219–220.

64. Peter Marsden, *Afghanistan, Aid, Armies & Empires* (London: I. B. Tauris, 2009), 112–113.

65. Germany outlined its ISAF–OEF position in December 2001: *Times*, "Britain Sets Time Limit on Peacekeeping," December 20, 2001.

66. *Daily Telegraph*, "I Am Not Convinced, Fischer Tells Rumsfeld," February 10, 2003.

67. The Defense Policy Guidance of April 2003 divided German forces into combat forces, stability and reconstruction forces, and support forces. Germany has since emphasized expeditionary capabilities even more; Timo Noetzl and Benjamin Schreer, "All the Way? The Evolution of German Military Power," *International Affairs* 84/2 (2008), 211–221 at 217.

68. For the debate on the NRF see Marco Overhaus, "In Search of a Post-Hegemonic Order: Germany, NATO, and the European Security and Defence Policy," *German Politics* 13/4 (December 2004), 551–568 at 557. For the Struck Hindu Kush comment see *Focus Magazin*, "Portraet: Zivil bis in die Knochen," July 14, 2003.

69. Sebastian Merz, *Still on the Way to Afghanistan? Germany and Its Forces in the Hindu Kush*, SIPRI Project Paper, November 2007; available at www.sipri.org/ research/conflict/publications/merz, 9.

70. *Washington Times*, "Pullout in Afghanistan Worries Germany," July 17, 2003; *Taz*, "Afghanistan: Struck stürmt voran," August 9, 2003; *Der Spiegel*, "Angst vor Überdehnung," August 25, 2003.

71. *International Analyst Network*, "A True Challenge for Leadership," interview with Lieutenant General Goetz Gliemeroth, October 20, 2003; available at www .analyst-network.com/article.php?art_id=713.

72. *Descent into Chaos*, 351.

73. *Le Monde*, "La crédibilité de l'OTAN érodée," March 24, 2003 ; "L'OTAN prend le commandement de l'ISAF en Afghanistan, hors de sa zone naturelle," April 18, 2003.

74. Jaap de Hoop Scheffer took office on January 1, 2004. In an op-ed column later that month he wrote, "I have come into the job with my eyes open. I know that NATO has had a bruising year. . . . It's time to get back to business. . . . If we want to win the war on terrorism, we must win the peace in Afghanistan"; Jaap de Hoop Scheffer, "A Bruised Alliance Marches On: NATO," *International Herald Tribune*, January 30, 2004.

75. Sean M. Maloney, "Afghanistan Four Years On: An Assessment," *Parameters* 35/3 (Autumn 2005), 21–32.

76. *Le Monde*, "Donald Rumsfeld appelle l'OTAN à s'engager davantage en Afghanistan," February 9, 2004.

77. *Le Monde*, "L'Eurocorps pourrait prendre, au cours de l'été, la tête des opérations de l'OTAN en Afghanistan," February 6, 2004.

78. "Berlin Plus" was a formula approved in 1999 to specify the ways in which the EU could be assisted by NATO. Given Turkish–Greek disputes, the formula has been activated only twice (Macedonia in 2003 and Bosnia in 2004; Kosovo is next in line). On "Berlin Plus in reverse" see Michèle A. Flournoy and Julianne Smith, who suggested a new arrangement to "provide NATO access to EU civilian and constabulary capabilities for crisis management operations," *European Defense Integration: Bridging the Gap between Strategy and Capabilities* (Washington, DC: CSIS, 2005), 70. See also Paul Cornish, *EU and NATO: Co-operation or Competition?* European Parliament briefing paper, October 2006; available at www.chathamhouse.org.uk/ files/3379_nato_eu.pdf.

79. *New York Times*, "How the 'Good War' in Afghanistan Went Bad," August 12, 2007.

80. U.S. Army, *A Different Kind of War*, 251.

81. Colonel Ian Hope, *Unity of Command in Afghanistan: A Forsaken Principle of War*, (Carlisle, PA: U.S. Army War College, Strategic Studies Institute, November 2008), 9.

82. "The benefit of physical colocation of senior military and diplomatic leaders and their staffs cannot be overemphasized," writes Tucker B. Mansager, the CFC-A Political-Military Division chief, 2003–2004; "Interagency Lessons Learned in Afghanistan," *Joint Forces Quarterly*, 40, 1st Quarter (2006), 80–84.

83. U.S. Army, *A Different Kind of War*, 253.

84. Khalilzad and Barno formally recommended to Secretary of Defense Rumsfeld the change to counterinsurgency in December 2004; Rumsfeld, *Known and Unknown*, 686.

85. Bradley Graham, *By His Own Rules: The Ambitions, Successes, and Ultimate Failures of Donald Rumsfeld* (New York: Public Affairs, 2009), 501–504.

86. Rumsfeld, *Known and Unknown*, 685.

87. *New York Times*, "NATO Runs Short of Troops to Expand Afghan Peacekeeping," September 18, 2004.

88. *New York Times*, September 14, 2005; *Guardian*, September 15, 2005; *New York Times*, "How the 'Good War' in Afghanistan Went Bad," August 12,2007.

89. *SACEUR OPLAN 10302 (Revise 1)*, unclassified version, November 8, 2005. The political end state is defined in section 1.d; the military end state in section 3.b.9.

90. There are five phases in NATO's plan: Phase 1 was assessment and preparation for Kabul; phase 2 is ISAF expansion; phase 3 stabilization; and phases 4 and 5 transition and redeployment, respectively.

91. OPLAN, section 3.b.2.c and Annex C.

92. OPLAN, sections 3.b.3 and 3.b.4 as well as Appendix 1, section 2.

93. OPLAN, Annex A—Supplementary Concept of Operations for Transitional Operations. This point is corroborated by the observation of a background source who indicates that the main text of the OPLAN foresees an "offensive air-ground campaign." This is not apparent from the sanitized version of the OPLAN to which I have had access.

94. This is based on a background interview with an officer who worked at SHAPE's J5 (Plans and Policy) at the time. The interview was conducted in November 2009.

95. Author's interview, February 2010.

96. Vincent Morelli and Paul Belkin, *NATO in Afghanistan: A Test of the Transatlantic Alliance*, CRS Report for Congress, RL33627, July 2, 2009, 16–17.

97. Interviewed at ISAF headquarters, Kabul, October 1, 2009.

Chapter 5

1. Canada suffered four casualties that day, a small figure by the annals of the fight in Afghanistan but a dramatic and eye-opening loss that day in September 2006. Brigadier-General Fraser's decision to advance the attack was controversial and an often-cited source of the failure of the southern strategy. Fraser has defended his position with reference to intelligence he received indicating that the Taliban was not ready for a fight and the necessity of adapting to the battlefield. See the three-part investigation by journalist Adam Day, "Operation Medusa: The Battle for Panjwai," *Legion Magazine*: part I, "The Charge of Charlie Company," from September 1, 2007;

part II, "Death in a Free Fire Zone," from November 1, 2007; and part III, "The Fall of Objective Ruby," from January 26, 2008; available at www.legionmagazine.com.

2. *The Globe and Mail*, "Conquering Canadians Take Stock; With the Taliban Having Melted Away, Commander Reflects on Lessons Learned," September 13, 2006.

3. On the intent of the Taliban, see Fraser in Part I of "Operation Medusa" (note 1); see also Captain Edward Stewart, forward PAO for Operation MEDUSA, "Op Medusa: A Summary"; available at www.theroyalcanadianregiment.ca/history/1992-present/1rcr_op_medusa_summary.htm.

4. *Christian Science Monitor*, "Taliban Turn to Suicide Attacks," February 3, 2006.

5. Bernd Horn, "No Small Action: Operation Medusa, Panjwayi, Afghanistan," in Bernd Horn, ed., *Fortune Favours the Brave: Tales of Courage and Tenacity in Canadian Military History* (Toronto: Dundurn Press, 2009), 361-416 at 366.

6. See especially the work of Antonio Giustozzi, *Koran, Kalashnikov and Laptop* (London: Hurst, 2007); *Empires of Mud: The Neo-Taliban Insurgency in Afghanistan 2002-2007* (New York: Columbia University Press, 2009); and the edited book *Decoding the New Taliban: Insights from the Afghan Field* (Columbia: Columbia University Press, 2009).

7. Antonio Giustozzi finds the evidence ambiguous but ultimately in favor of a jihadist interpretation: *Koran, Kalashnikov and Laptop*, chapter 4. See also *Christian Science Monitor*, "Taliban Adopting Iraq-Style Jihad," September 13, 2006. Thomas H. Johnson and M. Chris Mason believe that the Taliban is an agile actor exploiting its enemy's weaknesses akin to a "war of the flea"; "Understanding the Taliban and Insurgency in Afghanistan," *Orbis* 51/1 (Winter 2007), 71–89. Ali A. Jalali finds the classical insurgency movement important but also just one part of a complex campaign; "Afghanistan: Regaining Momentum," *Parameters* 37/4 (Winter 2007), 5–19. For more on the Taliban's role as a kind of shadow government, see *Christian Science Monitor*, "Taliban Kidnappings Rise, but Style Differs from Al Qaeda," March 20, 2007.

8. *Globe and Mail*, "Conquering Canadians Take Stock"; also, "Taliban 'Eliminated' from Pivotal District; Canadian Forces Declare Victory in Panjwai, but Many Afghan Civilians Remain Skeptical," September 18, 2006; and "Inspiring Tale of Triumph over Taliban Not All It Seems; A Local Revolt against Police Abuse and Tribal Persecution Figured into Panjwai Showdown with Insurgents," September 23, 2006.

9. Gregg Mills, *From Africa to Afghanistan: With Richards and NATO to Kabul* (Johannesburg: Witts University Press, 2007), 207.

10. *Telegraph*, "Paras Strike Deep into the Taliban Heartland," June 19, 2006.

11. On the Canadian forces' involvement in Operation Mountain Thrust and preparation for Medusa, see Chris Wattie, *Contact Charlie: The Canadian Army, the Taliban, and the Battle that Saved Afghanistan* (Toronto: Key Porter Books, 2008).

12. Mills, *From Africa to Afghanistan*, 220–223.

13. I have relied in parts on my own background interview with General Richards for this overview, but see also his presentation of his thinking in an interview with *Frontline*; available at www.pbs.org/frontlineworld/stories/afghanistan604/interview_richards.html.

14. In interview with author, March 2010.

15. Ibid.

16. See the JCMB *Terms of References*; available at www.diplomatie.gouv.fr/en/IMG/pdf/JCMB_TOR_-_English.pdf.

17. For the U.S.–U.K. relationship, see *Guardian*, "Taliban Town Seizure Throws Afghan Policy into Disarray," February 4, 2007; for Karzai, see *International Herald Tribune*, "Peace Accord in Provincial Afghanistan Dividing Opinion," November 1, 2006.

18. For instance, on several occasions in 2007 British diplomats met with the Taliban's commander of the southern region, Mullah Mansoor Dadullah, to purchase peace. When exposed, Karzai expelled the diplomats and Mullah Omar, the Taliban's supreme leader, demoted Mullah Dadullah; *Times*, "Expelled British Envoys Tried to Turn Taliban Chief," January 6, 2008; also *The Long War Journal*, "Divide and Conquer: The British Strategy against the Taliban," January 15, 2008; available at www.longwarjournal.org/archives/2008/01/divide_and_conquer_t.php. In February 2008 Condoleezza Rice and David Miliband, Britian's foreign secretary, went through a "very troubling moment" during a Kabul visit as President Karzai, with reference to this incident, accused Britain of treachery; Condoleezza Rice, *No Higher Honor: A Memoir of My Years in Washington* (London: Simon & Schuster, 2011), 637.

19. NATO's anodyne and complicated language is as follows: "To that end, while recognising that NATO has no requirement to develop capabilities strictly for civilian purposes, we have tasked today the Council in Permanent Session to develop pragmatic proposals in time for the meeting of Foreign Ministers in April 2007 and Defence Ministers in June 2007 to improve coherent application of NATO's own crisis management instruments as well as practical cooperation at all levels with partners, the UN and other relevant international organisations, Non-Governmental Organisations and local actors in the planning and conduct of ongoing and future operations wherever appropriate"; NATO, *Riga Summit Declaration*, Press Release 2006/150, November 29, 2006; available at www.nato.int/docu/pr/2006/p06-150e.htm, paragraph 10. Shortly before the Riga summit, NATO, the United Nations, the World Bank, and non-NATO ISAF contributors met for the first time, informally and without issuing a declaration. They did appear at a press briefing, however; *Joint Press Point*, NATO Online Library, November 2, 2006; available at www.nato.int/docu/speech/2006/s061102d.htm.

20. Background interview by author, January 2010.

21. The comprehensive approach was vigorously promoted by Denmark. This small ally sought to put the CA on NATO's agenda in late 2004: It organized a high-profile NATO conference on the topic in Copenhagen in June 2005, and it sowed the seeds of the thinking that blossomed into the Riga conclusions of November 2006. However, multiple streams led to Riga. One was the obvious operational experience from the Balkans and now Afghanistan that NATO had too few tools to handle such conflicts. Another was the stream of experiences out in "comprehensive" planning that the United States along with the key RC/S allies—Great Britain, the Netherlands, and Canada—were advancing, not least based on their PRTs. A third stream concerned NATO's leadership and the issue of timing. The secretary general's office was not ready to take control of the issue in 2005–2006 because they were not convinced that it was a winning issue. The string of controversies related to the OPLAN of December 2005, the national approaches to the PRTs, and controversies related to force contributions made the issue look unattractive. In consequence, up until mid-2006 there was no proposal, no political decision, and no tasking for organizational work on the issue. On the Danish origins, see Peter Viggo Jakobsen, *NATO's Comprehensive Approach to Crisis Response Operations: A Work in Slow Progress*, DIIS Report 2008:15, October 8, 2008, 7; also Kristian Fischer and Jan Top Christensen, "Improving Civil-Military Cooperation the Danish Way," *NATO Review* (Summer 2005); available at www.nato.int/docu/review/2005/issue2/english/special.html. The wider assessment of national approaches and the secretary general's office draws on interviews with officials from NATO's Political Affairs and Operations Divisions.

22. *Daily Telegraph*, "NATO Troops Must Be Allowed to Fight in War Zones of Afghanistan," November 24, 2006; *Times*, "NATO Urges End of Right to Opt out of Afghanistan Combat," November 27, 2006.

23. John Deni, *Alliance Management and Maintenance: Restructuring NATO for the 21st Century* (Aldershot, UK: Ashgate, 2007), 95–96.

24. See for instance *International Herald Tribune*, "NATO Chief to Appeal for Troops," September 6, 2006; *Times*, "NATO Chief Fails to Win Additional 2,500 Troops," September 14, 2006.

25. Background interview in December 2009 by author.

26. Gade, interview with author, May 31, 2010.

27. Daniel Korski, "London Calling: How Britain Now Runs European Security," March 20, 2008; available at www.ecfr.eu/content/entry/commentary_london_calling_how_britain_determines_euroepan_security. Condoleezza Rice does not delve much into NATO politics in her memoirs but does note that the RC/S group of allies "bristled as they watched other countries restrict their military presence so their soldiers would be exposed to minimal conflict"; *No Higher Honor*, 635.

28. De Hoop Scheffer, interview with author, February 2010.

29. Under Secretary of State for Political Affairs R. Nicholas Burns, "Briefing on NATO Issues Prior to Riga Summit" (Washington, DC: U.S. Department of State, November 21, 2006); for the citation see America.gov, "United States Outlines 'Ambitious Agenda' for NATO Summit," November 3, 2006. See also Rebecca Moore, "NATO's Partners in Afghanistan: Impact and Purpose," *UNISCI Journal* 22 (January 2010), 92–115.

30. Burns, interview with author, April 2010.

31. On the Nuland speech and Burns's background, see Karl-Heinz Kamp, "'Global Partnership': A New Conflict within NATO?," *Konrad Adenauer Foundation Report* no. 29 (May 2006), 3. Senator John McCain in early 2006 urged NATO to continue its political transformation with the words, "In turning back the forces of tyranny and terror, and in helping to secure the blessings of liberty everywhere, we will embark on a project worthy of this grand alliance"; *NATO's Future Role in International Peace Keeping*, Munich Security Conference, February 4, 2006. Ivo Daalder, later NATO ambassador, together with James Goldgeier, published widely noted commentaries in favor of a global NATO around the time of the Riga summit; Ivo Daalder and James Goldgeier, "Global NATO," *Foreign Affairs* 85/5 (September/October 2006), and "NATO: For Global Security, Expand the Alliance," *International Herald Tribune*, October 12, 2006.

32. The summit in addition declared existing structures of partnership such as the EAPC to be of "enduring value"; *Riga Summit Declaration*, paragraphs 11–13.

33. David S. Yost, *NATO and International Organizations*, NATO Defense College, Forum Paper 3, September 2007, 59–64.

34. The document, dated September 23, 2008, is entitled *Joint Declaration on UN/NATO Secretariat Cooperation* and is published on various websites easily located via a search engine. It is a short document consisting of a brief introduction and five points that lay out the desire for cooperation and concrete issue areas where such cooperation could begin (specifically, "communication and information-sharing, including on issues pertaining to the protection of civilian populations; capacity-building, training and exercises; lessons learned, planning and support for contingencies; and operational coordination and support").

35. Background interview with author, May 2009.

36. *BBC Monitoring Former Soviet Union*, "Russia Says Agreement between UN, NATO Secretariats Illegitimate," October 9, 2008; Michael F. Harsch and Johannes Warwick, "NATO and the UN," *Survival* 51/2 (April–May 2009), 5–12.

37. *BBC Monitoring Europe*, "Russia Warns Poland against Hosting Missile-Defence Site," October 3, 2006; *BBC Monitoring Former Soviet Union*, "Russia Pledges to Respond to US Missile Defence Plans for Eastern Europe," October 26, 2006; *Daily Telegraph*, "Arms Race Fears as Putin Attacks US Missiles Plans," February 2, 2007;

New York Times, "Russian Criticizes U.S. Plan for Missile Defense System," February 10, 2007.

38. De Hoop Scheffer, interview with author, February 1, 2010.

39. *Los Angeles Times*, "US Calls Iraq the Priority," December 12, 2007; *New York Times*, "Afghan Mission Is Reviewed as Concerns Rise," December 16, 2007.

40. See *Statement to the House Armed Service Committee by Secretary of Defense Robert M. Gates Tuesday, December 11, 2007*; available at http://armedservices.house .gov/pdfs/FC121107/Gates_Testimony121107.pdf; for the later Gates comments on allies and counterinsurgency, *Los Angeles Times*, "Gates Says NATO Force Unable to Fight Guerillas," January 16, 2008; for McNeill and the RC/S situation, *Washington Post*, "Gates Hits NATO Allies' Role in Afghanistan," February 7, 2008.

41. On the contrast between Rumsfeld and Gates, see Bradley Graham, *By His Own Rules: The Ambitions, Successes, and Ultimate Failures of Donald Rumsfeld* (New York: Public Affairs, 2009), 667–669.

42. Craddock, interview with author, November 2009.

43. The 2008 Resolution renewing the mandate breaks the UNAMA mandate down into no fewer than nine points for prioritized and comprehensive action; *U.N. Security Council Resolution 1806 (2008)*, March 20, 2008; available at http://daccess-dds-ny.un.org/doc/UNDOC/GEN/N08/279/31/PDF/N0827931.pdf?OpenElement, paragraph 4. The preceding resolution renewing the mandate, UNSC Resolution 1746 (March 23, 2007), merely stressed the role of UNAMA in coordinating the international effort.

44. *U.N. Security Council Resolution 1401*, March 28, 2002; available at http:// daccess-dds-ny.un.org/doc/UNDOC/GEN/N02/309/14/PDF/N0230914.pdf?Open Element.

45. For "got on well" see Sherard Cowper-Coles, *Cables from Kabul: The Inside Story of the West's Afghanistan Campaign* (London: Harper Press, 2011), 136. For "downbeat" see Chris Alexander, *The Long Way Back: Afghanistan's Quest for Peace* (Harper Collins, 2011, kindle edition), location 2724.

46. *Reuters*, "Ashdown Accepts job as U.N. Afghan Envoy," January 16, 2008; available at http://uk.reuters.com/article/idUKL1664024720080116?feedType=RSS& feedName=worldNews; *Times*, "Ashdown Pulls out of UN Post after Losing Afghans' Support," January 28, 2008.

47. Alexander, *Long Way Back*, location 3106.

48. Western diplomats in Kabul noted that "This is very much a US-led initiative," and that "it is not being pushed internally within the UN. It is the US and Nato that are pushing it." See *Daily Telegraph*, "Ashdown Wins US Backing to Be Afghan 'Super Envoy,'" December 4, 2007; also *Guardian*, "Brown and Bush Line up Ashdown for Role in Linking Afghan Aid and Military Effort," December 5, 2007. On Bush and Karzai, see Cowper-Coles, *Cables from Kabul*, 136.

49. President Karzai is said to have favored Turkey's Hikmet Cetin, who for a full two and a half years (January 2004–August 2006) was NATO's senior civilian representative in Afghanistan. Cetin could hardly leave much of a footprint in Kabul, given the conditions and mandate at the time, and he did not. Karzai might likely have had this permissive experience in mind when pointing to Cetin; *Independent*, "Bid to Resolve Stalemate on UN Envoy," February 6, 2008.

50. North Atlantic Council, *Final Communiqué*, June 14, 2007; available at www .nato.int/cps/en/natolive/news_47011.htm, paragraphs 4–8.

51. For McNeill's past record, see Giustozzi, *Koran, Kalashnikov, and Laptop*, 189–191. For 2007 worries, see *Economist*, "A Double Spring Offensive—Afghanistan's War," February 24, 2007; *Observer*, "Up to 80 Dead after US Air Strikes in Afghanistan," July 1, 2007; *Economist*, "Policing a Whirlwind—Afghanistan," December 15, 2007.

52. For these numbers, see the ISAF Placemat Archive, available at www.isaf.nato .int/en/isaf-placemat-archives.html.

53. Craddock, interview with author, November 2009.

54. Jason Burke, *The 9/11 Wars* (London: Allen Lane, 2011), 371.

55. *New York Times*, "Pakistanis Aided Attack in Kabul, U.S. Officials Say," August 1, 2008; also Burke, *9/11 Wars*, 587 (note 101).

56. U.S. Department of Defense News Transcript, *DoD News Briefing with Gen. McNeill from the Pentagon*, February 6, 2008; available at www.defense.gov/Transcripts/ Transcript.aspx?TranscriptID=4138.

57. David Kilcullen in interview with *Sunday Times*, "Lawrence of Arabia Takes on the Taliban," March 11, 2007.

58. References to the contents of the CSPMP and the CA Action Plan were obtained in background interviews.

59. The four pillars of the CAAP are (a) the planning and conduct of operations; (b) education, training, exercises and lessons learned; (c) cooperation with other international actors; and (d) public messaging.

60. The major track of ongoing work concerns the "bible" of NATO operational planning—the Military Committee's guide for operational planning, or MC133. Getting the comprehensive approach inserted here has been a very time-consuming and complicated matter, according to observers interviewed by author.

61. From interviews by the author: de Hoop Scheffer in February 2010 and Martin Howard in March 2010.

62. This and the next paragraph are based on author's interview with Martin Howard, March 2010.

63. *Le Figaro*, "La France est prête à envoyer des renforts en Afghanistan," February 11, 2008, and "La France renforce sa présence en Afghanistan," March 24, 2008.

64. Once the NAC decided that NATO needed to do something, the military authorities would define a strategic concept of operations (CONOPS) that, following more NAC deliberation, would lead to the development of an operations plan (OPLAN). Once the NAC approved hereof, NATO was ready to go.

65. The comitology of NATO is extensive, but the basic idea is this: NATO's Operations Division runs the PCG to oversee operations; the Political Affairs Division runs an equivalent Political Committee to structure political relations (for instance, to set up partnership agreements or to arrange transit); while the military staff runs the Executive Working Group, which deals in military issues. The secretary general and his assistant secretaries general coordinate, and matters for political attention or decision can be lifted either to the Senior Political Committee (composed of the deputy permanent representatives) or all the way up to the North Atlantic Council.

66. *American Forces Press Service*, "Gates Arrives in Scotland for Afghan Meetings," December 13, 2007; available at www.defense.gov/news/newsarticle.aspx?id= 48407.

67. Howard, interview with author, March 2010.

68. Ibid.

69. De Hoop Scheffer, interview with author, February 2010.

Chapter 6

1. *Press Conference with Secretary Gates and Adm. Mullen on Leadership Changes in Afghanistan From the Pentagon*, Department of Defense News Transcript, May 11, 2009; available at www.defense.gov/transcripts/transcript.aspx?transcriptid=4424.

2. *New York Times*, "Pentagon Outs Top Commander in Afghan War," May 12, 2009, and "Switch Signals New Path for Afghanistan," May 13, 2009; Max Boot, "Obama's Right on Target in Afghanistan," *Los Angeles Times*, May 13, 2009; *Wall Street Journal*'s Peter Spiegel in web report, "The Reasons Behind McKiernan's Firing," available at http://online.wsj.com/video/the-reasons-behind-general-mckiernan-firing/106A9B31-800F-4BFC-B371-3BFD430281AC.html; and *Washington Post*, "Pentagon Worries Led to Command Change: McKiernan's Ouster Reflected New Realities in Afghanistan— and Washington," August 17, 2009.

3. Bob Woodward, *Obama's Wars: The Inside Story* (London: Simon and Schuster, 2010), 82–83.

4. *Guardian*, "Trumpeting the New Consensus on Afghanistan," August 31, 2009.

5. General Stanley A. McChrystal, *COMISAF's Initial Assessment*, August 30, 2009; available at http://media.washingtonpost.com/wp-srv/politics/documents/Assessment_ Redacted_092109.pdf.

6. NATO's public mandate that prepared the ground for General McChrystal's command was the broad and engaging Strasbourg-Kehl *Summit Declaration on Afghanistan*, April 4, 2009, NATO Press Release (2009) 045.

7. Author's interview with Brigadier General Davis, February 7, 2010. Some points were clarified in another interview, February 27, 2012.

8. *New York Times*, "Dash to Baghdad Left Top U.S. Generals Divided," March 13, 2006.

9. *New York Times*, "US Army Chief in Europe to Run NATO Afghan Unit," January 15, 2008.

10. Davis, interview with author, February 7, 2010.

11. The overall U.S. OEF command for Afghanistan (CFC-A) had been folded when ISAF took over security operations in the entire country, thus in 2006, but the United States maintained a division level headquarter in RC/E to run both ISAF and OEF operations. In 2008 this headquarter was Combined Joint Task Force 101 (named after the 101st Airborne Division). It thus reported both to ISAF headquarter (the double-hatted security deputy) and CENTCOM.

12. Interview with author, February 7, 2010.

13. *Washington Post*, "Pentagon Worries Led to Command Change: McKiernan's Ouster Reflected New Realities in Afghanistan—and Washington," August 17, 2009.

14. Kai Eide, *Høyt Spill om Afghanistan* (Oslo: Cappelen, 2011), 53.

15. Author's interview with Colonel Claus Wessel-Tolvig, ISAF liaison to PAG in 2008, April 12, 2010.

16. Eide, *Høyt Spil*, 41 and 51.

17. Wessel-Tolvig, interview with author, April 12, 2010.

18. "My impression was that the Afghans couldn't quite figure out where UNAMA was heading with this"; Wessel-Tolvig interview.

19. For Eide's remark see Chris Alexander, *The Long Way Back: Afghanistan's Quest for Peace* (Harper Collins, 2011, Kindle edition), location 3229.

20. *Høyt Spil*, 24.

21. Kai Eide devotes very little—too little—space to the case of JCMB reform and thus UNAMA-ISAF disputes. Going by his memoirs, the new UNAMA design got off to a good start in late 2008 but then in 2009 encountered the Obama surge, which militarized the conflict, and also the fraudulent elections; *Høyt spil*, 131 and 230–234; on Bush, 40–41.

22. For this delay in interaction I rely on the Davis interview, February 27, 2012.

23. Background interviews are the single best source for piecing together this sequence of failed Western diplomacy. Eide does not really address the controversies in his memoirs, *Høyt Spil*, though he is up front about his decision to go with President Karzai. UNAMA deputy Chris Alexander, who allegedly did not always align with Eide, treads carefully in his *The Long Way Back*.

24. Davis interview with author, February 7, 2010.

25. The joint conference ran for a day and a half, and half a day was set aside for ISAF only, it should be noted.

26. General McChrystal's highly visible embrace of COIN thinking and planning in 2009 would help convince NATO allies that COIN was acceptable. As we shall see later, the allies then put in motion the work that in January 2011 would result in NATO's first COIN doctrine. ISAF's embrace of COIN came with OP TOLO, however. See Catherine Dale, *War in Afghanistan: Strategy, Military Operations, and Issues for Congress*, Congressional Research Service R40156, January 23, 2009. This is based also on the OP TOLO CONOPS Brief dated October 16, 2008 (classified NATO/ISAF Secret), which I have been able to read.

27. *New York Times*, "Taliban Free 1,200 Inmates in Attack on Kandahar's Main Prison, Killing 15 Guards," June 14, 2008; *Washington Post*, "Taliban Seizes Seven Afghan Villages," June 17, 2008.

28. Davis interview with author, February 7, 2010.

29. Anonymous interview with author, November 23, 2009.

30. Jim Hoagland, "Poppy vs. Power in Afghanistan," *Washington Post*, December 23, 2007.

31. There were four conditions for such concerted action: (a) that the Afghan government request it; (b) that it fall within the ISAF–U.N. mandate; (c) that the action take place within the existing OPLAN; and (d) that the individual ally's government provide authorization; NATO, *NATO Steps up Counter-Narcotics Efforts in Afghanistan*, October 10, 2008; available at www.nato.int/docu/update/2008/10-october/e1010b.html. The Afghan forces ISAF aimed to work in concert with were not the regular Afghan police but a special counternarcotics police force that took aim not least at corrupt police officials. NATO's ambition was therefore to "neutralize" the impact of drugs on the insurgency; it was not about counternarcotics as such but about arresting the flow of money and resources into the insurgency.

32. Counternarcotics remained a "key supporting task" for NATO and did not become a "key military task," an enhanced emphasis that required the renegotiation of the OPLAN. By sticking to "key supporting task," NATO could lay out the new counternarcotics policy in a ministerial guideline, leaving the OPLAN intact. Interviews at ISAF HQ, September 27, 2010.

33. *New York Times*, "Under Pressure from U.S., NATO Agrees to Take Aim at Afghan Drug Trade," October 11, 2008.

34. *New York Times*, "2008 Becomes Deadliest Year for U.S. in Afghanistan," September 11, 2008; George W. Bush, *Decision Points* (London: Virgin Books, 2010), 217–218.

35. Woodward, *Obama's Wars*, 25.

36. *BBC Monitoring South Asia*, "NATO Will Not Attack Insurgents in Pakistan, Secretary-General says," July 24, 2008.

37. General McKiernan's campaign has been criticized for neglecting the city of Kandahar and especially the Taliban advance on the city from the north through Ar-

ghandab district, which they secured in late 2008 to enable an offensive on the provincial capital. ISAF's forces in RC/S were at this point predominantly focused to the east in Helmand and to the south in the border area to Pakistan. See Carl Forsberg, *The Taliban's Campaign for Kandahar*, Afghanistan Report 3, Institute for the Study of War (Washington, DC: December 2009).

38. Woodward, *Obama's Wars*, 44. President Bush writes that he chose not to make the Lute review public because the incoming Obama team preferred it that way; *Decision Points*, 218. Vice President Cheney confirms this point, noting that the request came from incoming security advisor James Jones and also noting that White House Chief of Staff Rahm Emanuel was wrong to give the impression that the Bush team left behind no plan; Cheney, *In My Time: A Personal and Political Memoir* (New York: Threshold Editions, 2011), 500–501. This chapter will shortly engage the Obama team's view of the Lute review.

39. Barak H. Obama, *Remarks by the President on a New Strategy for Afghanistan and Pakistan*, The White House, March 27, 2009; available at www.whitehouse.gov/the_press_office/Remarks-by-the-President-on-a-New-Strategy-for-Afghanistan-and-Pakistan/.

40. This summary is made from President Obama's speech (ibid.). The White House issued a six-page summary of the strategy fleshing out these points: *White Paper of the Interagency Policy Group's Report on U.S. Policy toward Afghanistan and Pakistan* (no date); available at www.whitehouse.gov/assets/documents/afghanistan_pakistan_white_paper_final.pdf. For other summaries, see the briefing by National Security Advisor James Jones, *Foreign Press Center Briefing*, March 27, 2009; available at http://fpc.state.gov/120965.htm; and the briefing by Bruce Riedel, Richard Holbrooke, and Michelle Flournoy—respectively chair and vicechairs of the Obama strategic review—*Press Briefing*, March 27, 2009; available at www.whitehouse.gov/the-press-office/press-briefing-bruce-riedel-ambassador-richard-holbrooke-and-michelle-flournoy-new-.

41. The 21,000 new troops came about in a sequence of two steps. The president approved of a reinforcement of 17,000 troops in mid-February, in response to a force request of three fresh brigades filed by General McKiernan in mid-2008. As the president remarked in his strategy speech later in March, "I've already ordered the deployment of 17,000 troops that had been requested by General McKiernan for many months." As part of the March review, the president added another 4,000 troops for the training mission, bringing the total to 21,000.

42. NATO, *Summit Declaration on Afghanistan*, Press Release (2009) 045, April 4, 2009.

43. The OMLTs' mission was to train operationally: to embed with Afghan army battalions (*Kandaks*) moving into the field, to mentor them, and to help them call in air support or medical evacuation as needed. In 2009 ISAF had around fifty-nine

such OMLTs, and France both provided a national OMLT and contributed to several others.

44. Woodward, *Obama's Wars*, 325.

45. NATO also committed another 3,000 troops for security operations in relation to the Afghan presidential elections scheduled for August 2009; NATO, *Summit Declaration on Afghanistan*; also *New York Times*, "Europeans Offer Few New Troops for Afghanistan," April 4, 2009; and *Sunday Times*, "NATO Summit: The Truth behind the Troops Heading to Afghanistan," April 6, 2009.

46. NATO Secretary General Jaap de Hoop Scheffer, *Press Conference*, June 12, 2009; available at www.nato.int/cps/en/SID-DB30D745-DEB726B1/natolive/opinions_55630.htm.

47. NATO, *Summit Declaration on Afghanistan*.

48. Interview with author, December 2009.

49. For Biden see The White House, *Opening Remarks by the Vice President to the North Atlantic Council*, March 10, 2009; available at www.whitehouse.gov/the_press_office/Remarks-by-Vice-President-Biden-to-the-North-Atlantic-Council/. For Clinton, see *Secretary of State Clinton's Remarks after NATO Meeting*, March 5, 2009; available at www.cfr.org/publication/18708/secretary_clintons_remarks_after_nato_meeting_march_2009.html.

50. This is from President Obama's March 27, 2009 speech.

51. This latter statement is from Biden's opening remarks to the North Atlantic Council meeting: The White House, *Opening Remarks by the Vice President to the North Atlantic Council*. The press conference was covered by *Washington Post*, "Biden Asks NATO for Aid in Afghanistan," March 11, 2009.

52. Woodward, *Obama's Wars*, 135.

53. Bruce Riedel, "Al Qaeda Strikes Back," *Foreign Affairs* May/June 2007; and *The Search for Al Qaeda: Its Leadership, Ideology and Future* (Washington: Brookings, 2010). The book, originally published in 2008, contains a short postscript regarding President Obama's request to Riedel to chair an Afghanistan review.

54. Riedel, interview with author, October 25, 2010.

55. Woodward, *Obama's Wars*, chapter 10. The Rahm Emanuel quote is from p. 104.

56. Reidel, interview with author, October 25, 2010.

57. It had been called by Secretary of State Clinton in early March, it gathered around ninety countries, and it asked them to commit them to the new comprehensive (civil–military) and regional focus of the Obama administration. The Hague conference may have contained "more bark than bite," as the German weekly the *Spiegel* noted, and this perhaps because it had been hastily convened, but it conveyed the message of the new presidency and connected to NATO's summit three days later, April 3–4; *Spiegel Online*, "More Bark than Bite: Afghanistan Conference Yields

Few Concrete Results," April 1, 2009; available at www.spiegel.de/international/
world/0,1518,616736,00.html.

58. Jaap de Hoop Scheffer, interview with author, October 27, 2010.

59. Ibid.

60. The White House, *Remarks by President Obama and NATO Secretary General Jaap de Hoop Scheffer after Meeting*, March 25, 2009; available at www.whitehouse.gov/the-press-office/remarks-president-obama-and-nato-secretary-general-jaap-de-hoop-scheffer-after-meet.

61. Jaap de Hoop Scheffer, interview with author, October 27, 2010.

62. The NAC, meeting in the format of heads of state and government, issued a Declaration on Alliance Security (DAS) that served as a precursor to the Strategic Concept review process, setting a type of agenda for the work. The DAS is short, though, and contains the usual staged emphasis on, first, Article 5, then Europe and enlargement, and finally global security issues. This was the standard "geographic approaches" view of the Alliance (allied territory/the Euro-Atlantic region/the world): Depending on where you put the emphasis, you can foresee distinct Strategic Concepts, which is to say that the secretary general had considerable leeway in drafting one. See NATO, *Declaration on Alliance Security*, Press Release (2009) 043, April 4, 2009.

63. Fogh Rasmussen, interview with author, October 29, 2010. On his appointment in April, Fogh Rasmussen resigned as prime minister.

64. See also Ryan Hendrickson, "NATO's First Prime Minister: Rasmussen's Leadership Surge," *RUSI Journal* 155/5 (October–November 2010), 24–30.

65. Background briefing, Kabul, October 2009.

66. In January 2009 ISAF stood at approximately 55,000 troops; the United States provided 23,000, or 42 percent; non–U.S. NATO provided around 55 percent (the remaining 3 percent being provided by non-NATO ISAF countries). In October 2010 ISAF stood at 130,000, with the United States providing 69 percent and non-U.S. NATO another 28 percent. Compare ISAF's force placemats from January 2009 and October 2010 at www.nato.int/isaf/docu/epub/pdf/placemat_archive/isaf_placemat_090112.pdf and www.isaf.nato.int/images/stories/File/Placemats/25OCT10%20Placemat%20page%201,2,3.pdf.

67. No official declaration was issued following the informal meeting, but Secretary General Rasmussen stated this in his press briefing: "What we did today was to discuss McChrystal's overall assessment, his overall approach and I have noted a broad support for all Ministers of this overall counterinsurgency approach"; *Press Conference*, 23 October 23, 2009; available at www.nato.int/cps/en/natolive/opinions_58469.htm. See also *New York Times*, "NATO Ministers Endorse Wider Afghan Effort," October 24, 2009.

68. The doctrine is *Allied Joint Doctrine for Counterinsurgency (COIN)*, AJP 3.4.4. It was finalized in January 2011.

69. For the Task Force mission statement, see NATO's Military Committee, *Terms of Reference (TOR) for the Counter Insurgency Task Force (COIN TF)*, MCM-001 7-2010, NATO Unclassified, January 29, 2010. For General Ramms, see *ISAF Training Requirements for a COIN Environment*, 1170/JBKEPB/194/10, NATO Unclassified, June 17, 2010.

70. In London on October 1, 2009, General McChrystal notoriously spoke out against the scaled-back strategic option favored by Vice President Biden. McChrystal spoke in support of his own strategic assessment but then in the Q&A session went against other options. He was summoned the next day by the president to a meeting in Copenhagen, Denmark, aboard Air Force One, and called to order. For the McChrystal speech and comments, see IISS, *General Stanley McChrystal Address*, October 1, 2009; available at www.iiss.org/recent-key-addresses/general-stanley-mcchrystal-address/. See also *New York Times*, "McChrystal Rejects Lower Afghan Aims," October 1, 2009; *Daily Telegraph*, "White House Angry at McChrystal Speech on Afghanistan," October 5, 2009.

71. The terms are reprinted in Bob Woodward, *Obama's Wars*. The Pentagon originally wanted to draw down the reinforced military effort—the surge—in 2016; President Obama insisted that this effort begin already in mid-2011, though within the context of an assessment of local conditions. In his speech laying out the results of the fall 2009 review, President Obama said that "I have determined that it is in our vital national interest to send an additional 30,000 U.S. troops to Afghanistan. After 18 months, our troops will begin to come home. These are the resources that we need to seize the initiative, while building the Afghan capacity that can allow for a responsible transition of our forces out of Afghanistan"; *Remarks by the President in Address to the Nation on the Way Forward in Afghanistan and Pakistan*, December 1, 2009; available at www.whitehouse.gov/the-press-office/remarks-president-address-nation-way-forward-afghanistan-and-pakistan.

72. General McChrystal, *Commander's Initial Assessment*, August 30, 2009; available at media.washingtonpost.com/wp-srv/politics/documents/Assessment_Redacted_092109.pdf?sid=ST2009092003140, 2-1 and 2-2.

73. *New York Times*, "U.S. Is Seeking 10,000 Troops from Its Allies," November 26, 2009.

74. As stated to *Economist*, "The Beginning or the End? The Surge in Afghanistan," December 5, 2009; also *Washington Post*, "McChrystal's Afghanistan Plan Stays Mainly Intact," December 7, 2009.

75. Ryan Hendrickson notes quite correctly that the secretary general was urging allies to support the campaign commander, General McChrystal; Hendrickson, "NATO's First Prime Minister," 28.

76. Rasmussen, interview with author, October 29, 2010.

77. The timetable of the Obama surge thus differed from that of the Bush surge in Iraq. President Obama justified this compressed timetable with reference to "reasonable cost" and "what we need to achieve to secure our interests. Furthermore, the absence of a time frame for transition would deny us any sense of urgency in working with the Afghan government"; *Remarks*, December 1, 2009. Perhaps not unsurprisingly, former Vice President Cheney saw a lack of "military rationale" and a path to "catastrophic consequences"; *In My Time*, 501–502.

78. Stanley A. McChrystal, "The New Face of War: It Takes a Network," *Foreign Policy* March/April 2011; available at www.foreignpolicy.com/articles/2011/02/22/it_takes_a_network?page=full.

79. *PBS Frontline*, "Kill/Capture: Inside the military's secret campaign to take out Taliban and Al Qaeda fighters," May 10, 2011; available at http://video.pbs.org/video/1917910631.

80. *Irish Times*, "Dutch Cabinet Near Collapse over Afghan Mission Row," February 20, 2010; *Guardian*, "Dutch Government Collapses after Labour Withdrawal from Coalition," February 20, 2010; *Financial Times*, "Dutch Open to Afghan Return," October 14, 2010. One of the issues that contributed to the government's malaise was the release of commission report criticizing not only the legality of the Dutch participation in the Iraq war but also sitting Prime Minister Balkanende's truthfulness on the matter. The report was issued in January 2010 and fanned the flames of the Afghan debate. See the Rapport Commissie van Onderzoek Besluitvorming Irak, January 12, 2010; available at www.nrc.nl/multimedia/archive/00267/rapport_commissie_i_267285a.pdf.

81. *Globe and Mail*, "U.S. to Press for Canada to Keep Troops in Afghanistan; Pending Request for up to 600 Troops Threatens to Start Standoff in Parliament over 2011 Withdrawal Date," March 25, 2010; *Star*, "Ottawa Turned Down NATO Request for More Afghan Troops," August 22, 2010; and *Star*, "Stephen Harper Rebuffs Talk of Afghan Role after 2011," June 4, 2010.

82. Stephen M. Saideman, "Canadian Forces in Afghanistan: Minority Government and Generational Change while Under Fire," in Theo Farrell, Frans Osinga, and James Russell, eds., *Fighting the Afghanistan War: States, Organizations, and Military Adaptation* (Stanford, CA: Stanford University Press, forthcoming)

83. *Daily Telegraph*, "US Wants British Troops to Leave Helmand," April 24, 2010; and *Guardian*, "British Troops May Leave Helmand as Tension Grows over Afghan Role: Shift to Kandahar Proposed for UK Soldiers as US Plans 'Final' Surge," April 22, 2010.

84. Among the focal points for this debate were small outposts in upper Helmand, such as Musa Qala and Sangin. More than 100 British troops had died in Sangin since 2001, about one-third of the total British losses, and as a place invested with that level of blood and effort, it was not easily abandoned by the British. Yet they handed it over

to the United States in September 2010. Afghan Defense Minister Abdul Rahim Wardak was among those who found the British footprint too light, observing that British forces came to "a really difficult province in Afghanistan with just Land Rovers, which are not much different than the ones driven in the streets of London"; *New York Times*, "British Forces Leave Deadly Afghan District," September 20, 2010. See also *New York Times*, "U.S. Tests British Resolve On War in Afghanistan," June 10, 2010; *Washington Post*, "U.S. Marines, British Advisers at Odds in Helmand," September 4, 2010; and *Belfast Telegraph*, "British Hand over Sangin after Four Years of Bitter War," September 21, 2010.

85. *Le Figaro*, "Sarkozy fixe à 2013 le retrait d'Afghanistan," January 27, 2012. For the earlier position of France, see Nicolas Sarkozy, *Discours du Président de la République sur la base de Tora en Afghanistan*, July 12, 2011; available at www.elysee.fr/president/les-actualites/discours/2011/discours-du-president-de-la-republique-sur-la-base.11720.html. For Panetta's announcement, see *New York Times*, "US Plans Shift to Elite Units as It Winds Down in Afghanistan," February 4, 2012.

86. *Spiegel*, "Westerwelle wagt sich an die Wahrheit über Afghanistan," February 10, 2010; *Spiegel*, "Guttenberg spricht von Krieg in Afghanistan," April 4, 2010.

87. *Spiegel*, "Regierung will neues Afghanistan-Mandat im Eiltempo durchpeitschen," February 9, 2010; *New York Times*, "Germany Will Begin Afghan Exit Next Year," December 17, 2010; *Spiegel*, "Nightmare in Afghanistan: Merkel Visits Troops Amid Tense Atmosphere," March 13, 2012.

88. The twenty-five PRTs in Afghanistan were notoriously uncoordinated, and the PRT Executive Steering Committee (ESC), which dated back to 2003, was not up to the job of steering. An effort to reinvigorate this body was made in 2008—following the collapse of the viceroy/Paddy Ashdown model—but the effort had come to naught. The ESC was chaired by the Afghan government with a triumvirate of international cochairs from the United Nations (the UN SGSR), the military chain of command (COMISAF), and NATO's civilian representative (SCR).

89. *Kabul Conference Communiqué*, July 20, 2010, 2–3; available at www.mfa.gov.af/FINAL%20Kabul%20Conference%20%20%20Communique.pdf.

90. The *Inteqal* paper itself has not been published, but the Prioritization and Implementation Plan regarding the Afghan National Development Strategy issued at the Kabul conference contains a detailed overview; see pages 35–37 of *The ANDS Prioritization and Implementation Plan*, Mid-2010–Mid-2013, Volume I, Kabul International Conference on Afghanistan, July 20, 2010. I have had access to the *Inteqal* paper, which is formally entitled *Joint Framework for* Inteqal: *A Process for Strengthening Peace and Stability in Afghanistan and the Region*.

91. Project on National Security Reform, *Forging a New Shield*, November 2008; available at http://pnsr.org/data/files/pnsr_forging_a_new_shield_report.pdf; in January 2009, two months ahead of the Af-Pak review, Secretary of Defense Robert Gates

concluded that the United States needed to improve its "soft power" to build indigenous institutions and provide for rule of law, reconciliation, and good governance: "Doing so requires exploring whole-of-government approaches for meeting complex security challenges"; Department of Defense, *Quadrennial Roles and Missions Review Report*, January 2009; available at www.defense.gov/news/Jan2009/QRMFinalReport_v26Jan.pdf, foreword.

92. *United States Government Integrated Civilian Military Campaign Plan for Support to Afghanistan* (ICMCP), August 10, 2009; available at www.comw.org/qdr/fulltext/0908eikenberryandmcchrystal.pdf.

93. Riedel, interview with author, October 25, 2010.

94. In making this overview I have benefited from discussions with national diplomats who shall remain anonymous.

95. *New York Times*, "British Diplomat, Bonding with U.S. Commander, Takes Key Afghan Role," May 16, 2010. Various background interviews confirm this tight relationship.

96. Conducted variously with officials within NATO's organization and national officials assigned to NATO.

97. In a secret but leaked memo ambassador Eikenberry writes that "the proposed counterinsurgency strategy assumes an Afghan political leadership that is both able to take responsibility and to exert sovereignty in the furtherance of our goal . . . Yet Karzai continues to shun responsibility for any sovereign burden, whether defense, governance, or development"; *New York Times*, "Ambassador Eikenberry's Cables on U.S. Strategy in Afghanistan," n.d.; available at http://documents.nytimes.com/eikenberry-s-memos-on-the-strategy-in-afghanistan#p=1.

98. *Times*, "Low-Profile Diplomat to Take over 'Mistrusted' UN Mission: Appointment Seems to Rule out a Leading Role," January 27, 2010. The assessment of di Mistura is drawn from background interviews.

99. *Rolling Stone Magazine*, "The Runaway General," July 8–22, 2010; available at www.rollingstone.com/politics/news/17390/119236.

100. Interview with various national officials, October 31, 2011.

101. The Kabul conference in July 2010 backdated this "Kabul process" to have begun with President Karzai's inauguration speech in November 2009 following his reelection in August 2009. This comes close to whitewashing the fraudulent electoral process, however, and the international community seems to prefer to talk of a process of transition that began notably with the London conference in January 2010. Compare the *Kabul Communiqué*'s preamble (available at www.mfa.gov.af/FINAL%20Kabul%20Conference%20%20%20Communique.pdf) to the overview provided by UNAMA, *Kabul conference*, July 20, 2010; available at http://unama.unmissions.org/Default.aspx?tabid=4482.

102. Urging a more proactive United States and also allied policy on reconciliation is Gilles Dorronsoro, *Afghanistan at the Breaking Point* (Washington, DC: Carnegie, 2010). With U.S. policy turning around, a road map has become necessary. James Shinn—an assistant secretary of defense and also Afghan strategy review contributor under President Bush—and James Dobbins—the U.S. negotiator to the 2001 Bonn conference—provide one in *Afghan Peace Talks: A Primer* (Santa Monica, CA: RAND, 2011).

103. Reconciliation was put on NATO's agenda as early as December 2007 in the context of a NATO defense ministers' meeting, notes former defense minister Søren Gade, but he continues that the debate did not really take root in NATO because the Alliance as a whole lacks doctrines or structures for driving these debates; Gade, interview with author, May 31, 2010.

104. Sun Tzu, *The Art of War* (London: Penguin, 2003), chapter 3, "Strategic Offensive," 14–19.

105. Anders Fogh Rasmussen first set out this vision (which had floated in the NATO debate before this point, it should be mentioned) on October 8, 2010, stating that "the time has now come for NATO 3.0. . . . The Strategic Concept is the blueprint for that new NATO"; *The New Strategic Concept: Active Engagement, Modern Defense*, speech at the German Marshall Fund, Brussels, October 8, 2010; available at www .nato.int/cps/en/natolive/opinions_66727.htm. For Ivo Daalder, see *Foreign Policy*, "Get Ready for NATO 3.0," October 29, 2010; available at http://thecable.foreignpolicy .com/posts/2010/10/29/get_ready_for_nato_30.

106. This is lifted from the *Lisbon Summit Declaration*, NATO Press Release (2010)0155, November 20, 2010, and the new Strategic Concept, *Active Engagement, Modern Defense*, November 20, 2010. Both documents are available at www.nato.int/ cps/en/natolive/events_66529.htm.

107. In August 2010 NATO set up a new Emerging Security Challenges Division (ESCD) at its headquarters, directing it to focus on terrorism, the proliferation of weapons of mass destruction, cyber defense, and energy security.

108. *Declaration by the North Atlantic Treaty Organisation (NATO) and the Government of the Islamic Republic of Afghanistan on an Enduring Partnership Signed at the NATO Summit in Lisbon, Portugal*, November 20, 2010; and *Declaration by the Heads of State and Government of the Nations Contributing to the UN-mandated, NATO-led International Security Assistance Force (ISAF) in Afghanistan*, November 20, 2010; both available at www.nato.int/cps/en/SID-D52452D0-EE856634/natolive/ news_68728.htm.

109. These three pillars define the 2010 *Strategic Concept*. They make up the body of the Concept following a statement of NATO values and purposes and a description of the security environment..

110. Rasmussen, interview with author, October 29, 2010.

111. In Bratislava, in October 2009, the secretary general asked to meet separately with the defense ministers, leaving the permanent representatives outside the door. It was a cause of some concern and controversy (and not only because the representatives felt snubbed: Ministers do not always possess adequate knowledge of issues to negotiate them) but also a clear signal of change. Secretary General Rasmussen also does not cultivate the meetings on Tuesdays during which ambassadors discuss Alliance matters and prepare for the regular Wednesday Council meeting. There used to be two Tuesday meetings: first a morning coffee meeting hosted by the secretary general and for which records were kept, then a luncheon hosted by one of the ambassadors and for which no record was kept. The Tuesday morning coffees have been canceled under Fogh Rasmussen, and the luncheons now take place at the headquarters, hosted by the secretary general, and in more formal format to set up the Wednesday agenda. This is done perhaps because the ambassadors' informal Tuesday luncheons began (in the 1960s) as a reaction to weak leadership from the secretary general, but likely also to define the ambassadors as a kind of civil servants. Information here has been obtained in various background interviews, but see also Hendrickson, "NATO's First Prime Minister." Hendrickson notes that Secretary General Rasmussen tends to work at home every once in a while, which naturally also decreases his availability.

112. Defense and foreign ministers coming to NATO headquarters have always met with the secretary general, but under new and revised guidelines defined in 2010 they have been informed that the secretary general's availability can be assumed but not guaranteed.

113. Inside the North Atlantic Council, in whatever format it met, Afghanistan used to always figure on the agenda—typically with an operational briefing following by a discussion of topical issue—but this changed from August 2009. Operational issues have been pushed down to the Military Committee, and the Council addresses Afghanistan only when there are major and principled issues to be decided on—such as the training mission and the COIN strategy as a whole but also key issues such as the judicial implications of partnering with Afghan forces, and the transition strategy (*Inteqal*).

114. Rasmussen, interview with author, October 29, 2010.

115. Visit the *Secretary General's Corner* at http://andersfogh.info/.

116. President Obama, *Nobel Lecture*, December 10, 2009; available at http://nobelprize.org/nobel_prizes/peace/laureates/2009/obama-lecture_en.html.

117. Secretary of Defense Robert Gates's parting shot took aim at the European allies: They have 2,000,000 men and women in uniform but have trouble sustaining 25,000 to 40,000 in Afghanistan, and they have been lukewarm in Operation Unified Protector in Libya where a handful of allies have done much but more have done little or nothing at all. It comes down to a question of muscle, Gates continued: "Frankly, many of those allies sitting on the sidelines do so not because they do not want to

participate, but simply because they cannot. The military capabilities simply aren't there." This capability gap, Gates finally warned, is undermining U.S. support for the Alliance; Robert Gates, *The Security and Defense Agenda (Future of NATO)*, speech delivered in Belgium, June 10, 2011; available at www.defense.gov/speeches/speech .aspx?speechid=1581.

Conclusion

1. Sun Tzu, *The Art of War* (London: Penguin, 2003), 14–19; Hans Morgenthau, *Politics among Nations: The Struggle for Power and Peace* (Boston: McGraw-Hill, 1993), 30.

2. Chris Alexander, *The Long Way Back: Afghanistan's Quest for Peace* (Harper Collins, kindle edition, 2011), location 3471.

3. Jason Burke, *The 9/11 Wars* (London: Allen Lane, 2011), 444.

4. For the suggestion that the United States anchor its policy in Afghan security forces build-up and support, see Bing West, *The Wrong War: Grit, Strategy, and the Way Out of Afghanistan* (New York: Random House, 2012).

5. Max Weber, "The Profession and Vocation of Politics," in Peter Lassmann and Ronald Speirs, eds., *Weber: Political Writings* (Cambridge, UK: Cambridge University Press, 2000), 309–369.

6. Rynning, "Realism and the Common Security and Defence Policy," *Journal of Common Market Studies* 49/1 (January 2011), 23–42; Calleo, *Follies of Power: America's Unipolar Fantasy* (Cambridge, UK: Cambridge University Press, 2009).

7. To live for politics, in Weber's words, is to enjoy the "naked possession of the power" one is able to exercise or to gain self-esteem from the "meaning and purpose" inherent in politics. Weber, "The Profession and Vocation of Politics," in Peter Lassmann and Ronald Spiers, eds., *Weber: Political Writings* (Cambridge, UK: Cambridge University Press, 2002), 318.

8. For the ultimate task of statesmanship, see Henry Kissinger, *On China* (London: Allen Lane, 2011), 13.

INDEX